THE LISTENING BIENNIAL READER, VOL. 1: WAVES OF LISTENING

EDITED BY BRANDON LABELLE

THE L:STEN:NG BIENNIAL READER

VOL. 1: waves of listening

ERRANT BODIES PRESS, BERLIN

CONTENTS

BRANDON LABELLE

Intro — ductory Waves

What leads us to listening? And how does listening lead us? Where does it take us, and what does it enable? It is our interest to stay close to listening, and to stay close to the ways in which listening brings one into a process of discovery, negotiation, sensitivity, sharing, transformation. Listening prompts a critical and creative curiosity, a receptiveness and responsiveness, to what one may hear or encounter, see and feel, and also what such listening may give way to, from knowing and meaningful exchange, lazy thoughts and critical attention, to social debate and poetic imagination.

If listening takes us somewhere it is into the ebbing and flowing of life, the deep pulse and resonant reach of becoming-with; it is toward intimacies and a world of touch, as well as to the edges of the familiar, what is unidentifiable yet no less present, from the invisible to the less-than-linguistic, the untold and the not-yet. Listening is so fragile, so tenuous and yet so powerful; it extends and stretches, it leaves one open and it opens space for others, from friends to strangers, the earthly to the cosmic. Listening can be beautiful, and it can be painful as well, whether in relation to the noises of the world, those voices and words that may hurt, that aim at hurting, or by way of the unlistenable cries of others, where listening is strained, made unbearable, or where we may miss hearing what we so long to receive or experience. Listening invades and it may control – it is clearly part of a greater set of techniques for monitoring the borders of states and communities, as well as what helps create a safe space for lonely feelings, for being alone, and with each other, slowly, considerately.

Listening takes us in all these different directions, and in this way it becomes important to consider where one places one's listening, and how one's listening is placed, positioned; what am I hearing around me, and what is left unsaid, unheard? Am I heard, and in what ways? Is listening given the time and space needed for its patient work? Can I refuse to be listened to, and does my listening also demand more than others can give? The sensorial politics shaping the flows of attention is deeply at play when it comes to listening, requiring a greater engagement with what listening may mean or do, and how it should question itself at times.

Following such complexity and curiosity, the Listening Biennial is posed as a framework for thinking further about listening and how we may come to foster its political and poetic potential, its material and imaginative shaping of things. To do so, the Biennial sets out to create experiences of listening as defined by participating artists whose works confront us with a complex range of performative expressions; through their works we encounter strategies and methods, questions and answers, localities and worlds, all of which speak toward ways of listening that are equally ways of thinking and living-with, where listening is never only about sound or the normative ear. Rather, it is made radically attentional, exuberant, tenacious and tender, inciting wayward paths and critical echoes in and around being-human.

Listening is put forward as what enables both localized, intimate, and communal relationships as well as global and planetary views, where listening may sense beyond the apparent and the legible. As Anna Tsing poignantly suggests, listening wields a power by which to attend and align with greater ecosystems of life and their polyphonies. The Biennial adopts such a transversal position in its curatorial approach. For the first edition launched in July 2021, this was articulated by way of a curatorial team whose international and regional perspectives allowed for assembling an extremely diverse group of participating artists. Including Budhaditya Chattopadhyay, Brandon LaBelle, Israel Martínez, and Yang Yeung, each was tasked with inviting artists based in particular regions of the world, and whose practices engage with questions and experiences of listening in interesting, provocative, thoughtful and surprising ways. This led to a range of conversations and collaborations, which contributed to nurturing the Biennial as a collective effort, one that might contribute to a transcultural story, to figure an aural weave of differing sonorities. In addition to the main curators, a number of key curatorial partners contributed by helping extend our knowledge, putting us in touch with other artists and institutions whose work and activities are equally involved in listening as a practice and as a proposition. Our curatorial partners included: Rayya Badran, Florencia Curci, Hardi Kurda, Gentian Meikleham, Alexandre St-Onge, Lucia Udvardyova, and James Webb.

In pursuing a transversal, polyphonic approach, the Biennial is further based on bringing together a constellation of collaborating organizations, spaces, and collectives as active partners, each of which were invited to create and present their own version of the Biennial in 2021. Sharing the works by participating artists, each partner responded by situating them within their own environments, and in relation to the communities or audiences they serve, often nesting the Biennial within diverse and dynamic settings, festivals, institutions and scenes – giving way to a multiplicity of listening experiences.

Through such an approach, the Biennial adopts a listening attitude or sensibility, creating opportunities and openings for others to join, to present and perform, to jam together, to craft localized expressions that also contribute to a greater network of exchange – a construct of rhythms and resonances passing across and between different worlds. In this sense, the Biennial poses an idea of "acoustic care," where attention may be given not only to the listening one may individually enact, but also to facilitating the particular conditions in support of the listening others may do, or that we may do together. Acoustic care cares for the timings and spacings, the social arrangements and bodily gestures, the languages and structures needed to support a sensitivity for listening, and a sense for what listening may enable or create; an acoustic care that is not only bound to the audible, and the sounded, but equally concerns itself with supporting a broader ecology of attention. From the vibrational commoning key to being-together, and becoming-with, to the reverberant circulation of voices and views, to the noisy intensities of creaturely and multi-species life, acoustic care emerges as a craft, a civility, a tactic, a pedagogy, and, further, an invitation. It is less a performative approach and more *conductive*, in terms of keeping our listening going, and keeping the (bio)diversity of our social adventure going as well.

It is these ideas and concerns that underpin the Listening Biennial, and which we offer as a proposition, a care-work, a scene, and a gesture of love. For listening is certainly there, as part of the passionate and enduring stories we may create together. Following these lines of thinking and doing, organizing and sharing, *The Listening Biennial Reader* presented here seeks to elaborate a discursive and reflective culture of listening. Capturing some perspectives and experiences from the presentation of the first Biennial, as well as inviting contributions from key scholars, artists, and cultural practitioners whose thinking and research afford greater critical and creative understandings of listening, we hope the *Reader* can contribute to forms of transdisciplinary knowledge sharing, as well as to keep the vitality of working (and playing) at listening in motion. In this regard, we are deeply grateful to the authors and artists who have contributed their time and work, giving us the opportunity to publish so many engaged and insightful words and initiatives, voices and views.

Through the collected essays here, it is our concern to recognize listening as a method of research and inquiry, as well as a topic that traverses multiple critical contexts, that is there like a current flowing under and around experience, relations, technology, lands and the air we breathe. The notion of *Waves of Listening* is therefore put forward as a soft organizing figure, where waves become suggestive for how listening is a movement, a living process, an intensity that flows along with time and space, history and society. As the essays presented here capture, listening extends itself, passes across contexts and communities, attending to time and space, people and place, and then it recedes, comes back into the body, pulling all that it touches or encounters inward, toward an arena of reflection, affection, discourse, thinking. Along the way, listening affords critical questioning, sensorial engagement, experiential knowledge; it flows along, in an endless proliferation of relational action and acknowledgment, working its way into the difficult and enriching tasks of care and concern, compassion and debate. It also punctuates, intensifying the pace, at times, of what it means to be held in the momentum of a greater force or system or collectivity. Listening may be an act, but it is also pulled by events; it may direct itself, but it is equally directed.

To follow waves of listening is to move across and with past and present, thought and action, oneself and others, a movement or oscillation that figures along the way a plethora of important contact zones and experimental practices – ways of attuning to and dealing with and caring for all that is submerged, unheard, as well as all that may arise, persist, ripple. It is to go over and over again, along a liquid, oceanic, and tidal course, the difficult, joyful, and complex ongoingness of history and daily encounter, moving in and along, then through and against, to nurture a flow and force of affinities, narratives, other movements and voices.

As we continue to work at and through the ongoingness of social, political, and ecological struggles, a lot of which brings into sharp display the challenges undermining open dialogue today, and the ability to stay with the complexity of a globalized conversation – to create the conditions for a more sustainable set of encounters – we hope that by nurturing greater attention to listening the Biennial may participate in both the small and wider movements that aim for a more planetary world.

EXHIBITING ARTISTS:

Octavio Aguilar & Diego Martínez Guillén (Mexico), Khyam Allami (Iraq/UK), Wah-yan Au & Yannick Dauby (Hong Kong/Taiwan), Georges Azzaria (Canada), Tania Candiani (Mexico), Antoine Chessex & Mélia Roger (Switzerland/France), Michele Chu (Hong Kong), Cyclops (Carlos Amorales & Enrique Arriaga) (Mexico), Bidisha Das (India), Emcsi (Hungary), Julie Faubert (Canada), Yolande Harris (UK/US), Jeph Jerman (US), Orsolya Kaincz (Hungary), Nandita Kumar & Joseph Kamaru (India/Kenya), Isuru Kumarasinghe & Sara Mikolai (Sri Lanka), Bárbara Lázara (Mexico), Sharon Lee (Hong Kong), Sandra Monterroso & Manuel Estrella Chí (Guatemala/Mexico), Ziad Moukarzel (Lebanon), Alecia Neo (Singapore), Angel Nevarez & Valerie Tevere (US), Jocelyn Robert (Canada), Ish S (India), Tao G. Vrhovec Sambolec (Slovenia/NL), Surabhi Saraf (India/US), Mene Savasta (Argentina), Wantanee Siripattananuntakul (Thailand), Alexandre St-Onge (Canada), Fernando Vigueras (Mexico), Raheleh (Minoosh) Zoromodinia (Iran/US).

PARTICIPATING ORGANIZATIONS, VENUES, AND COLLECTIVES:

1983, Hong Kong / The Cube Project Space, Taipei / Ayer, Guadalajara / National Arts Festival, Makhanda / aerial, Bergen / Space21, Kurdistan / École d'art Université Laval, Quebec City / Liquid Architecture, Melbourne / AMEE, Madrid / Klank.ist, Istanbul / Culture Monks, Kolkata / TAFMA, Nagaland / Investigaciones del Futuro, Buenos Aires / Generator Projects, Dundee / Noise N' Roses, Budapest / Errant Sound, Berlin

CURATORS:

Budhaditya Chattopadhyay, Brandon LaBelle, Israel Martínez, Yang Yeung

CURATORIAL PARTNERS:

Rayya Badran, Florencia Curci, Hardi Kurda, Gentian Meikleham, Alexandre St-Onge, Lucia Udvardyova, James Webb

ARTISTIC DIRECTOR:

Brandon LaBelle with Octavio Camargo, Annette le Fort

ISRAEL MARTÍNEZ

Searching stealth, not silence

I understand stealth as a condition, a state or a situation even that allows a mild flow of information that is intimate, vital, almost secret, regularly clear. I link it to the territories that legendary Mexican writer Juan Rulfo shared with us, portraying with unlimited clarity the noises of silence between death and life, thus breaking the (useless? conceited?) binary thinking between "noise" and "silence," between what is and what's not music that has been the basis of numerous essays, for example, on "the silent piece" by John Cage, and its many remakes and covers. Literature has, undoubtedly, a greater imaginative potential around sound than what has been developed by focusing on its physical production in several other fields.

I conceive of stealth, quietness, as an "enabler" or "maximizer" of experiences and sensations: to listen and talk (the most logical conceptions), but also to get closer to literature, to cook, to taste food and drink, to smell with greater concentration, to wander and "get lost," to be critical, to self-evaluate, to sharpen our sight, to encourage imagination, to rethink our relationship with time, to appease thoughts, to feel our bodies, to become sexier (as Einstürzende Neubauten proposed in its only concert in Mexico twenty years ago). This might sound banal and even somewhat new agey, but bear with me: It could be necessary in our grizzly present which is neither characterized by a rebellious nor a radical stridency, but trivialized by the extreme saturation we receive and partake in one way or another at all times, and that usually only flows towards the economic benefit of the big capital owners.

I intuit stealth as a political tool, as part of a resistance methodology, as a bridge to listen and share better, that allows us to act bluntly after that necessary pause, especially nowadays when we have no answers to more urgent questions, or citing the Chto Delat collective, that the questions have been changed when we thought we had the answers. I think about the Mexican March of Silence on September 13, 1968, or The Silent March of the Zapatista Army of National Liberation (EZLN) on December 21, 2012.

It is not true that silence only denotes apathy, repression or defeat, nor that megaphones, shouts and public demonstrations are the most effective forms of protest. Thinking that is falling into the "noise vs. silence" dichotomy. Stealth inserts those critical and often contradictory possibilities that we need to assume to deliver new ideas. Stealth can be an alternative to binary thinking: heterosexual or homosexual, white or black, capitalist or communist, good or bad, etc., criticized by Spanish philosopher Paul B. Preciado for wreaking havoc on the way we process any matter.

Stealth, I believe, is an option today.

LUÍSA SANTOS

Calls for Listening — a tribute to untold micro-narratives

In "calls for listening: a tribute to untold micro-narratives," the path of the *4Cs: From Conflict to Conviviality through Creativity and Culture*, a European Cooperation Project co-funded by the Creative Europe Programme of the European Union, will be told. To tell the path of the 4Cs is to tell its stories, which unfolded in various formal, organizational and conceptual layers that, in turn, embodied micro-narratives that have been systemically and systematically shadowed and silenced.

WHAT IS THE 4CS?

The *4Cs: From Conflict to Conviviality through Creativity and Culture* was a European Cooperation Project co-funded by the Creative Europe Programme of the European Union, which began in 2017 and ended in December 2021. Throughout its existence, the 4Cs sought to understand how training and education in art and culture might constitute powerful resources to address the issue of conflict as well as to envision creative ways in which to deal with conflictual phenomena. The project aimed at advancing the conceptual framework of intercultural dialogue and enhancing the role of public arts and cultural institutions in fostering togetherness through cultural diversity and intercultural encounters. In other words, or following its title, in its inception, the 4Cs' initial intention was to move from Conflict to Conviviality.

Our path, nevertheless, wasn't quite like that. In our first meeting as a consortium of institutions, in July 2017 in Berlin, Professor Arjun Appadurai predicted that, in the end, we would move from Conflict back to Conflict, rather than to Conviviality. I agree. I'd say that we moved – or that we are still moving – from Conflict to (ex)Change. I'll come back to this in the end.

To tell of the path of the 4Cs is to tell its stories. All stories – like curatorial practices – have a time, a space, and characters. In research practice, atop these elements, there is always a problem to be solved; a way (a method) of solving it, and, hopefully, some knowledge is produced along the way, leading to (some sort of) a conclusion. The 4Cs' story (or stories) unfold(s) in various formal, organizational, and conceptual layers that embody micro-narratives, which I have adopted for the structure of text in a series of short-stories as follows: i) when the shadow(ed) is highlighted, when the silen(t)(ced) acquires a voice; ii) listening as a speculative practice; iii) mutability and (ex) change, which is, in fact, the last story told by the 4Cs and will hopefully produce an echo in the near future. These three micro-narratives are tied together by a fourth element, which is the collective of institutions and individuals that make up the 4Cs. In other words, the characters of the story, which I will briefly introduce in the first part.

I WHEN THE SHADOW(ED) IS HIGHLIGHTED, WHEN THE SILEN(T)(CED) ACQUIRES A VOICE

Let's start by contextualizing the 4Cs within its own time and geo-cultural location: 2017–2021, Europe. When we started thinking about the 4Cs, a year before its inception, in 2016, the notion of conflict was undergoing decisive transformations and Europe was more than ever providing a center-stage for these changes. From the Ukraine crisis to Brexit, from the refugee emergency to new migration flows, from the threat of terrorism to increasing nationalist feelings, Europe became a site where new conflicts take shape, challenging once stable ideas of belonging, cohesion, and hospitality. Founded in the aftermath of a destructive war, Europe created the institutional, political, and legal frameworks necessary to sustain a project of peace, solidarity, and mutual relief. Under these conditions, however, Europe was faced with trials and challenges posed by new forms of conflict that endanger this legacy and demand urgent interrogation.

In 2020, the circumstances of the Covid-19 pandemic challenged even more the once stable ideas of belonging, cohesion, and hospitality that lay at the foundation of the European project and social differences became even more evident in the continent while all humans, across the world, faced the pandemic. In the moment of the writing of this text, in April 2022, Europe is undergoing the largest war since World War II and the urgent nature of the policy response to it shows deeply racialized and gendered underpinnings. Again, it became clear that the risk exposure to conflict is clearly uneven across diverse genders and races. In other words, many voices remain silent(ced) while others are given center stage.

As contemporary art institutions become increasingly global/ international/ transnational in their scope, they face tremendous responsibilities, such as showing the (hidden) multi micro-narratives told by the many who make up the world. Alike speculative realism (Harman, 2018),[1] and while challenging the multipolar Western institutional structures (grand-narratives told by few) that they inhabit (Gupta and Watson, 2016),[2] the responsibilities of contemporary art institutions appear to imply a spirit of collaborative networks, imaginative audacity, and (ex)change, integrating both human and non-human experiences, knowledge, and stories.

The 4Cs was created precisely to reflect and act upon these responsibilities, which entail considering the danger of the hegemonic absorption of dissonant practices into canonical art historical and curatorial discourses. While contemporary challenges undoubtedly require the formulation of new questions and solutions, the 4Cs project also looks at Europe as a project far from being exhausted, quite the contrary. Europe's desideratum of peaceful coexistence is, clearly, still to be fulfilled, but in need of urgent re-articulation. It is also important to understand that art, as a creative form, is inherently conflictual as it involves rupture and the collision of differences as methodologies to perceive, reflect upon, and visually translate (alternative proposals to) the world we live in.

Grounded in the belief that we need a different institutional strategy, in the universities and in contemporary art centers, a strategy which would understand audiences not as passive consumers, but as constituent members of a plural community in permanent becoming, the 4Cs aimed at developing a new cultural production institutional strategy. This was done by departing from the premise that knowledge production is possible via theoretical research as much as it is via doing, in artistic practices.

So by exploring the challenges of the first decades of the 21st century, through a program of conferences, exhibitions, and experimental mediation, the eight 4Cs partners – 4 Faculties of arts and cultural studies (Faculdade de Ciências Humanas-Universidade Católica Portuguesa, Royal College of Art, Vilnius Academy of Arts, École Nationale Supérieure des Arts Décoratifs), and 4 contemporary art centers (Fundació Antoni Tàpies, SAVVY Contemporary – The Laboratory of Form-Ideas, Tensta konsthall, and Museet for Samtidskunst) – aimed at developing a new institutional strategy to reflect and act upon social challenges. On our path to develop this new strategy, we adopted the multiplicity of methodologies that we came across through the guest artists, cultural producers, researchers, and students we collaborated with.

One of the methodologies shared by most of the 4Cs' activities was speculation, a concept that was taken on by various artists, particularly in the last two years. The word speculation has two main different applications: high risk-high gain economic activities such as real estate; and making conjectures without grounded evidence. Artists use the second of these meanings, both as an empirical and as a listening practice. In many respects it reflects the ethos of art practice, the notion of art itself conveys an openness to the possibilities that may come with a dynamic complex world where constraints (like the limitations of materials and technologies) may be viewed as both limiting yet – to some degree – also very much enabling. Speculation – as derived from Alfred North Whitehead's exhortation "Philosophy can exclude nothing"[3] and taken up to gain prominence of late within the social sciences particularly by Isabelle Stengers (2002) –, is a notable response, or a set of responses, to phenomena that cannot be held, observed, and acted upon without either the taking of risks or the experiencing of consequences.

In their explorations, artists attempt to make apparent the systemic failure and the loss of knowledge experienced through the silencing instigated by the mainstream processes of constructing the grand-narratives that make up what we know as History. In other words, while sometimes speculation connotes an activity of anticipation and even exploitation of expectations, it is also adopted under an approach remindful of speculative design, which might be described as a tool to present visions of possible futures as a means of critique of hegemonic narratives and provocation of such futures (Smyth and Helgason, 2020).[4] In order to present their visions, they rely on their observations and in listening to what others have to say.

An example of the power of speculation and storytelling can be found in Rouzbeh Akhbari's exhibition *por ser a terra muito calmosa*, which shows how perception plays a role in the ways we learn, unpack, and act upon narratives. *por ser a terra muito calmosa* turns close attention to micro-histories rather than the grand political and cultural narratives that became accepted as the historical colonial relationship between early 17th century anti-colonial warfare in the Persian Gulf and a multitude of approaches to temporality in political Islam. In Akhbari's narrative, a result of the intersection of his imagination and the speculations of his collaborators – such as an amateur archaeologist who manages the historical cisterns in Qeshm and Hormuz or his grandfather via inherited drawings –, gossip and speculation mostly via oral (hi)stories, and written historical facts cross and are given equal relevance. In this case, such a methodology is particularly relevant considering how a massacre during the reconquest of the island in the 16th century led to the erasure of many stories, making it difficult to tell what is truth and what is fabricated in the grand-narratives that make up history as we know it. In his fabricated micro-narratives, Akhbari offers a critical lens to unpack the specters of various mythologies in the upkeep of neo-imperial hegemonies and continued proxy battles over ancient trade networks. To be able to counter-tell grand-narratives, Akhbari offers a counterintuitive model to the academic research that makes up what becomes known and validated as History: he listens to ordinary people, their stories and their hopes and gives them the same center stage as historical facts from textbooks.

Ana Vidigal, in her series *A mulher do soldado desconhecido* (2020), produced for the exhibition *Silence in Pieces: 4 acts*, one of the 4Cs activities co-created with the MA and PhD students in Culture Studies of The Lisbon Consortium alongside artists and senior researchers, has also used speculation as a trope. The work consists of four large-scale prints of photographs depicting anonymous women, with their heads surrounded by deep-red circles, which were added by the artist. The images show women standing in front of the camera, gazing directly at the lens. Vidigal's work invites observers to dedicate a moment to wonder about the stories behind the old photos. Who did their eyes hope to meet? What were they trying to tell that nobody cared to listen to? Vidigal chose to place the anonymous woman at the very center of her work. The red circle – also the color of blood, of violence, and of war – urges the visitor to look, observe, and focus on their faces. Red. These portraits were taken at the time of the Portuguese Colonial War, during the 1960s and 70s, and were

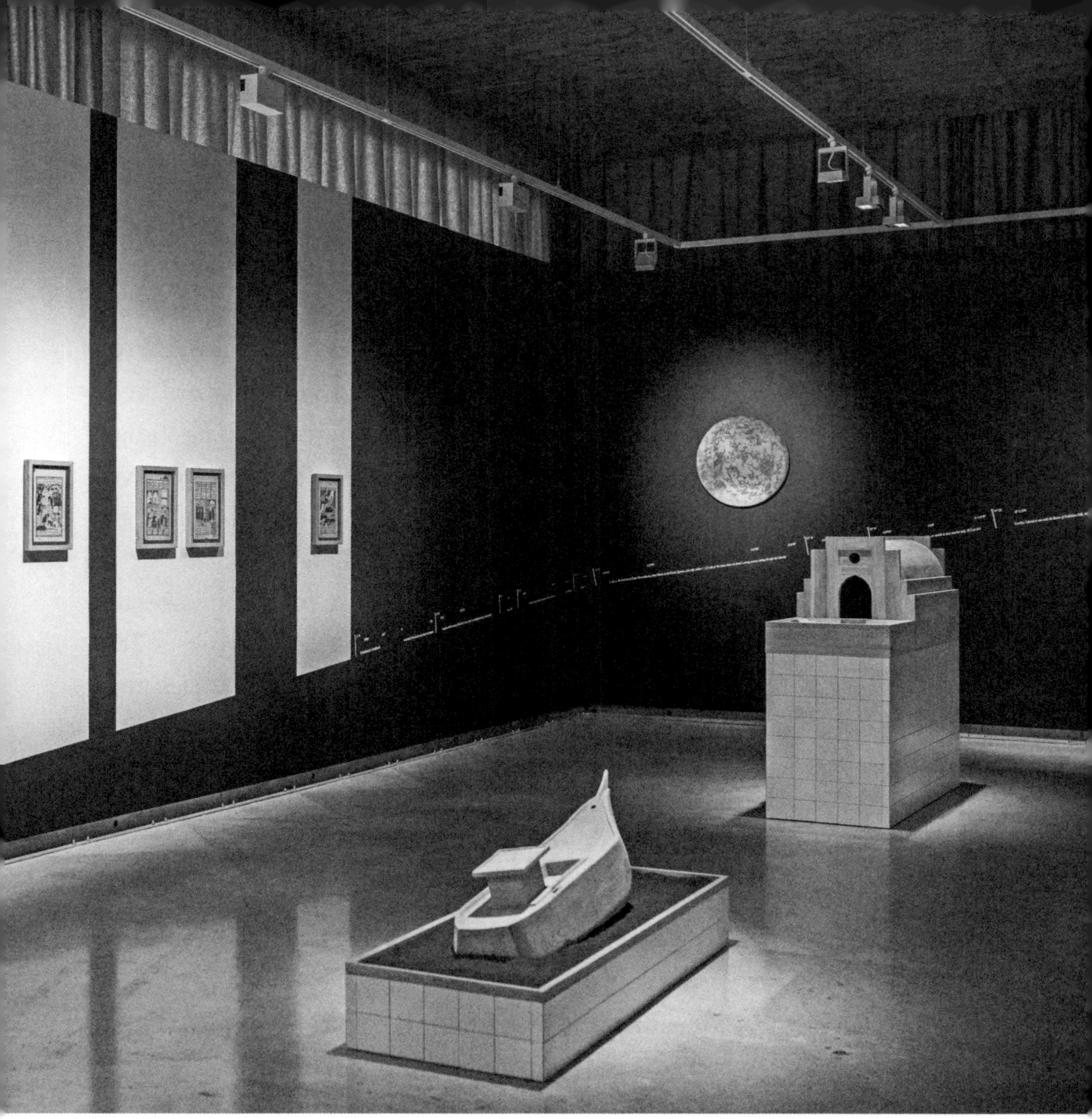

Rouzbeh Akhbari, *Por Ser A Terra Muito Calmosa* (2021) installation view, Galeria Fundação Amélia de Mello, Universidade Católica Portuguesa. Photograph by João Matos.

found by the artist in Lisbon's flea market, Feira da Ladra, in the neighborhood of Alfama, five decades later. No one knows exactly who these women are, but the artist created a narrative for them. In Vidigal's story, they were "Madrinhas de Guerra" (Godmothers of War) and they took these photos in order to send them to the soldiers that fought overseas. Vidigal enlarged these images to transform them from being little women in a family album into large-scale representations to be hung in a gallery space, highlighting what remained invisible and mute in the found material. In this fabricated narrative, Ana Vidigal speculates about a reality in which the often-forgotten role that women played during the war is highlighted. As in Akhbari's work, there's a call for looking at and listening to the stories that remain shadowed and silenced.

The third and last example that I'll speak about to tell of how speculation and storytelling were used in the 4Cs activities is Ângela Ferreira's *Talk Tower for Forough Farrokhzad*, the 4Cs' mediation lab in Lisbon. Designed to broadcast poetry, the work is a tribute to the modern poetess and Iranian director Forough Farrokhzad (1934–1967). Born into a military family, she experienced what one would call a traditional upbringing – she studied painting and sewing, married at the age of 16, and moved to Ahvaz with her husband. After her divorce and having been forced to give up her only child, Farrokhzad published her first book of poetry, "The Captive," in 1955, featuring influences from poets such as Fereydun Tavallali, a poet from the second generation (*nowpardaz*/ New Wave poets) of Iranian modernists and also a political commentator. In 1963, she published her fourth volume of poetry, "Another Birth," the poem given voice to by Ângela Ferreira's *Talk Tower*, and perhaps the most renowned for its pioneer role in Persian modern poetry. Known for her protest poetry, she gave voice to and shone a light onto the feminine world, its secrets, intimate desires, sorrows, and yearnings, hitherto considered taboo. With this sculpture-installation, Ângela Ferreira wonders about what happens when a once silenced voice is given center stage. In other words, more than giving voice, Ferreira listens and asks the audiences to listen to Farrokhzad's voice, which, in turn, is a call to listen to the many micro-narratives that have been – and still are – systemically silenced across History(ies).

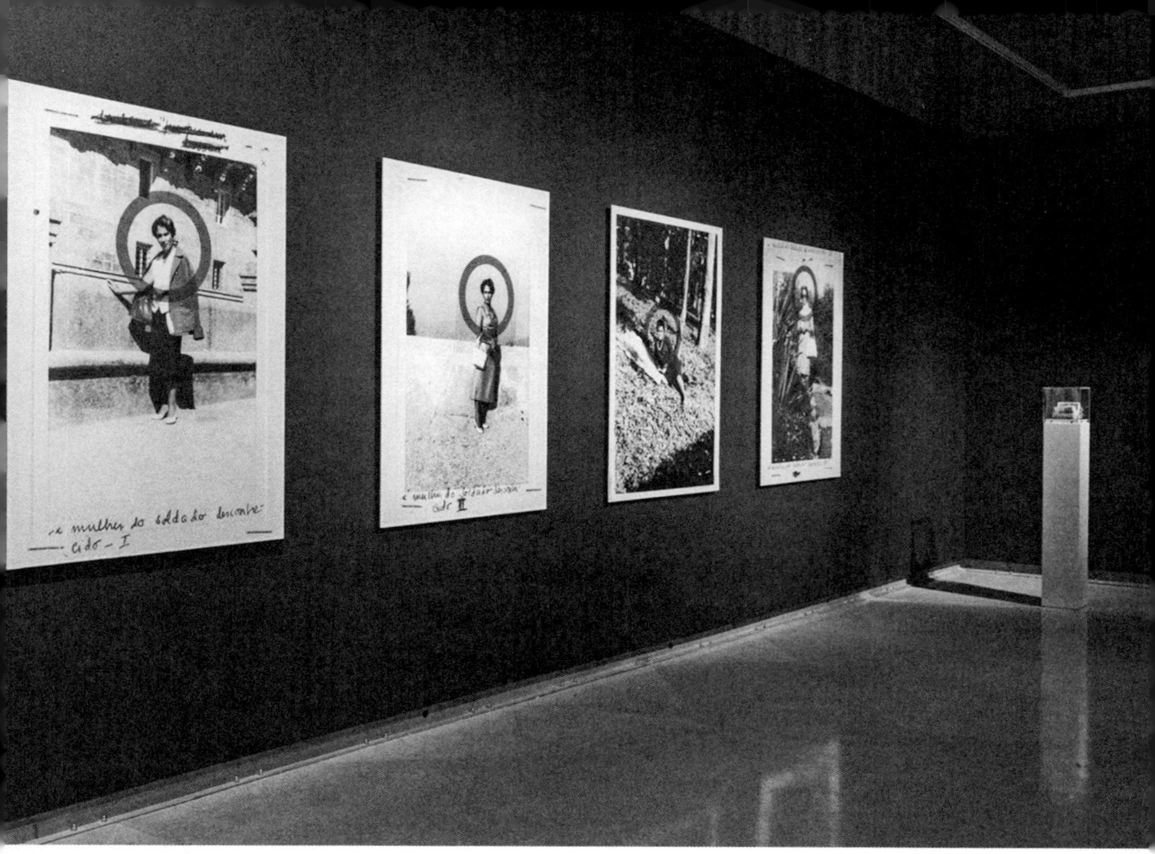

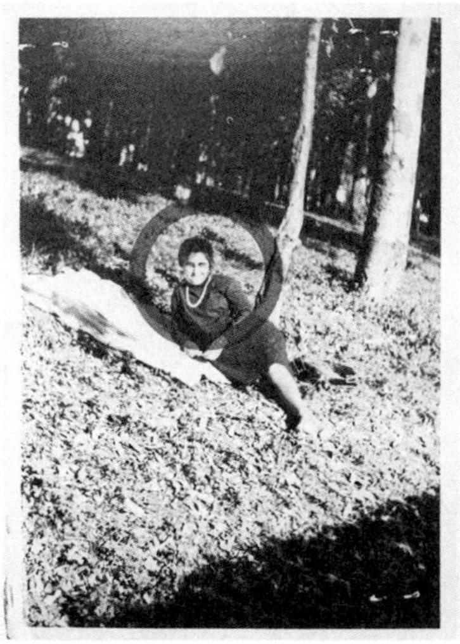

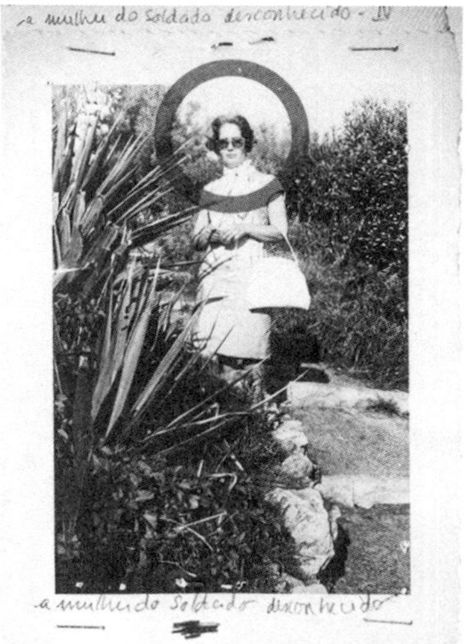

Ana Vidigal, *A mulher do soldado desconhecido* (2020), photographic series. Exhibition view, Galeria Fundação Amélia de Mello, Universidade Católica Portuguesa. Photograph by Alfredo Brant.

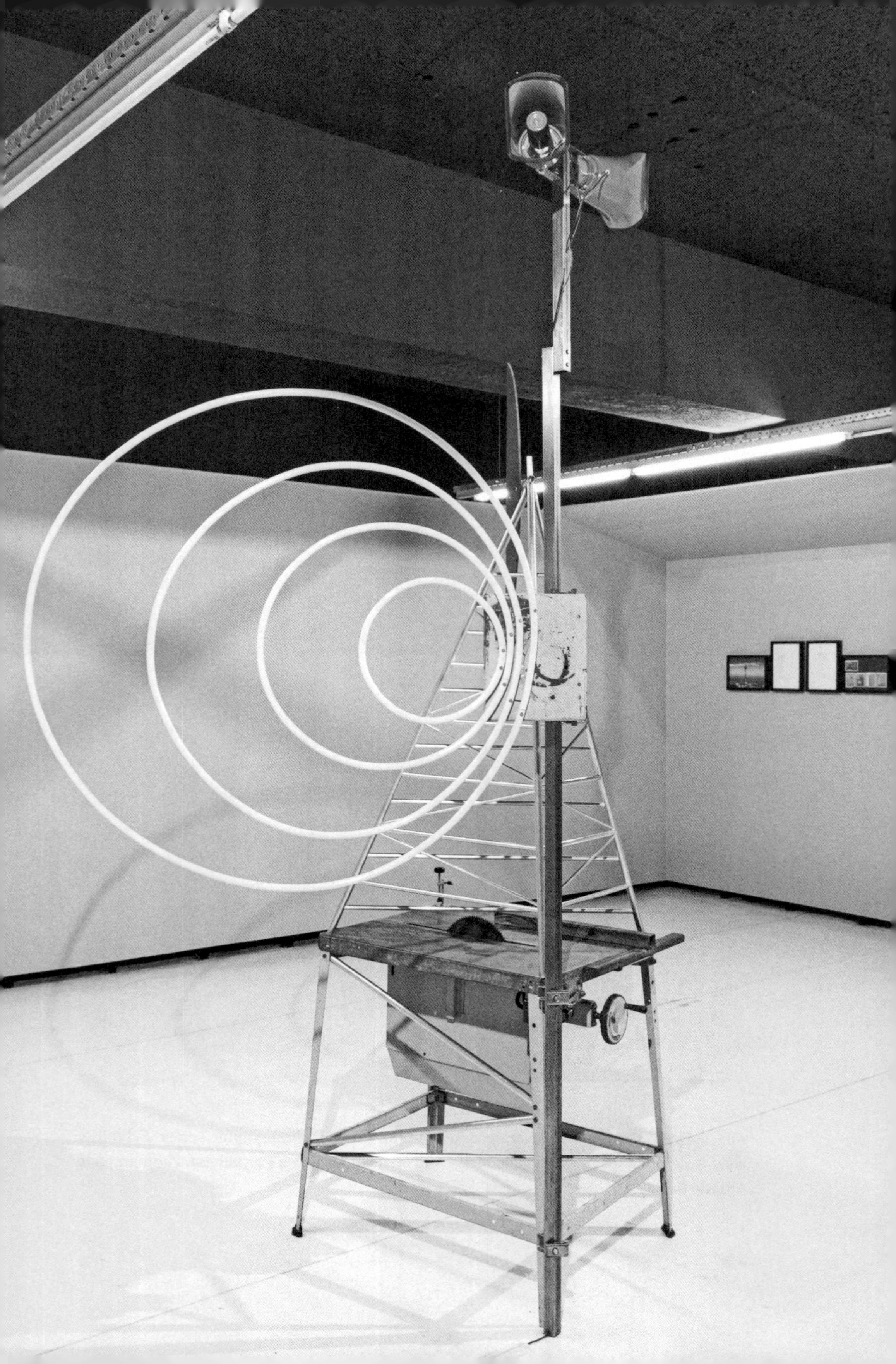

The threads that run through the aforementioned engagements with the speculative are, on the one hand, a transformed interest in the possibility of extracting from the present certain immanent potentialities that may be capable of opening up a transition into otherwise unlikely futures and, on the other hand, through their open-ended format, the uncovering of untold or not listened to – and, therefore, unknown but existing – narratives. Furthermore, in these examples, speculation works as a particular way of engaging with the dynamic and transformative nature of "things" in order to explore their situated and contingent characteristics as well as their capacities to affect and be affected.

Much like architectural projects such as *The Continuous Monument* (1969) by the Superstudio,[5] which never aspired to be realizable buildings, the focus rested primarily on the effect the stories produced on the viewer. Their goal – as of the 4Cs – was to be a catalyst for thought; a pledge for individual and collective change. The stories told in the three examples were deliberately ambiguous, left to the imagination of the viewer to make their own assumptions about its meanings and effects. In this way, these stories were both a translation of conflict and of conviviality. Conflict because they take place on a material, lived dimension, but also on the plane of imagination and representation. The work of imagination, as professor Arjun Appadurai has suggested,[6] is pivotal for conflict to take shape, to produce effects, but also to be understood and dealt with on an everyday level. The circulation of images, voices, stories, and affects in the form of artistic representation was fundamental within the 4Cs as a means to promote an informed visibility about new and emerging conflicts taking place around the globe. The stories told (or speculated about) in the 4Cs also translate conviviality as a model of intercultural dialogue. As the most recent recommendations by the European Commission put it: "Intercultural dialogue is, essentially, the exchange of views and opinions between different cultures. Unlike multiculturalism, where the focus is on the preservation of separate cultures, intercultural dialogue seeks to establish

Ângela Ferreira, *Talk Tower for Forough Farrokhzad* (2020), installation. Exhibition view, Appleton BOX, Oct. 2021. Photograph by Alfredo Brant.

linkages and common ground between different cultures, communities, and people, promoting understanding and interaction."[7] Conviviality has emerged precisely as a model of intercultural dialogue that wishes to move beyond multicultural segregation. Conviviality fosters everyday processes of coming together, mutual recognition, negotiation of difference, and shared transformation (Gilroy 2004),[8] thus representing a model of "experiencing life together" (Arizpe 1998)[9] instead of living side-by-side. What the three above described works seem to tell us is that if we are to live together, we have to learn how to look and how to listen rather than giving light or giving voice. Living together in mutual respect means that we have equal rights despite our enriching differences and, as such, all of our narratives are equally relevant and deserve the same center stage, the same listening ears and the same seeing eyes.

III THIRD NARRATIVE: MUTABILITY AND (EX)CHANGE

Mutability and exchange – across and beyond geographies, cultures, disciplinary discourses and methodologies, political contexts and histories – seemed key in the development of a new cultural production institutional strategy for coming together in our plural world.

Various large-scale European cooperation projects besides the 4Cs have been created since the early 21st century, addressing ideas of collaboration among different cultures, which go much beyond the political frame of Europe. By this idea of the political framing of Europe, I mean to say the difference between what it means to be a political and a physical entity, as expounded by Jimmie Durham in his *Eurasian Project* of 2002. In his words:

> And why is Europe considered a continent, when in fact it is a political entity that has the strangest and most fluctuating boundaries. Even now, especially now, no one agrees to where Europe might be, because it's always only a political not a geographic entity. And the fact that Europe is known as a continent, and Eurasia, the continent, is not known

> as a continent, means that we are taught to think politically, never physically. I can be Eurasian just by living on this continent but I can never be European, because to be European you have to be born into one of these nation states that form its political history. To be European, you have to be French or Italian or German or English, but to be Eurasian you can be anything.

In face of current challenges, Europe cannot exist without recognizing the presence of others. While European cooperation projects confirm this, their very existence might be regarded as problematic going no further than their naming – European. We faced this challenge from the very beginning when designing the consortium of partners previously to the application for funding – some institutions refused to join because they did not want to be pigeonholed as places where conflict was arising while some artists refused to participate in the 4Cs because it was co-funded by the European Union, a Union that they refused to be part of. Examples of large-scale European cooperation projects include the *CreArt* (2012–21), the *L'Internationale* (2009–20), *Contested Desires* (2019-22), and the *Our Many Europes* (2019–22). The main goals of these endeavors have revolved around the so-called priorities of audience development, transnational creation, and capacity building (EC, 2016: 3).[10] However, the methodologies for collaborating transnationally within contemporary art institutions that produce, show, and collect works from various parts of the world remain underdeveloped and an area of concern for much more internal and external / micro and macro organizational and cultural conflict than conviviality. This became even more evident under the COVID-19 conditions, which were felt very differently across the globe.[11] An example which was widely discussed was that of the Tate Modern, in which "as many as 200 jobs are at risk in its commercial arm (...) where a higher proportion of staff are BAME, according to the PCS union" (Quinn, 2020).[12]

While European Cooperation projects – the 4Cs included – claim to have a transnational scope and advocate for international collaboration and co-creation among artistic and cultural institutions, the application of the concept of the transnational remains underdeveloped and an area of conflict at the internal / external, micro / macro organizational and conceptual levels. Indeed, there is a scarcity of research and practices which aim at and provide for the development of effective methods for overcoming the danger of the hegemonic absorption of dissonant practices into canonical art historical and curatorial discourses – which would imply the deactivation of conflictual questions that may defy Western notions of power, quality, influence, originality, work of art vs. artifact, etc.

Despite their transnational scope, these European-based (and European co-funded) projects may become tempted to consider European schools of thoughts and practices rather than the multiple methods, tools, and works from various cultures on a given premise – inter and trans(nationalisms and cultures) – and principles underlying them. The transforming potential of these projects lies in the power they have to give voice to the manifold silenced micro-narratives and views of conceptualizing exchange, collaboration, and mutability across individual practices and emerging methodologies, such as that of speculation.

In her calls for imagination, Azoulay points towards a collective and collaborative endeavor of cultural and arts experts in recognizing that the existing knowledge and skills needed to create cultural artifacts and projects do not work in our contemporary world:

> Imagine artists, photographers, curators, art scholars, newspaper editors, museumgoers, or art connoisseurs going on strike and refusing to pursue their work because the field of art sustains the imperial condition and participates in its reproduction.[13]

Now, the hypothesis that lies in the existing tools and literature to overcome such a recognition of failure can be related to the space given to showcase the work of the artists and cultural producers that remain underrepresented, to give them visibility and a voice. The idea, how noble it may sound, doesn't quite dissect the existing methods neither the current global challenges, which are felt unevenly across the world. At the CIMAM's 2009 annual conference in Mexico titled "Fair-trade: The Institution of Art in the New Economy," Natalia Majluf, Director of the Museum of Art in Lima, Peru, explored questions related to the locality of culture and its confrontation with the global market. As Majluf observes, "the inclusion we fought for was as necessary as it was blind to the consequences of what it proposed, although in the process we forgot the sites of production, the locality of culture, and the place of institutions like museums in this new field of production and exchange."[14] The engagement of local artists with the international market often translates, in fact, as noted by Majluf, into a rise of prices that inhibits local institutions from acquiring and showing the works. This is just an example of how the existing responses for the current challenges don't quite work and each narrative has its own characters, time, and space and, as such, its own circumstances.

IV THINKING AHEAD, A PROPOSAL

Let's go back, for a minute, to the concept of conviviality – it represents a model of intercultural dialogue that has been proposed as a possible answer to the limits of multiculturalism.

Even though "intercultural" is commonly used to describe the state of our contemporary world, in arts, communication, education, and business, Wolfgang Welsch criticizes interculturalism as approaching from "a conception of cultures as islands or spheres" creating a separatist character of cultures.[15] In "Transculturality: The Puzzling Form of Cultures Today," he refers to the complexity of modern societies and how the traditional concept of culture fails to deal with this inner complexity. As Welsch explains, cultures today are interconnected and entangled in each other. Lifestyles go beyond national cultures and concepts. Local realities and cultural identities are linked globally. Ever-increasing global communication technologies and tools make it more possible for all kinds of information to be available from all points in the globe – available and accessible aren't, however, the same thing. As our history shows, different regions of the world face global phenomena in very uneven ways. While having access to the internet might be taken for granted by a few, if we move a bit away from our own neighborhoods we will see that this is not the case everywhere, not even within the same country. What, then, can we – artistic and cultural institutions – do?

I'll end with a series of questions rather than an answer:

- What would happen if we operated within an intersectional approach rather than an old, separatist, and exclusive one? How could we offer interaction and exchange with the diversity of different cultures and life-forms, each arising from transcultural permeations in a network mechanism?
- What if, much like the transcultural notion of Berry and Epstein (1999); Kravagna (2013); and Welsch (2009), we worked as open and mutually transforming organisms rather than monolithic, self-sufficient entities?
- What would happen if we listened and read History from different perspectives? Could we then transcend art-historical boundaries and its hierarchies?

I might not have one definite answer to offer. However, I would like to speculate that the path towards answering these larger questions – like the path of the 4Cs and of any large-scale cooperation project embracing diversity – is grounded in conflict. And that's a constructive, rather than a destructive, path. Assuming the existence of a common ground among the cultural networks between the different people that make up the globe can be vastly damaging if unchecked as it will likely imply the erasing and the silencing of the many micro-narratives that make up the totality of the world we live in. While a symbiotic integration into a single dominant system (Kim, 2002) entails the idea(l) of multiple and equal systems co-existing for mutual benefit while maintaining individual cultural integrity, the globalized world has demonstrated to be a place where a few narratives – of financial, political, and cultural dominance

– prevail over the others. Just as the notion of the (trans)cultural, institutions can be conceived of as in constant relation to each other, fluctuating in an ongoing flux of confluences and (ex)change. How we listen to others and change – individuals and institutions – throughout our encounters, packed with both conviviality and conflict, is our own full responsibility.

NOTES, REFERENCES

1. Harman, Graham. 2018. *Speculative Realism: An Introduction.* Polity: Cambridge.
2. Watson, Grant, and Gupta, Sunil. 2016. Panel convened by Nada Raza. Transnationalism In Practice: Strategies Of Affect, Tate Research Centre: Asia, Tate Britain, London, December 7, 2016.
3. Alfred North Whitehead, *Modes of Thought.* Toronto: Macmillan. 1966 [1938]. p. 2.
4. Helgason, Ingi and Smyth, Michael (2020). "Ethnographic Fictions: Research for Speculative Design." Conference on Designing Interactive Systems (Companion Volume): 203–207.
5. The purely theoretical drawings from The Continuous Monument series illustrate Superstudio's conviction that by extending a single piece of architecture over the entire world they could "put cosmic order on earth." The white, gridded, monolithic structures span the natural landscape and assert rational order upon it. Superstudio saw this singular unifying act, unlike many modern utopian schemes, as nurturing rather than obliterating the natural world.
6. Appadurai, Arjun (1996) *Modernity at Large. Cultural Dimensions of Globalization.* Minneapolis: University of Minnesota Press.
7. See http://ec.europa.eu/culture/policy/strategic-framework/intercultural-dialogue_en.htm.
8. Gilroy, Paul (2004): *After Empire. Melancholia or Convivial Culture?* New York: Routledge.
9. Arizpe, Lourdes (1998): *Convivencia: The Goal of Conviviability.* Paris: UNESCO (World culture report: culture, creativity and markets).
10. European Commission. CREATIVE EUROPE Culture Sub-programme SUPPORT FOR EUROPEAN COOPERATION PROJECTS GUIDELINES. Brussels: European Commission Publications, 2016, 3.
11. And again today, with the current war. However, since the project has ended in December 2021, I've decided not to delve into the current context.

12. Quinn, Ben (2020). "Tate faces protests over impact of job cuts on BAME staff". *The Guardian*, July 26, 2020. https://www.theguardian.com/artanddesign/2020/jul/26/tate-faces-protests-over-job-cuts-impact-on-bame-staff Last accessed January 22, 2021.
13. Azoulay, Ariella Aïsha (2019). *Potential History: Unlearning Imperialism*. London: Verso Books, 338.
14. Natalia Majluf in "Fair-trade: The Institution of Art in the New Economy", CIMAM 2009 Annual Conference, Ciudad de Mexico, Museo Tamayo, MUAC, November 9–10, 2009. Conference Report, p.58. https://cimam.org/documents/49/Publication_CIMAM_2009_Annual_Conference1.pdf / Accessed: November 16, 2020.
15. Wolfgang Welsch, *Transculturality-The Puzzling Form of Cultures Today, Spaces of Culture: City, Nation, World*, ed. By Mike Featherstone and Scott Lash, London: Sage, 1999, 194–213.

SARA MIKOLAI

Listening — Sound Narratives of a Dance

Through a practice of listening, I engage with manifold layers, which inform, influence and shape my approach to dance. Actively listening to dance encourages to perceive movement not only through the eyes, but through the sense of hearing. By doing this I learn to stay present, unlearn and relearn meanings attached to the sound source, as the practice of listening requires an openness towards what is being listened to. Not seeking one particular answer, this practice developed from my continued engagement with epistemologies of dance: a field in particular pressured by questions of representation and gaze, as it is an art form dealing with what is closest to us: the body. The foundation of my dance training is Bharatanatyam, a descendant of the temple and court dances of India.[1] These practices of the Devadasis – the temple dancers –, which is referred to as the origins of this dance, has gone through a complex history of diverse local contexts and realities, to the abolishment through the colonial powers and is today performed as this reinvented form known as Bharatanatyam. Today it is learned in many regions of South Asia and the diaspora. After training and performing this form since childhood, I took a break to comprehend the meaning of a form being developed from a ritual dance to what is today called a classical dance and the confusing contradictions it comes with.

This writing addresses how a listening practice enables me to re-enter the vocabulary, music, philosophy, mythology and somatics of the dance, to more deeply comprehend what it teaches about the body, as well as the body's inner and outer relations in dance and everyday life. The writing makes space for thinking about how this listening practice can be understood as a proposal to critically, openly and poetically engage with passed on knowledge through decolonial strategies, queer reclamations and ecological reflections. Insisting on a commitment to this dance and practices close to it and staying with the trouble, not only in theory but within an artistic practice, is a response to the prejudiced dichotomies of tradition[2] and progress and the consequences of past and present day marginalization and discrimination of *othered* bodies, practices and methodologies of knowledge production. In the sections that follow, I introduce the different modes of listening central to my practice: listening to dance itself as a sonic experience; listening to the sounds of the environment; listening to music/sound compositions; listening to personal and historical narratives.

ON SOUNDS OF TREES AND TRANSFORMING SKINS

Each time I go for a walk and the wind blows through the branches of a tree – in the urban space with a strangely measured distance to another – I listen to those branches beginning to wave and the leaves clapping against each other. It is my favorite song, my favorite dance. Hundreds of little tingling sounds played by foliage, a collective consisting of single leaf members, reflecting colors of themselves, of each other, of the sun and what is around them. I have noticed that this way of listening pulls me to the present and helps me to breathe. It tingles under my skin, which feels as if it expands into the space. It is as if the boundary between my body and the space it is surrounded by softens. I feel how the space breathes through me and I through the space. It makes me feel small and wide at the same time: small as I realize how much more I need this exchange than the tree does and wide as I begin to feel not separate, but part of it. A blurring of entities in space, recognizing the commonalities while embracing the differences. When stepping into waters it is a particularly vibrant version of space getting in touch with my skin. Kindly carrying my body, splashing drops into my eyes and eardrums, changing my experience of sound as a child of the city and its constant urban drone. I would take walks in the forest with occasional dips into lakes, listening to organisms I am surrounded by and notice that by listening I could understand better. Not necessarily by defining the sound of what I am listening to and aiming to put it into a human-made word, but by letting be what is and letting me be what I am. And in doing so, the visual sense, which so quickly cognitively links with the habit of defining what is thought to be seen and the judgment it comes with, has changed for me. This may as well be what the practice of meditation does. If I think of it, I can call this a kind of meditation, that allows movement and activates a certain mindfulness towards the environment, my body and situating one in the other.

The feeling in my body and skin while doing this practice of listening also guides back to mythological stories and the language of Bharatanatyam. Stories and dances my mother has taught me. And so I relate the experience of the forest walks to South Asian myths of celestial beings represented as mountains, waters, plants and curious hybrids of beings. Already in the *namaskaram*, a small sequence before each dance, Bhūma Devi, representing Mother Earth, is saluted, by guiding a touch from the ground to the eyes with the hands. A simple gesture of acknowledgement. Listening to trees may just be something like that.

OF SONGS, FLUID BODIES, TEACHINGS OF A MOTHER AND BLURRED BORDERS

lalita lavanga latA pariSeelana kOmala malaya sameerE
A cool breeze of spring season
from clove bushes is gently blowing

Ashtapadi, song 3

I remember when my mother taught me the Asthapadis of the *Gita Govinda*: a poetry work of songs and hymns about Radha, "a subversive and all-too human emblem of mortal and divine love" (Lal, Malashri; Gokhale, Namita, 2018, p.1) and Krishna, a forest cowherd and deity countering hegemonic masculinity, composed in the 12th century by the poet Jeyadeva: here I have learned for the first time to not only use the *mudras*[3] used in dance as separate movements in order to narrate a story, but to move them fluidly through space, depicting for example a leaf going from one, to the next, to another. Connected, not disrupted. This way of fluidly moving through space, even if only with the hands, within this rather rigid and geometrical form Bharatanatyam has become, has shifted my understanding of *abhinaya*[4] – the emotive telling of a story. It opened up more flexible possibilities of connecting the imaginary (the leaf in the story), the real (my present body) and blurring the two. If I apply this mode of being fluid in a *nritta* (abstract dance) moment, even this moment gets filled with emotion. By doing this, I experience that not directly representing or telling a story does not mean that emotion is absent. We experience this especially in instrumental sound and music works. Using a *mudra* fluidly rather than rigidly, opens up space in my joints. Space, which is more than mere anatomy. Space that is filled with energy and emotion. And so *abhinaya* begins to emerge, even without a direct acting out of a story line, which *bhava* (expressive technique in the performing arts), is often reduced to. I am curious to explore these moments, by being present through an interplay of moving, listening, pausing, resting and how that transforms, transmits and becomes what is called *rasa*,[5] an intangible emotive space. Even though my first encounter with the Ashtapadi was around

17 years ago, it deeply impacts my practice of today more consciously within an embodied philosophy of being fluid in dance and life. In conventional trainings body and gender fluidity within our dance traditions are neither discussed, nor linked. But it is very much there, right in front of us, in the many mythologies of transforming, multi- and cross-hybrid deities, where set categorizations of gender and fluid forms of intimacies are absurd. To me this multiplicity of fluidity as both imaginary and lived are deeply connected.

The popularity of the Ashtapadi songs crosses states from the deep South to the North and East of the subcontinent. I imagine that this has to do with the sensuous quality of the narration, as well as the sound of the music compositions, which merge and melt from one tone and word to the next. I wonder if this compositional fluidity is connected to the local practices of where the *Gita Govinda* was written, in Orissa. In their local dance practice Odissi I observe a sensual fluidity of the body curving through sculptural postures, unlike in Bharatanatyam, where sensuality is rather frowned upon, which can be traced back to the abolishment of the dance as the Devadasis were stigmatized as sex-workers. With the reinvention in the early 20th century, spine movements were quite literally stiffened for acceptance. Reflecting on the latter has helped me to rethink the boundaries created through the borders of the colonial and neocolonial idea of the nation state, by looking at the commonalities and influences of the different dance and music practices, while embracing the differences.

When I began to allow the fluidity learned through the Ashtapadi sink into my chest and hips, it began to curve my spine, which soon felt like throwing a stone into the water – a cause and effect of waves and shifts until it is time to rest. Listening to these compositions with the same intention as I do to trees and waters, expands possibilities of working with the movement vocabulary of this dance background. It becomes less about set choreographies, but more about ephemeral moments of a body in motion. To me, a sense for fluidity has become crucial for my listening: both defy hierarchical and categorizational conditions. I can't listen unbendingly if I genuinely want to listen. And further I can't move rigidly, if I genuinely do listen. Metaphorically, but also quite literally in terms of how to hold, position or move my body when I listen and vice versa. Sitting on a chair or lying on a floor completely changes the way the sound reaches the ear and hence the whole experience. The same would apply to a moving body. Adding fluid qualities to this practice is certainly not a requirement, but it makes the somatic experience of both listening and dancing so much richer.

LISTENING TO DANCE

A ball, inside a ball. Thrusting, stroking, banging, rolling, falling. Standing still. A metal ball, inside another ball of brass. Moving when the body moves and continuing to stroke the coating even if the body pauses. A matter of microseconds. It is like hearing one's pulse in stillness. Or hearing the waves of the water in the distance, when one just quiets down for a moment. Or the birds, or the clapping of leaves on each other on a windy day. Or hearing the absence of it. The bird not present, the trees not present. Other beings – not present. The *Salangai*, footbells, used in many Indian dances are a sound signifier of movement. The experience of dance with and without the bells is of tremendous difference. The soundscape created by dance through the bells creates an incomparable sensorial experience, not only to the outside, but already from the interior experience of being the dancer. In early years I have often been disappointed by the rare usage of the footbells being reserved for moments of public performances. But as an instrument to me the *Salangai* offer more than a mere amplification of movement in hours when a piece has been trained to perfection. The relationship of instrument and body suggests that the dance is not only a dance, but a sonic experience, a music piece in itself, as part of a dance. It expresses that the dance becomes more present and alive, through its sound and not only through an added music piece. This is especially noticeable in northern Kathak dance and its intense footwork creating vast soundscapes. It indeed can be understood as a direct translation of movement into sound, but at the same time it has its own life, resonating back to the body in a way that has its own response, like all acoustic instruments do, in particular those in close proximity to the body. This

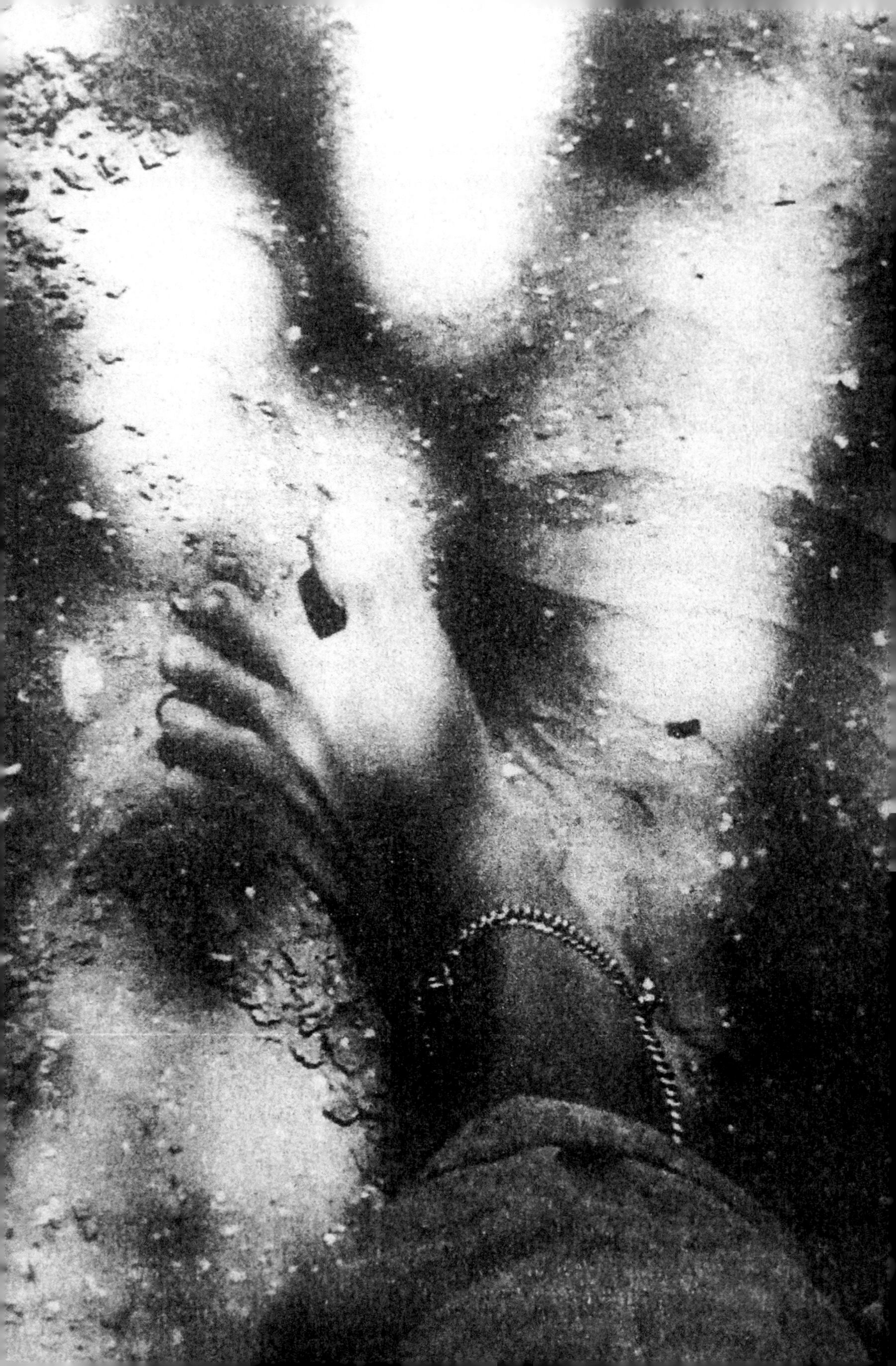

can be well heard in the use of the northern Thai instrument *phin pia*, a string zither, where the chest is used to resonate the sound. When the body is still, the bells tied around the ankles still resonate to minor movements of the muscles, little cracks in the ankle joints and pulsation of the blood. This tells me tales of presence and absence, of silence and noise, of movement and stillness.

What if I do not only dance in set rhythms? What if the way I move the hand *mudra* in the Ashtapadi resonates into my foot and initiates another movement, another sound? What if a curved spine sounds different in the ankle bells? What are the different volumes at play: the volume of the body, the volume of movement, the volume of sound, the volume of space? How can I explore the different types of resonances: the resonance of the bells and the resonance of the body? What if a dance is a song and a song is a dance? How does hearing myself dance affect the movement? And why is a dancer in these dance practices both dancer and musician? The traditional training involves not only dance, but also the study of *sollukattus* – the rhythmic language for dance and percussion –, singing the compositions and understanding the *ragas* and texts in various languages, mostly Tamizh, Sanskrit, Telugu, Kannada and Hindi. I indeed understand the content better with the information through language, but why is sound and voice in a performance today conventionally given to another person? Why have all these entities, being part of one dance practice, been separated in the performance? Why has it become something to remain in studio and study chambers and the musical arrangements fully been given to an orchestra? I understand the beauty of the collaboration between musician and dancer. But is that so that the dancer has more capacity to perfect the form and if so, is this for reasons of entertainment aesthetics as part of the modern era of dance, influenced by ideologies and staging of ballet? If my reasons to dance are not the latter – entertaining –, can I find new meanings within old strategies and practices, which approached all the described layers as a whole? This is not a question of authenticity. But as a dancer I seek to re-enter the *traditions* I have learned in ways, which do not copy alterations to the dance I perceive as unnecessary or even violent, while giving space for explorations. And understanding what is *traditional* about a reinvented form in the first place.

When exploring dance within a listening practice, I sense a resemblance to moments in the forest to dancing the Ashtapadi: skin tingling, breath changing, moving, resting, activating, acknowledging, feeling small and wide, being fluid. When I listen, I give up repetitive ways of directing and controlling my body and movement and negotiate to explore the space with the help of the bells and the sound of movement. This experience expands my understanding of time: set minutes, set rhythms and sequences morph into a rather fluid understanding of time, where the body is given space to find a relation to what the body is surrounded by, through exploring, activity, resting – b e i n g . To find out what the movement sounds like and what it tells me about space, as well as time versus timing. The perceived expansion of time can be well heard in the Dhrupad and Thumri singing practices: both distinct, but having in common durational, meditative and almost trance-like qualities. As an admirer of these music practices it would be wrong to deny their influence on my listening and dancing, despite the different contexts they come with.

INTERSECTING MANIFOLD MODES OF LISTENING AS A DECOLONIAL STRATEGY

There are many existing approaches to listening, which are mainly dealt with from the perspective of sound art, meditation and healing practices. And in this last section of the writing I share selected voices of practitioners and researchers, who attend to the same and similar topics and respond to them through my own writing voice. The artist Salomé Voegelin writes in her book dedicated entirely to listening:

> Seeing always happens in a meta-position, away from the seen, however close. And this distance enables a detachment and objectivity that presents itself as truth. Seeing is believing. The visual "gap" nourishes the idea of structural certainty and the notion that we can truly understand things, give them names, and define ourselves in relation to

> those names as stable subjects, as identities. By contrast, hearing is full of doubt: phenomenological doubt of the listener about the heard and himself hearing it. Hearing does not offer a meta-position; there is no place where I am not simultaneous with the heard. However far its source, the sound sits in my ear. I cannot hear it if I am not immersed in its auditory object, which is not its source but sound as sound itself. Consequently, a philosophy of sound art must have at its core the principle of sharing time and space with the object or event under consideration (Voegelin, 2010, p. xii).

As a dancer, listening to me is a practice for the sake of the practice itself: experiencing different qualities of sounds and body and their relation in effect and affect. I am interested in how sounds involve me as a listener, move me emotionally, but also physically. And further understanding the body and dance as the sound source within this practice, while engaging with the sound itself as its own entity as a result of movement. It is an interest in abstraction, where I leave out narration, in order to stay present with the sounds and refrain from attaching meaning and hence judgment on them, which is where a deeper experience of sound and hence its source, usually ends. I leave it up to an exploration to navigate through an open interplay of movement creating sound and sound bouncing back to the ear: the sound stops (at least in a generalized volume perception) when the body is in stillness. This silence however, I understand as part of the movement and soundscape that explores perception of time and space as well as contractions and expansions of sounds. Perhaps this can be imagined similar to moments between inhalation and exhalation or the contractions of muscles. However, as abstract as this mode of listening is, it is also a response to a gaze othering from an orientalist point of view. A dance that proposes listening hence asks the listener to challenge their gaze and be present in an audio-sensorial situation.

As Voegelin writes:

> Listening, in this sense, is an aesthetic activity that challenges the philosophical tradition of the West, which, according to film theorist Chris-

> tian Metz, is based on a hierarchy between the senses which positions sound in the attributal location, sublimated to the visual and its linguistic structure. In that position sound is left to describe and enhance but never to do and become (Voegelin, 2010, p. 13).

Similar to this position of sound, dance practitioners not coming from a Western lineage of art are continuously denied entry to ontologies of *doing* and *becoming*: we are left to represent, justify and describe to either sceptics of *traditions* or to curatorial concepts of empowering an othered body with sometimes genuine, but often pretentious charitable grandiosity, seeking to satisfy a fetishizing eye within the markets of art. Both situations – are gut wrenching. With the burden of a colonial past, which in this case led to the abolishment of local dance practices, to the reinvention of them as constructed traditions, used for false propagation of an ancient past, class and cast divides for performers, our positions as dancers today remain complicated. The reinvented tradition is both problematic and eminent in the attempt of repair for the idea of a postcolonial nation. It is its' exclusiveness and disregard for the rightful lineage of the temple dancers, that remains disturbing. The term *tradition* (Hobsbawm, Ranger 1983) is of course loaded, but too complex to be abandoned with simple one-sided argumentation and the same applies to *ritual* as a term and idea. It is not a secret anymore that Bharatanatyam is a reinvented form and the label of *tradition* a strategic marker.[6] In theory it is perhaps easy to take one position, but as a practitioner this is a much more complicated reality, as we do not only deal with theoretical terms, but with practices. The term *classical* attached to the dance is even more problematic, as it copies ideologies and aesthetics of Western classical art: all that, which modern and contemporary dance movements oppose, was imposed and at the same time strategically glorified from within. As a practitioner today, who seeks to critically reflect through practice and can not rely on theory alone, it has been and most likely will continue to be a challenging journey to withstand unreflected and uninformed interventions and demands to explain more than being encouraged to deepen a practice, that seeks to find genuine decolonial strategies, rather than to either carry on a recent lineage of conceited classicism, or simply move to the obliviousness of Western contemporary dance and its equally constructed idea of *progressiveness* (Bhambra, 2007), which is likely more than partially based on non-Western ideas and philosophies. I do not share the same fear of form and old teachings towards a never-ending search for originality. Chaos, color, improvisation, drone, durational and meditative qualities, to name a few, are not new to many artistic practices labeled as *classical* and *traditional* in many regions of South Asia today – in dance and music. But both ideologies – *classical/traditional* – have deeply changed exactly those qualities. However, remaining in a constructed category of *tradition* as a result of a past as described, is an equally discontented experience. With consideration of the history and strategic usage of the categorization of *traditional*, *classical* and *contemporary* as conflicting and hierarchical, I stand critical towards all of them as terminologies. In view of these constructed boundaries, I seek to explore possibilities of working with the material openly, but mindfully. I resonate with the words of dancer and choreographer Chandralekha:

> I have increasingly been disturbed by current Western critical opinion which so effortlessly glamorizes and valorizes Eastern 'traditions' in an uncritical manner entirely from an orientalist' and patronizing perspective. For us, in our Eastern contexts, both our 'traditionality' and our 'modernity' are complex and problematic areas which are not abstract theoretical categories but real every day concerns – both of life and of performing arts (Chandralekha 2010, p. 378).

The same applies to diasporic contexts and perhaps becomes even more complicated, as in my experience an unreflected critique on authenticity on the location of voice continues to censor diasporic communities. In my case, the shared Dravidian, Tamizh culture of Tamizh Nadu and the island of Sri Lanka, where my mother would fall in love with Bharatanatyam and like other comrades would bring it passed the forts of Europe to Germany, seeking new hope, which got lost to a war in her homeland. With all this in mind – both in cognitive and physical memory – this listening practice is an act of resistance in a world where the constant drone of the ongoing colonial project of capitalism/progressive modernity drowns voices and narratives of people and countless species in a never-ending machinery, where the body is fully mechanized in order to be part of it: to quiet down and listen with depth and care to subtleties, silences and noises alike and dance, is empowering to me, with or without putting a narration or a loud political statement on top. It proposes to be a soft resistance within a harsh world. And when I write of silence I make a difference between a sonic silence within an artistic practice, to staying silent in unjust situations.

Language in particular holds a desolate place in my heart. I feel deprived of a language that I can confidently call my mother tongue. Even though Berlin is known as an extremely multicultural city today, 80s and 90s Berlin was still getting used to this. Pressured by the German side of the family, my mother did not speak Tamizh with us at home, so that we would not become "outsiders." Having grown up in a single-parent household this of course had an effect on how one feels at home and secure in a language and society: emotions such as humor, love, sadness, anger, as well as expressions, sarcasm, idioms and literature communicated and taught by a parent eager to follow German integration politics, while still learning that very language herself, of course compromises on a lot. Until today I have to focus hard trying to avoid to stutter when speaking in German. And though I understand and can speak broken Tamizh having grown up in the community, all this leaves constant feelings of inadequacy and seclusion towards both cultural contexts I belong to. I know many first-generation migrant kids feel the same. And it was during the times of deepening my listening when I have thought back to our dance classes and realized how the sounds of the nattuvangam cymbals, the mridangam drums, the violin, flute – the vibration of brass and woods –, the abstract *sollukattus* (rhythmic syllables) and *svaras* (musical notes) have always been more impactful to me than the text. Though largely understanding and studying their meanings, words are much more abstract to me than rhythms and melodies. The latter always seem so clear in what they communicate and which emotions they speak to. How they resonate in the body and how the body responds and is moved by them. In the heart, mind, from fingers to toes – the *abhinaya* and *mudras* move with the

sound. *Lāsya* and *tāṇḍava*, the feminine and masculine qualities and motions in one body moved by rhythm, melody and tanpura drone. As well as all which goes much beyond that. That, which may not be able to be condensed into words.
________________ I can feel how my troubled relationship to language significantly influences my listening. And so that feeling of seclusion invites to other captivating places. Places of frequencies and resonances. Of body, sound, immediate and distant surrounding, further appealing to cosmic connection. And so after all, in the vastness of it all, words seem as fascinating and crucial as they seem limiting and insufficient.

In the wider context of the construct of national umbrella languages, inconsiderate of the many local differences of the use and function of the word, is in itself violent. And further forcing people to adopt the languages of the colonizer and ideologies they come with (objective, scientific, rational, heteronormative), this plays a major role in the erasure of various local epistemologies. Here I propose listening, even before language enters, as a decolonial strategy applying it to various modes. Using this practice to spend time with organisms and living beings, listening to mountains, winds, waters, plants and other beings, can be used as an approach to unlearn anthropocentric points of views.

> Knowledge of the colonized world, and its increasingly transformed nature, was intrinsic to colonial domination (Pratt, 1992; Drayton, 2000). (...) The 'Orientalist' discourses of colonialism (Said, 1978; Moore-Gilbert, 1997) took as their subjects both people and nature. Indeed, the two were commonly linked in loosely theorized (and deeply racist) discourses that dismissed as unordered, undisciplined, worthless and uncivilized the 'wildness' of exotic and remote peoples and landscapes. For indigenous peoples, colonialism reached 'into our heads' (Smith, 1999), and it did the same (with very different implications) for the colonizer: colonization changed the very categories within which nature and society were conceived (William M Adams and Martin Mulligan, 2003, p. 4).

To engage with the environment through modes of listening requires an openness towards what is being listened to in flexible and humble ways and proposes to assist in rethinking the notions of human and nature as separate and the latter being subordinated to the first. Even if it does not offer practical solutions necessary to act against the environmental crises, it intends to contribute to the conversations around the issues through an embodied philosophy as part of this listening practice, not only through cognitive, but kinaesthetic learning. It can be as simple as taking a walk in a forest or by the sea, taking a deep breath and feeling transformed, even healed. I perceive this as a dialogue between various beings: rather through words, through breathing, being together, listening. Incorporating this into my dance practice certainly informs the dance by stimulating somatic awareness, mindful sensing and decision-making, as well as physical fluidity. And I further link this with fluidity in gender: not necessarily as an explicit gender category as often described in more Eurocentric queer discourses. There are many subtle hints in mythology, but also clear evidence in various texts and it is important to note that my writing is not a modern queering of texts but a re-entering of abandoned ones under colonial rule. Many precolonial societies and groups of people have embraced queer existences not only in myths, but through their own terminologies and even legal protections. The Kamashastra, the book of love and desire (written between 3rd and 1st centuries BCE), refers to people of third nature, as *tritya-prakriti* and it is stated in the Arthashastra, an Indian treatise on politics, economics, the function of the state and social organization (written between 3rd century BCE and 2nd century CE), that nobody can insult or do an act of cruelty against them, for which a specified punishment under law existed. With the use of religion as part of the colonial project, the notion of queer identities was strategically labeled as *unnatural*. And so decolonizing relationships of *natural* and *unnatural*, whether plant bodies or queer bodies, by reclaiming and rereading passed on knowledge is essential to the fluid listening explorations within my body practice. In her writing the scholar Ruth Vanita wonderfully makes sense of how she uses mythologies to reclaim queer, as well as interspecies inclusions within precolonial agreements of sharing an ecosystem and life on this planet:

> The single most remarkable feature of medieval stories of the deities is their multiplicity and variability. Almost any variation that can be imagined exists somewhere. Capable of taking on any form, the divine is made available in multiple ways (...) as infinitely flexible and available – as male, female, neuter; as animal, bird, tree, jewel, river; as present in all elements and all forms of life. The Puranic gods are not just celebrated as omnipresent in a philosophical sense; the stories of their doings represent them as taking on all forms, incarnating as different types of creatures (for instance, Vishnu is incarnated as a boar and a fish) including humans of different ages, castes and genders. The absence of any clearcut philosophical boundary between gods and humans, or indeed gods and other living beings, allows for the deifying of all actions and every way of life (Vanita, 2000, p. 58–59).

And lastly, I experience the tremendous healing effects of listening on the body, as various listening practices propose. Here, it is necessary to point out again the issue of the Euro-Americentric lineage of art. When writing about a practice that can be clearly linked to sound art, the first people one might think of are John Cage and Pauline Oliveros, who undoubtedly are important figures in their contexts. But it is necessary to give balance to an imbalance and misconceptions of a narrative dominated by Euro-America continuously announcing itself as the pioneers of innovation, progressive and contemporary ideas. Hence it is important to clarify that their work has not been influential to mine. It is no surprise to get to know that Oliveros, who coined the term *Deep Listening*, was influenced by Native American ritual, meditation and music practices, and Cage by the work of Sri Lankan philosopher and historian Ananda Coomaraswamy and the Indian musician Gita Sarabhai, who taught him of the depiction of eight emotions in the concept of *rasa* aesthetics, as well as Zen Buddhism, having profound influence on his approach to music. Due to my interest in sound and performance I am often asked how Cage's work influenced my listening practice, rather than for example Chandralekha or even the idea of *rasa*. And I want to answer this here explicitly: not at all. I draw from the idea of *rasa*, trees in forests, waters, the idea of morning and evening *ragas*, diasporic bubbles, the people I am referencing, as well as wonderful colleagues, Krishna and other hybrids, Thumri songs rupturing my heart, Druphad vocal drones and a lifelong engagement with dance and music. And so I am particularly excited to have come across Nada Yoga, which links body and sound in one practice. The precision already of the description from a practice that thinks about sound from the body and not from an external instrument, of course fascinates me, as this is also what my work reflects about. And probably not as deep as this yogic practice already does.

> Nada Yoga is about sounds. It is the knowledge of the quality of sounds and the way they affect people. The word Nada comes from the Sanskrit root, Nad. Nad means to flow. The etymological meaning of Nada is a process or a stream of consciousness. Generally, the word Nada means sound. In Tantra, it is thought that sound occurs in four dimensions – four levels of sound relating to frequency, degree of fineness and strength. 1. The coarse (ordinary audible, material) sound, 2. the mental sound, 3. the visualised sound and 4. the transcendent sound. According to Nada Yogis and scriptures dealing with Nada Yoga, the original and transcendent sound is the seed from which the whole of creation has grown. The Nada Yogi experiences the macro cosmic universe as a projection of sound vibrations; the whole world as having developed from sound alone (Janakananda, 2009 / 2016).

I do recall how the beginnings of this listening practice quickly synchronized with my Yoga routines, not in a matter of simultaneity but frequency. Listening after aligning, specific and conscious breathing, activating, stretching, sweating, meditating and resting undoubtedly enhances and deepens my hearing experience. I have neither experienced nor learned a Nada Yoga practice. But in the spirit of both – exploring practices deepening listening as a bodily experience, as well as decolonizing a Euro-Americentric lineage of progressive (here sound) art, I can't wait to find my way towards this Nada Yoga practice in the future.

The different modes of listening inform each other on essential levels: diving into different modes of listening to sounds, stories and dances is a process of learning and reflecting, being present, responding, exploring, embodying and giving visibility to them in a process of rethinking a methodology of making visible: rather than proposing a voyeuristic experience, a situation of sound involving the listener and asking them to engage, be present and reflect on the way they digest the heard – here a dance. For me this is an ongoing process of wondering, listening, imagining, dancing, asking, repositioning, renegotiating, exploring, clarifying, unpacking, insisting, trying out and letting go.

This text was first published in *Many Forms of Learning, Year Four*, 2020, curated by Alexander Graham Roberts and published through the Iceland University of the Arts, LHI. It has been edited for the *Listening Biennial Reader*. Image on page 41: print by Sigurður Atli Sigurðsson.

NOTES

1. The term *India* is a "historical construct of relatively recent origin" (Vanita, 2000, XV) and compresses a tremendously wide geographical area with an enormous variety of languages, practices and groups under one national umbrella and it remains a challenge to use one word which simplifies this complexity. However, for reader friendly purposes I will use it in consideration of the content and frame of this text.
2. The invention of the terms *tradition* and *progress* as terms themselves are largely responsible for this dichotomy. This is a critique scholars fortunately have attended to for several decades already. There is a complex back and forth of well-formulated arguments and equally exclusions in this debate, such as indigenous practices.
3. *Mudra* means to seal, mark or gesture in Sanskrit and are hand gestures used in many Indian dances used for both abstract dance and story telling (*hasta mudras*). Yogic and tantric practices also include mudras to intensify the effects of yoga or meditation, enhancing the flow of energy. Today's use of mudras in dance, yogic and practices are not linked and a comparison requires a study of its own.
4. The Natya Shastra, a Sanskrit text on performing arts, explains abhinaya as *abhi* – towards, and *naya* – to carry: to carry the spectator towards the meaning.
5. "Rasa is an Indian concept of aesthetic flavour and an essential element of any work of visual, literary, or performing art that can only be suggested, not described. It is a kind of contemplative abstraction in which the inwardness of human feelings suffuses the surrounding world of embodied forms." (Britannica)
6. The research and writings of Davesh Soneji bring a lot of light to this complex history of Bharatanatyam, which are not the focus of this writing, but nevertheless a matter I continue to deal with from within my practice.

Adams, William (Bill), and Mulligan, Martin. *Decolonizing Nature: Strategies for Conservation in a Post-Colonial Era. Taylor and Francis*, 2012.

Bhabha, Homi K. *The Location of Culture*. W. Ross MacDonald School Resource Services Library, 2012.

Bhambra, Gurminder K. Rethinking Modernity: *Postcolonialism and the Sociological Imagination*. Basingstoke, Hampshire: Palgrave, 2009.

Britannica. Rasa. https://www.britannica.com/art/rasa (accessed June 20, 2020).

Chandralekha. *Reflections on New Directions in Indian Dance*, in Davesh Soneji's Bharatanatyam, *A Reader*. Oxford University Press, 2010.

Doshi, Tishani. *Everything Begins Elsewhere*. Copper Canyon Press, 2013.

Fukuoka, Masanobu. *The One-Straw Revolution*. New Yorck Review Books Classics, 1978/2010.

Gaztambide-Fernández, Rubén. *Decolonial Options and Artistic/AestheSic Entanglements: An Interview with Walter Mignolo*. Decolonization: Indigeneity, Education & Society 3 (1), 2014.

Gopalakrishnan, Paravur. *The Gita Govinda*, (translation) as The Song Celestial. Sanbun Publishers, 2008.

Gulan, Varun, and Anoop Mythili. *Contemporary Women's Writing in India*. Lexincton Books, 2014.

Gupt, Bharat. *Hindu View on Homosexuality: Dr Bharat Gupt India Inspires Views*. Youtube. https://www.youtube.com/watch?v=x8V6WzOoqeM (accessed June 24, 2020)

Hastings, Rachel N. *Performative Decolonization: Critical Performance Ethnography, Rize and the Battle to Articulate Race*. Edited by Eduardo Mendieta. Radical Philosophy Review 12 (1): 41–60, 2009.

Hobsbawm, E. J., and T. O. Ranger. *The Invention of Tradition*. Cambridge [Cambridgeshire]: Cambridge University Press, 1983.

Janakananda, Swami. *Nada Yoga – outer and inner*. yogameditation.com. https://www.yogameditation.com/reading-room/nada-yoga/(accessed June 19, 2020)

Lal, Malashri and Gokhale, Namita. *Finding Radha, A Quest for Love*. Penguin Books, 2018.

Mantillake Madamperum Arachchilage, Sudesh. *Colonial Choreography: Staging Sri Lankan Dancers Under British Colonial Rule From The 1870s – 1930s*. Ph.D., College Park, MD.: University of Maryland, 2018.

Miller, Barabara S. T*he Gita Govinda of Jeyadeva: Songs of the Dark Lord*. Columbia University Press, 1977.

Mikolai, Sara. *Listening – sound narratives of a dance*, performance and installation work at Iceland University of the Arts, 2020.

Mohapatra, Sujata. Sujata Mohapatra's Pallavi. Youtube. https://www.youtube.com/watch?v=Oqj3Y-hifoag (accessed June 1, 2020)

Mookerjee, Ajit, and Madhu Khanna. *The Tantric Way: Art, Science, Ritual*. Thames & Hudson, 2003.

Muni, Bharata. Translated by Ghosh, Manomohan. *The Natya Shastra. A treatise on Hindu Dramaturgy and Histrionics* (Volume I: Chapter I–XXVII). Calcutta, The Asiatic. Society, 1950.

Nandikesvarar. Translated by Coomaraswamy, Ananda. *The Mirror Of Gesture: Being The Abhinaya Darpana Of Nandikesvara* (1917). Kissinger's Legacy Prints, 2010.

Phillpotts, Bertha S. *The Life of the Icelander Jón Ólafsson, Traveller to India, Written by himself and completed about 1661 A.D: With a continuation, by another hand, up to his Death in 1679*. Volumes I–II. Taylor and Francis, 2017.

Reed, Susan A. *Dance and the Nation: Performance, Ritual, and Politics in Sri Lanka*. Madison: University of Wisconsin Press, 2010.

Shiva, Vandana. *Staying Alive: Women, Ecology and Development*. Zed Books, 1989.

Smith, Linda Tuhiwai. *Decolonizing Methodologies: Research and Indigenous Peoples*. Zed Books, 1999.

Soneji, Davesh. *Bharatanatyam, A Reader*. Oxford University Press, 2010.

Vanita, Ruth, Kirwai, Saleem. *Same-Sex Love in India. Readings from Literature and History*. St. Martin's Press, 2000.

Voegelin, Salomé. *Listening to Noise and Silence; Towards a philosopy of sound art*. The Continuum International Publishing Group Ltd. London, 2010.

Wilhelm, Amara Das. *Tritiya-Prakriti: People of the Third Sex: Understanding Homosexuality, Transgender Identity, and Intersex Conditions through Hinduism*. Xlibris, 2017.

DANIELA MEDINA POCH

The Land of Thunder and Lightning — Energy and Colonial Footprint

Territory is life itself and life is not to be sold, it is to be loved and defended. Territory is the place to dream our future with dignity!
Francia Márquez, environmental activist[1]

How are Germany and the Wayuu community in Northern South America interdependent? What is the Source of our everyday Resources, and in what ways is acknowledgment of these Sources an essential step in stopping the vertical relationship of exploitation between territories and communities? If colonization imposed a singular worldview, then listening could be a way to unveil a plurality of voices.

The association of noise and power has never really been broken in the human imagination argues R. Murray Schafer in his book *The Soundscape, Our Sonic Environment and the Tuning of the World*. "In earlier times, all natural events were explained as miracles."[2] Loud noises, such as the sound of thunder, evoked fear and respect back to the earliest times, seeming to be the expression of divine power. In the Modern era and beyond this fear and respect was transferred from natural sounds (thunder, volcano, storm) to the sounds created by industrial machinery, signifying a power shift. In a similar way, it can be argued that colonialism was the imposition of a monotonal and singular vocal structure which silenced the diversity of voices previously there. As Schafer posits, "Linguistic accuracy is not merely a matter of lexicography. We perceive only what we can name. In a man-dominated world, when the name of a thing dies, it is dismissed from society, and its very existence may be imperiled."

Every living being exists because all other living beings exist. Through euphonies and cacophonies of complex interconnections, life reverberates and echoes throughout the planet. There are connections that are more visible and easily imagined than others. The Amazon Rainforest may be so diverse because it nourishes itself from sand that travels on the wind from the Sahara Desert across the Atlantic Ocean. At the same time, the northernmost peak of South America is affected by Germany's energy consumption – why is that?

A possible starting point to answer this question might be by tracing Resources back to their Sources. A Source is where components originate; it is usually active, and its existence is often entangled within a complex environmental network. On the contrary, a Resource is understood as a means – an asset that functions efficiently. Resources are often extracted and manipulated and obey market regulation. The difference between a Source and a Resource lies in human intervention – humans transform Sources into Resources, adapting them to the demand of the market. Resources are therefore often understood in numbers. Through the transformation and numeric abstraction of Resources we often forget the Sources they spring from, and the workflow that lies behind them.

In a similar process of abstraction, in the neoliberal world we live in, the infrastructures and technologies that surround us have become deeply adopted by and adapted to our lifestyles, to the point of appearing ubiquitous – in effect, a background noise we have learned to ignore. From within these frameworks, we are unable to distinguish the apparatus that lies behind them, not only on a technical level but also in regard to the models they pursue and sustain. An equivalent on a smaller scale might be the energy that is powering this computer right now.

Where does our electricity come from?

> The three major categories of energy for electricity generation are fossil fuels (coal, natural gas, and petroleum), nuclear energy, and renewable energy Sources. Most electricity is generated with steam turbines using fossil fuels, nuclear, biomass, geothermal, and solar thermal energy.[3]

A TERRITORY FULL OF AURAL CONTRASTS

In the northern part of the South American continent lies the Guajira Peninsula, an extensive desert right on the Caribbean coast which is home to the largest aboriginal community in both Colombia and Venezuela. Originally a nomadic tribe, having migrated 3,000 years ago from the Amazon Rainforest and Antilles to the desert, the Wayúu and Afrowayúu have since preserved this territory as a communitary space.

La Guajira is filled with aural contrasts: In the background, the wind as a means of circulation, flowing with diverse speeds and intensities, roaring stereophonically across the territory. The wind shapes the paths of the sand and sculpts the sand dunes that give texture to the landscape. There are some places where the wind does not fluctuate, and that quietness and stillness corresponds with a funeral ritual, a celebration of life and death in the Wayúu community, at Cabo de la Vela. Along the coast, next to the infinite kilometers of sand and wind, almost as a surprise, a mass of salty water appears, caressing the coast. Waves rock incessantly, receding, absorbing, and exploding repeatedly – always different, but at the same time constant, mini-cyclical explosions, which

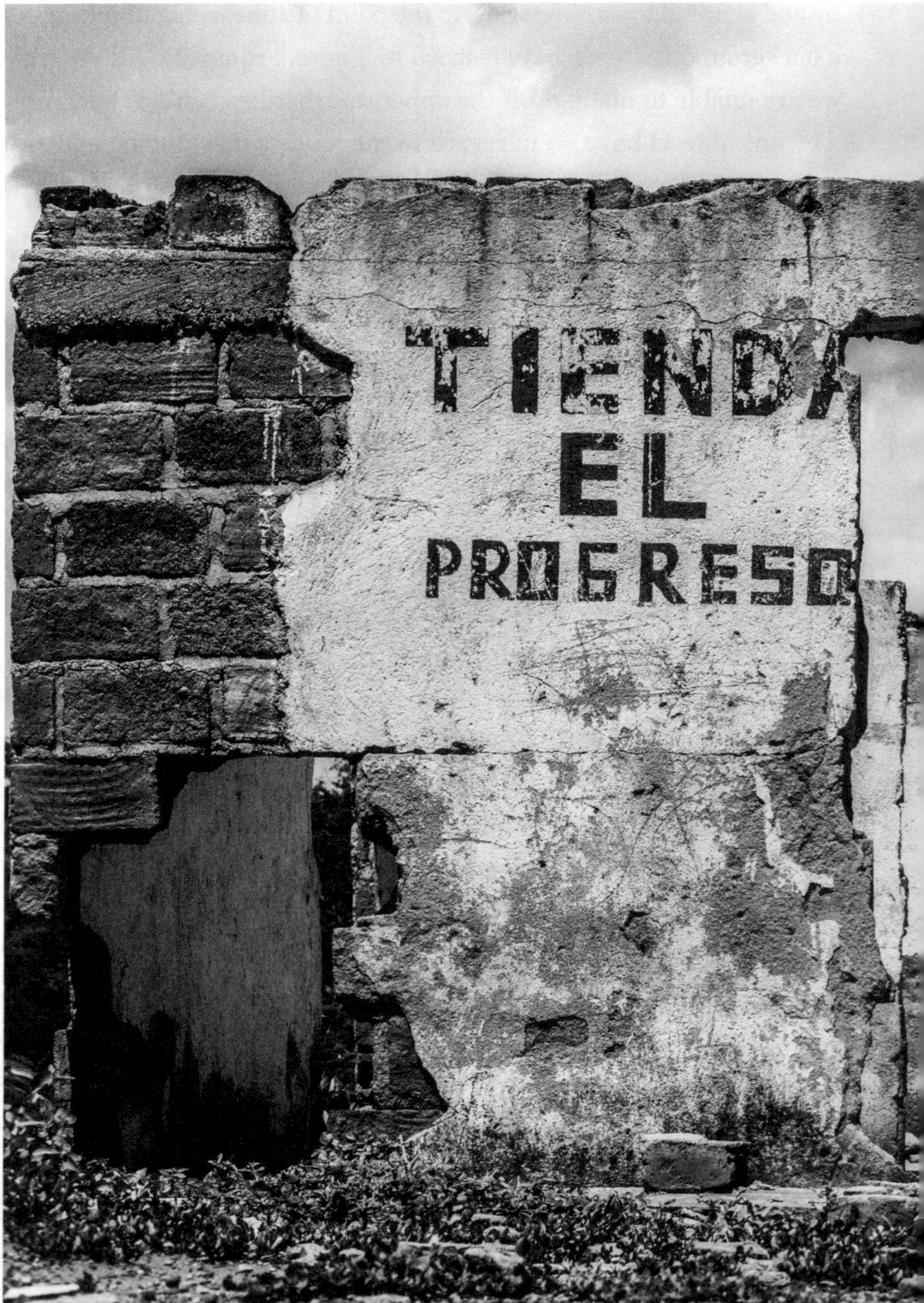
TIENDA
EL
PROGRESO

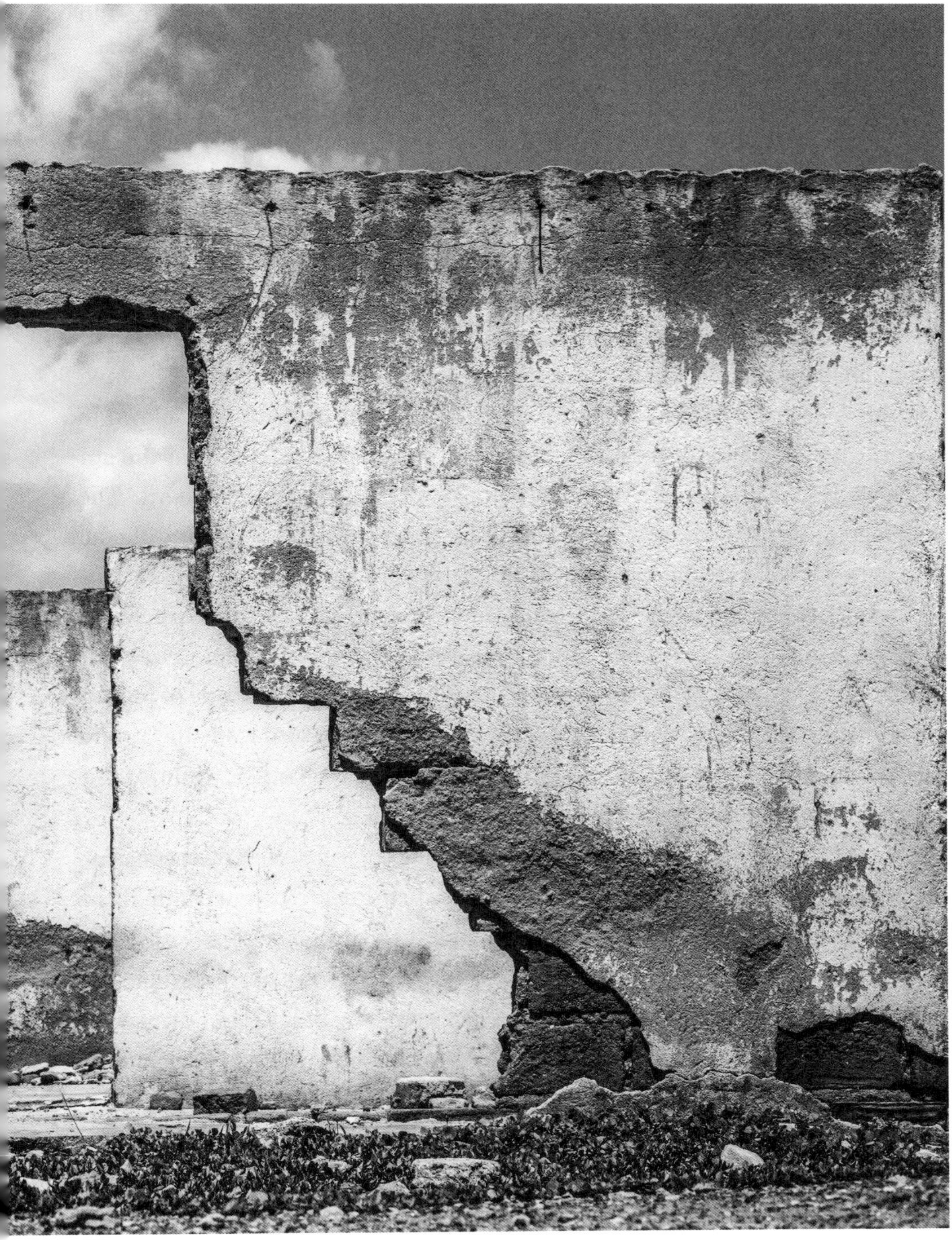

Fig. 1. Conrado Espitia, Sebastián, 2017. Retrieved from “Las Huellas del Cerrjón”.

despite their impotence generate tranquility by repetition, or at least the illusion of repetition.

Throughout the desert, there are Wayúu and Afrowayúu settlements or *rancherias* built from Trupillo tree and Yotojoro, the heart of a dried cactus.[4] Inside these rancherias, a hammock or *chinchorro* always hangs. Goats bleat, while women of the community weave colorful *mochilas* (saddlebags) and dresses – the needle traversing colorful threads, knotting, pulling, accompanied by some chit-chat. I wonder if those colors are a way to dialogue with the dry desert.

During their daily work, shepherds from these communities use aerophone instruments, in which the air vibrates mainly inside a tube. *Sawawa*, *Wootoroi*, *Maasi*, *Wa'wai*, *Kasha*, *Tropa* are all blown instruments, blown in reciprocal dialogue with the wind. Such instruments are used to lead the animals, while also serving as a means of sound expression for the shepherd.[5] The language of the Wayúu is Wayuunaiki.[6] The consonants are long, and the accent generally falls on the second syllable of the word. In rituals or celebrations – marking the first menstrual cycle of a Wayúu woman, for example – when a request for a dream or the healing of some disease is made, the Kasha – a bi-membranophone percussion instrument – is played. A type of drum made of pine or ceiba with a twisted goat hide at its ends, the instrument also leads the *Yonna Kasha* dance, two members of the community chasing each other, while extending their colorful dresses to the windy desert.

Nearby, one can hear the struggling engines of jeeps, with their considerable tires and traction, come from urban centers to the desert. From within these vehicles one can hear *vallenato* music ringing through the stereos – rhythms and melodies from the urban region of la Guajira that involve the accordion, the *guacharaca*, the *maracas* and the box. In fact, some say that it was German settlers who, in the mid 19TH century, brought the accordion to the municipality of Riohacha.[7] The *vallenata* box was an afro-colombian addition that, along with the *guacharaca* – an instrument from the aboriginal communities, gives *vallenato* its particular sound.

Colonial division of territories affected the Wayúu and Afrowayúu communities, because they came to belong to two nation states: Colombia and

Venezuela. While some borders have been shut down, despite geopolitical divisions, the communities strive for the preservation of this territory as a borderless living being with its own memory.

The Wayúu and Afrowayúu understand themselves as a tribe of about 56 families. The grandmother is the leader of the community – the *Piaachi* – and the person in charge of healing. The grandmother of the community is a self-taught healer who has dreamed of her role and the way to carry it out. She has a special channel of communication through which she can express what the territory needs and its goals.

According to the Wayúu worldview, the world was created by a romance between the Rain and the Earth; to make the Earth happy, the Rain chanted, and as it yodeled, Thunder and Lightning roared and released energy that allowed life to emerge: first the flora, then the fauna, and finally, humans.[8]

Despite this myth, since 2010 there has been no more energy-producing thunder or lightning, nor have there been raindrops chanting, as a result of which, in 2014 the territory was declared a region in crisis. "The *Macuira*, our territory, is not good for walking anymore, nor for growing crops or nourishing our animals. We are all thirsty and slowly malnourished. We are burning," the *Piaachi* said in a recent interview.[9]

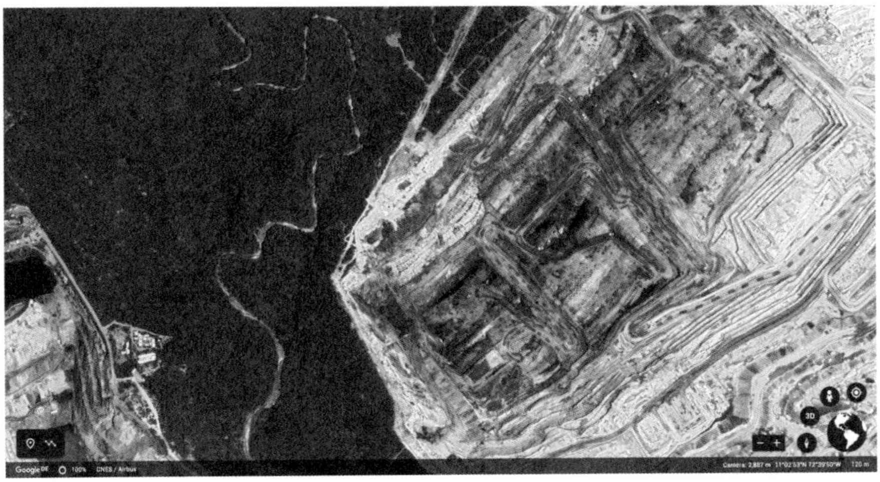

Fig. 2. Retrieved from Google Satellite Image.
Copyright 2020 CNES / Airbus, Maxar Technologies, Map data @2020.

In the midst of these conditions, Cerrejón, one of the largest open coal mines in the world, was founded.

The landscape changes from a palette of light orange, blue and green, to a vast, concave surface – a human valley of grey and black patches, in combination with heavy machinery. Backhoes carve the earth. Machinery reverberates, digging and extracting. A cacophony of minerals: industrial metal – a transformed mineral – and crashing and crumbling layers of earth in search of coal, an untransformed mineral. The operation is so big that no human noises surpass the acoustic presence and dominance of machinery. Huge wheels dig into the ground, crushing anything small. The sound of extraction is like that of something being forced out and, through this removal, immediately becoming something else. These incessant vibrations have dominated the landscape from 1976 until the present day.

Cerrejón was both a promise of employment and "development" and a tool to bring attention to the zone. Nevertheless, it has turned out to be one of the main sources of problems for both the region and the community. Being mostly owned by foreign companies (BHP, Anglo American and Glencore), 98% of what Cerrejón yields is exported with only 10% of total sales remaining as profit for the state.[10] On top of that, due to the centralized system of royalties as well as regional mismanagement, the community rarely receives any profit.

Beyond a disproportionate economic relationship, Cerrejón has had severe implications for the local Wayúu communities, depriving them of basic necessities and prioritizing the project's economic ambitions over the life of the community. Cerrejón has caused numerous cases of involuntary resettlement, affecting the community's traditional lifestyle and subjecting them to conditions imposed by the management company. Moreover, deep excavation and mining has caused severely unhealthy air pollution; due to inadequate consultation processes, the air is full of particles of coal which have already affected the health of newborn babies and also disrupted the balance of the aquifers across the whole zone. "Among the evidence submitted to the UN are photos of skin diseases and evidence of respiratory conditions in Wayúu children,"[11] says a recent note published by the *London Telegraph*. On top of that, official sources affirm the mine has financed illegal military groups during civil conflicts. "During this country-wide conflict the communities in the mining regions Cesar and in La Guajira suffered greatly. The role of mining companies during this period is subject to controversial allegations related to displacement and collaboration with paramilitary."[12]

The existence of an open coal mine in the desert is highly paradoxical and problematic: open coal mines require double the amount of water that closed coal mines do. Due to this structural conundrum, Cerrejón has privatized the Rancheria River, the main water Source in the desert. Furthermore, it has purposely dried out several of the streams that divert from the riverbed in order to extract coal from beneath them. In 2019 and 2020, after alerts from the community and deeper research carried out by the Universidad Nacional and United Nations, the Constitutional Court twice sued the company for causing life-threatening pollution and human rights violations. Today, Cerrejón is still operating, with a license to extract coal until 2034.

WHEN WILL WATER BE MORE VALUABLE THAN COAL?

To ask when water will have a higher value than coal is to ask when our collective survival will have a higher value than the accumulation of profit by a few. "While Wayúu children don't have a single drop of drinkable water, Cerrejón spends 17,000,000 L of water daily to extract coal, an economic activity which disproportionately benefits multinationals. With the 4700 members of the community whose life has perished due to the unbearable conditions, it seems as if the state is allowing an indigenous genocide. Is the life of these children less valuable than a gram of coal from these multinationals?"[13] *Telesur* asked in a report from 2017.

Despite efforts to penalize multinationals and compensate the affected communities, the mechanisms of compensation fail to acknowledge the complexity of the effects and consequences over a longer timeframe – not only environmental, but social, cultural and symbolic. As Arturo Escobar says, "the process of deterritorialization not only includes the dispossession of a population, but also the process of removing the territory from the population – the population is transformed."[14] Are there economic measures that account for this involuntary transformation?

What keeps Cerrejón in existence is the fact that, even with the penalties, their business is still highly profitable, which underlines the disproportionate value given to commercial interests. How to quantify the cultural and symbolic value of a river to an aboriginal community? Such values are hard to quantify, and most of the time they are not even recognized. But what if we were to devise a real accountability that includes social, cultural and environmental effects in both the immediate and the longer term? As Nataša Petrešin-Bachelez suggests, "By exploiting their natural Resources, and hence by durably damaging their environment, industrialized countries owe a huge debt to countries of the South. This ecological debt is much bigger than the financial debt the South supposedly owes the North. Taking it into account would completely transform the way we think about the global economy."[15]

A NEOCOLONIAL DISTORTION OF ETHICS

Between Berlin's abundant Spree river and Köpenicker Straße stands the Heizkraftwerk, a combined heat and power plant in the Mitte district. Despite the fact that energy company Vattenfall's Heizkraftwerk is visually so imposing – an industrial castle with two large chimneys and red lights that dominates the landscape of the Spree, its aural presence is barely perceptible. This absence of sound from such a large facility brings to mind an industrial deafness and the invisible trail that runs from Sources to commodities. The industrial processing of energy remains concealed within the headquarters of the factory, but what is commonly heard instead of industrial noises is the vibrations of the energy the plant produces, in the form of electronic music floating from nearby venues

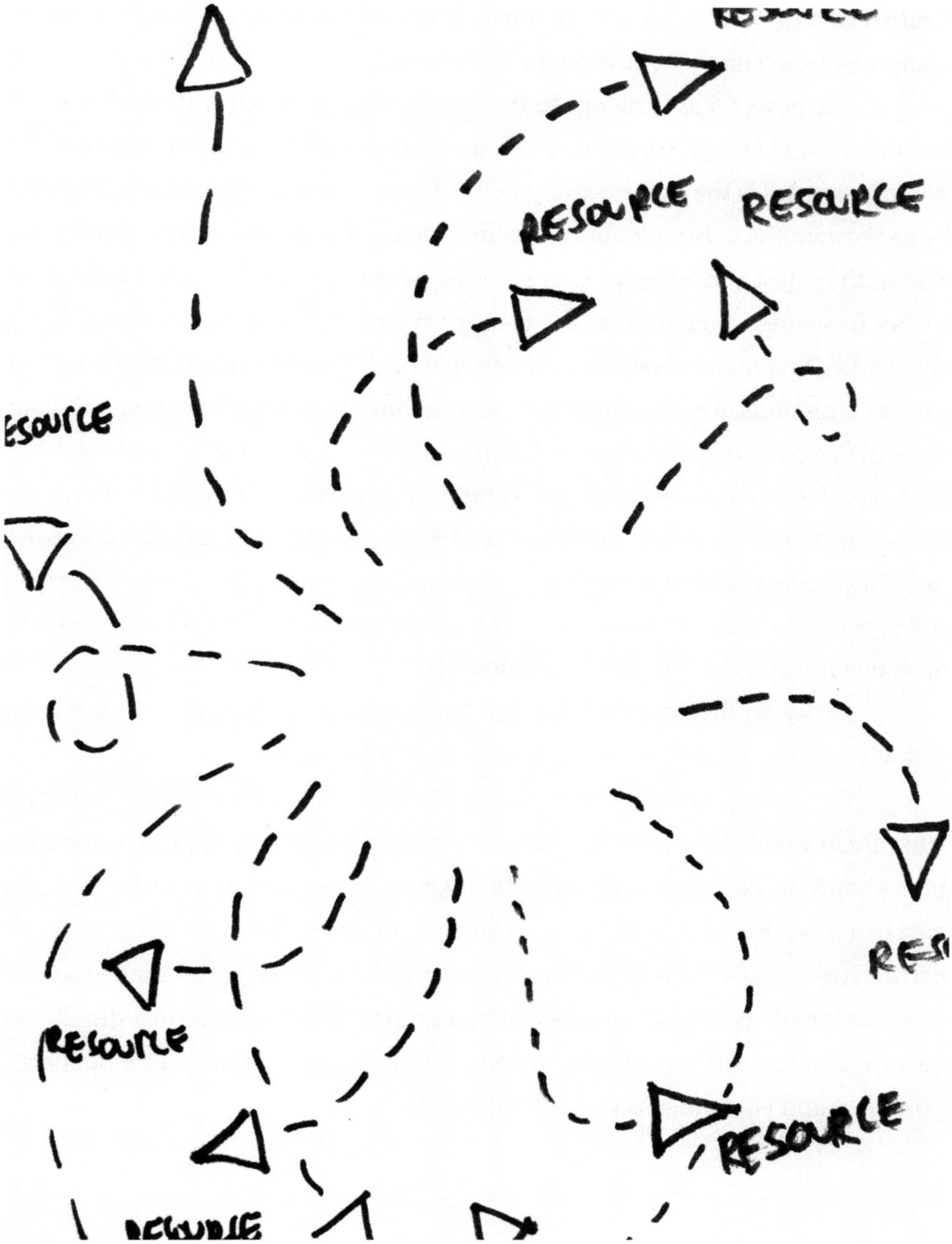

Fig 3. Medina Poch, Daniela, 2020. Sources and Resources.

Kraftwerk and Tresor. Electronic music is one of the first outcomes we can reclaim from such energy conversion.

The power plant belongs to the Swedish energy group Vattenfall Europe Wärme, which belongs to a German sub-group responsible for the operation of the plant. Vattenfall is the electric utility for the German states of Hamburg, Mecklenburg-Vorpommern, Brandenburg, Berlin, Saxony-Anhalt, Thuringia, and Saxony. The sixth largest consumer of energy in the world, Germany imports more than half of its energy. Nonetheless, the country claims it is on its way towards being "the world's first major renewable energy economy"[16] and has a reputation for low carbon emissions. These details notwithstanding, Vattenfall has taken the commercial decision to do business in Colombia. "Colombian coal is attractive for Vattenfall both from a commercial and technical perspective and enables us to maintain a diversified sourcing portfolio"[17] states the company on its official website, establishing its position towards the situation at Cerrejón. The official Cerrejón website affirms that "We generate social, environmental, economic and individual value for the Guajira region and Colombia."

In the land where thunder and lightning created life, there is not even water anymore. All this energy is now in the Global North.

Reviewing the national environmental indexes which makes countries such as Germany, Norway or Canada so proud, in relation to the Resources they import and the containers of waste they export, suggests that these indexes are part of a neocolonial strategy of the distortion of ethics. What is the use of green certificates if they only include the domestic activities and ignore the respective importation of resources and exportation of waste? Green certificates should not be a national award, but should include a real account of the quality of energy produced and consumed on a planetary scale.

WHEN WILL WE STOP PRETENDING THE PLANET IS NOT OUR COMMON TERRITORY?

When will we overcome the fiction of value determined by the market, in which a barrel of oil reached negative values in April of this year[18] but its extraction affected the ground, water, air, flora and fauna of its Source? When will we understand that we need each other for our planetary survival, and that environmental sustainability cannot happen at the expense of the lives of others? If Western concerns about climate change don't go hand in hand with a deep process of decolonialization, it's a one-sided struggle, incomplete and probably ineffective.

> *We have modern problems for which there are no modern solutions.*
>
> Boaventura de Sousa Santos[19]

Not until we embrace a borderless notion of territory which takes into account the specifics of local communities and also embraces interrelation can we attempt to really transform the notion of nature as solely a resource to extract, a direction aligned with the probability of human extinction. Borderless planetary awareness is not universalist, nor does it intend to standardize or reduce the complexities of communities. Instead, it puts in place horizontal exchange dynamics based on such particularities. Borderless planetary awareness acknowledges that making the Guajira a place that cannot support life and losing the Wayúu community as a consequence, like other communities devastated by resource extraction, is not only a national failure, but a planetary one.

Tracing Resources to their Sources acknowledges the living beings that are part of our planetary equilibrium. Tracing Resources to their Sources can contribute to a planetary society which is not based on production and consumption – a society in which we humans are also seen not as mere Resources, or a work force, but as Sources in our own right. If Resources have value as transformed Sources, let us claim back the value of Sources.

For some aboriginal communities, underground minerals such as coal, oil and gold resonate as Sources themselves – ritual Sources which, through their existence in specific places underneath the ground, trigger processes of rooting and consequent care for the territory.[20] Sources to be worshipped.

If colonization was an imposition of a homogenizing voice, and a consequent silencing of the rest, decolonization must be centered on listening. Only through deep listening can we begin to perceive the contingent composition of sounds and allow other worldviews to emerge. Perhaps it is time to listen – listen to Sources.

This text was first published in the Digital and Printed Publication of *Border Listening / Escucha Liminal*, edited by Alejandra Cárdenas. Berlin: Radical Sounds Latin America, October 2020.

NOTES

1. Márquez, Francia. *Situación que carcome mis entrañas. A propósito de la orden de bombardear el Cauca: Carta abierta.* April 18, 2015.
2. Schafer R. Murray. 1994. *The Soundscape, our Sonic Environment and the Tuning of the World.* Destiny Books.
3. EIA. 2019. "Electricity explained." Electricity in the United States is produced (generated) with diverse energy sources and technologies. Last modified March 2020.https://www.eia.gov/energyexplained/electricity/electricity-in-the-us.php#:~:text=The%20three%20major%20categories%20of,geothermal%2C%20and%20solar%20thermal%20energy.
4. Wooldridge, Anny. 2017. Culture trip. A Brief History of Colombia's Wayuu Tribe. Last updated 3 May, 2017. https://theculturetrip.com/south-america/colombia/articles/a-brief-history-of-colombias-wayuu-tribe/
5. Cultural, Colombia. INSTRUMENTOS MUSICALES WAYUU. concepto de instrumentos wayuu. https://sites.google.com/site/instrumentosmusicaleswayuu/home/concepto-de-instrumentos-wayuu
6. Omniglot. 2020. *The Online Encyclopedia of Writing Systems and Languages.* https://omniglot.com/writing/wayuu.php
7. Martínez, Juan. 2018. BBC Travel. "La sorprendente manera en que Alemania ayudó a crear el vallenato de Colombia." 9, March, 2018 https://www.bbc.com/mundo/vert-tra-43193906
8. Coronado Espitia, Sebastian. 2017. "Las Huellas del Cerrejón - Documental explotación de carbón mina El Cerrejón – La Guajira Colombia." 10 July, 2017 https://www.youtube.com/watch?time_continue=21&v=ryssy7pJhJI&feature=emb_logo
9. Coronado Espitia, Sebastian. 2017. "Las Huellas del Cerrejón – Documental explotación de carbón mina El Cerrejón – La Guajira Colombia." 10 July, 2017 https://www.youtube.com/watch?time_continue=21&v=ryssy7pJhJI&feature=emb_logo

10. Coronado Espitia, Sebastian. 2017. "Las Huellas del Cerrejón – Documental explotación de carbón mina El Cerrejón – La Guajira Colombia." 10 July, 2017 https://www.youtube.com/watch?time_continue=21&v=ryssy7pJhJI&feature=emb_logo
11. Gatten, Emma. 2020. "British lawyers launch UN bid to halt Colombian mine operations." Telegraph 17 June 2020. https://www.youtube.com/watch?v=_9WQjhhrYBo
12. Vattenfall. 2016. "Vattenfall's Hard Coal Procurement Explained Sourcing from Colombia." https://group.vattenfall.com/siteassets/corporate/who-we-are/sustainability/doc/updated_sourcing_from_colombia_130516.pdf May, 2016.
13. Hoyos, Lorena. 2017. "Colombia: indígenas de La Guajira mueren por hambre y falta de agua" teleSUR tv. 10 July, 2017. https://www.youtube.com/watch?v=_9WQjhhrYBo
14. Escobar, Arturo. 2018. Otro Posible es Posible. Caminando hacia las transiciones desde Abya Yala/Afro/Latino-América. Bogotá: Ediciones desde abajo
15. Petrešin-Bachelez, Nataša. 2017. "For Slow Institutions." e-flux journal #85. October, 2017.
16. Burgermeister, J. (n.d.). 2009. Germany: The World's First Major Renewable Energy Economy. RenewableEnergyWorld. Retrieved from https://www.renewableenergyworld.com/2009/04/03/germany-the-worlds-first-major-renewable-energy-economy/#gref. Last modified in March 2009.
17. Vattenfall. 2016. "Vattenfall's Hard Coal Procurement Explained Sourcing from Colombia." https://group.vattenfall.com/siteassets/corporate/who-we-are/sustainability/doc/updated_sourcing_from_colombia_130516.pdf May, 2016.
18. Sullivan, Brian. 2020. CNBC. https://www.cnbc.com/2020/04/26/why-oil-prices -went-negative-and-why-they-can-go-negative-again.html. Last modified on April 26, 2020.
19. Santos, Boaventura de Sousa. 2013. "Public Sphere and Epistemologies of the South". Promoting Access to African Research. African Journals Online. (AJOL). Last modified April, 2013. https://www.ajol.info/index.php/ad/article/view/87540
20. Santos, Bárbara. 2019. *Curación como tecnología Basado en entrevistas a sabedores de la Amazonía*. Bogotá: Instituto Distrital de las Artes.

BIBLIOGRAPHY

Alcoseba Fernandez, Hannah. 2020. Eco-Business. https://www.eco-business.com/news/if-the-philippines-banned-waste-imports-why-is-it-still-the-worlds-dumping-ground/ Last modified March 11, 2020.

Burgermeister, J. (n.d.). 2009. Germany: The World's First Major Renewable Energy Economy. RenewableEnergyWorld. Retrieved from https://www.renewableenergyworld.com/2009/04/03/germany-the-worlds-first-major-renewable-energy-economy/#gref. Last modified in March, 2009.

Cerrejón Main Page. https://www.cerrejon.com/

Coronado Espitia, Sebastian. 2017. "Las Huellas del Cerrejón – Documental explotación de carbón mina El Cerrejón – La Guajira Colombia." 10 July 2017. https://www.youtube.com/watch?time_continue=21&v=ryssy7pJhJI&feature=emb_logo

Cultural, Colombia. INSTRUMENTOS MUSICALES WAYUU. concepto de instrumentos wayuu. https://sites.google.com/site/instrumentosmusicaleswayuu/home/concepto-de-instrumentos-wayuu

EIA. 2019. "Electricity explained." Electricity in the United States is produced (generated) with diverse energy sources and technologies. Last modified March 2020. https://www.eia.gov/energy-explained/electricity/electricity-in-the-us.php#:~:text=The%20three%20major%20categories%20of,geothermal%2C%20and%20solar%20thermal%20energy.

Escobar, Arturo. 2018. Otro Posible es Posible. Caminando hacia las transiciones desde Abya Yala/Afro /Latino-América. Bogotá: Ediciones desde abajo https://tramasymingasparaelbuenvivir.wordpress.com/

Gatten, Emma. 2020. "British lawyers launch UN bid to halt Colombian mine operations." The Telegraph.17 June 2020. British lawyers launch UN bid to halt Colombian mine operations. https://www.youtube.com/watch?v=_9WQjhhrYBo

Hoyos, Lorena. 2017. "Colombia: indígenas de La Guajira mueren por hambre y falta de agua" teleSUR tv. 10 July 2017. https://www.youtube.com/watch?v=_9WQjhhrYBo

Márquez, Francia. 2015. Situación que carcome mis entrañas. A propósito de la orden de bombardear el Cauca: Carta abierta. April 18, 2015.

Martínez, Juan. 2018. BBC Travel. "La sorprendente manera en que Alemania ayudó a crear el vallenato de Colombia." 9, March, 2018 https://www.bbc.com/mundo/vert-tra-43193906

Omniglot. 2020. *The Online Encyclopedia of Writing Systems and Languages*. https://omniglot.com/writing/wayuu.php

Petrešin-Bachelez, Nataša. 2017. "For Slow Institutions." e-flux journal #85. October.

Santos, Bárbara. 2019. *Curación como tecnología Basado en entrevistas a sabedores de la Amazonía*. Bogotá: Instituto Distrital de las Artes.

Santos, Boaventura de Sousa. 2013. "Public Sphere and Epistemologies of the South". Promoting Access to African Research. African Journals Online. (AJOL). Last modified April 2013. https://www.ajol.info/index.php/ad/article/view/87540

Schafer. R. Murray. 1994. *The Soundscape, our Sonic Environment and the Tuning of the World*. Destiny Books.

Sullivan, Brian. 2020. CNBC. https://www.cnbc.com/2020/04/26/why-oil-prices-went-negative-and-why-they-can-go-negative-again.html Last modified on April 26, 2020.

Vattenfall. 2016. "Vattenfall's Hard Coal Procurement Explained Sourcing from Colombia." https://group.vattenfall.com/siteassets/corporate/who-we-are/sustainability/doc/updated_sourcing_from_colombia_130516.pdf May, 2016.

Wooldridge, Anny. 2017. *Culture trip. A Brief History of Colombia's Wayuu Tribe*. https://theculturetrip.com/south-america/colombia/articles/a-brief-history-of-colombias-wayuu-tribe/ Last updated 3 May 2017.

IMAGES

Fig. 1. Conrado Espitia, Sebastián. 2017. Retrieved from "Las Huellas del Cerrejón". https://www.youtube.com/watch?v=ryssy7pJhJI

Fig. 2. Retrieved from Google Satellite Image.
Copyright 2020 CNES / Airbus, Maxar Technologies, Map data @2020
https://www.google.com/maps/place/Cerrejon,+Barrancas,+La+Guajira,+Colombia/@11.0327963,-72.652702,438m/data=!3m1!1e3!4m8!1m2!2m1!1scerrejon!3m4!1s0x8e8ba638256a7e41:0x841b5c2916dd2914!8m2!3d11.0382555!4d-72.6525879

Fig. 3. Medina Poch, Daniela, 2020. Sources and Resources.

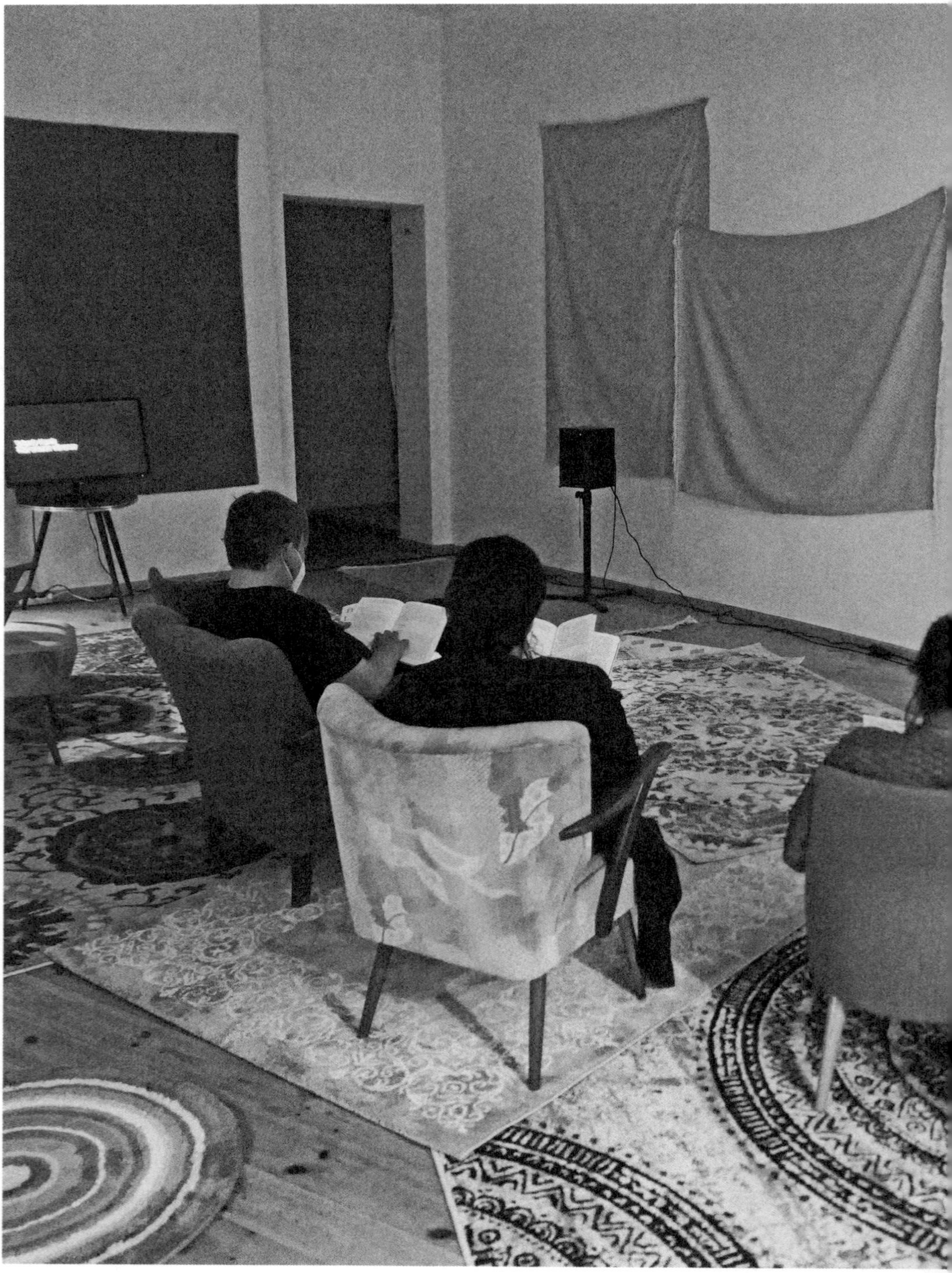

The Listening Biennial was presented across 14 participating institutions, spaces, and venues, each of which organized their own form of presentation along with related programs of activities and events.

AERIAL, BERGEN / presenting the Biennial over morning breakfasts, inviting visitors to share food, rest, listen together. Photography by Mila Larvoll. (p. 78, 81)

AYER, GUADALAJARA / exhibition presentation, as part of the center's program of video and media exhibitions. (p. 75)

ERRANT SOUND, BERLIN / gallery presentation of the Biennial, creating a listening lounge. (p. 72) / performance by Daniela Medina Poch, alongside the river Spree, Berlin. (p. 84)

GENERATOR PROJECTS, DUNDEE / listening within the context of an immersive installation by the artists Maria Tolia + Amos Newton. (p. 74)

INVESTIGACIONES DEL FUTURO, BUENOS AIRES / presenting and activating the Biennial through a series of events, talks, performances, often centered around an evening fire. (p. 80 / Tatiana Cuoco (aka TTCC) inviting the audience to experience one of her Festive Futures Fictions.) Photography by Florencia Curci. (p. 77, 83)

NOISE N' ROSES, BUDAPEST / organizing performance events at locations across the city, as part of weekend presentations of the Biennial. (p. 76, 86) (p. 86: performance by Lévai Viola; Photo: Bence Kollányi)

SPACE21, KURDISTAN / installing the Biennial within a public bus and inviting passengers to listen, to explore listening together. (p. 82)

1983, HONG KONG / hosting, sharing, creating intimate workshops on listening, the Biennial is turned into a participatory space for care practices. (p. 88)

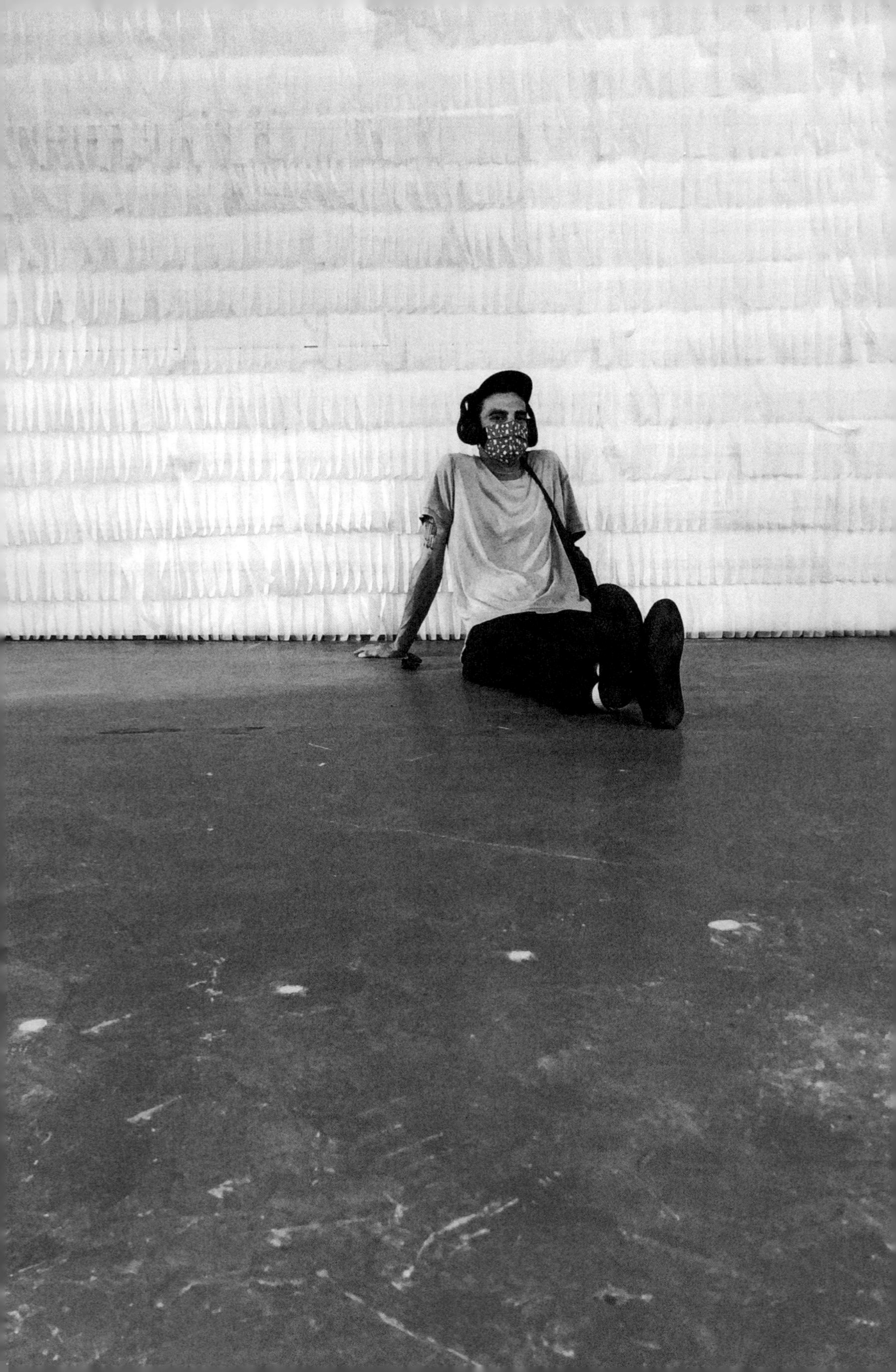

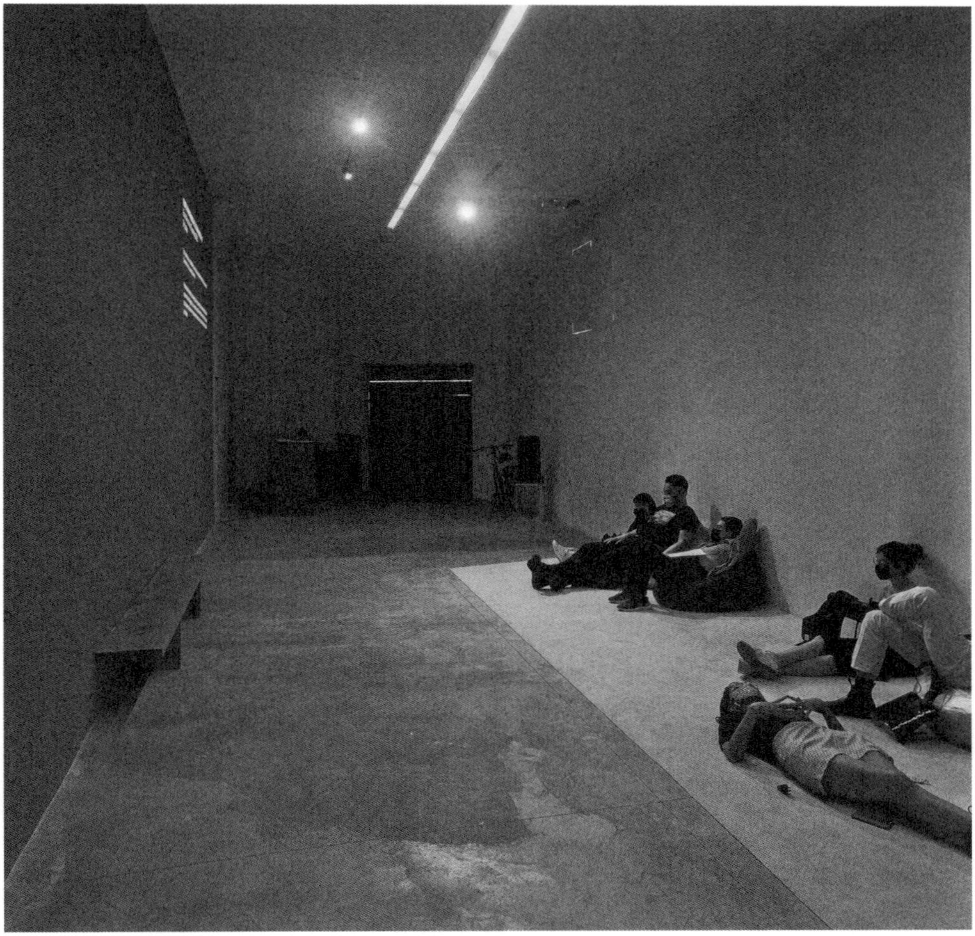

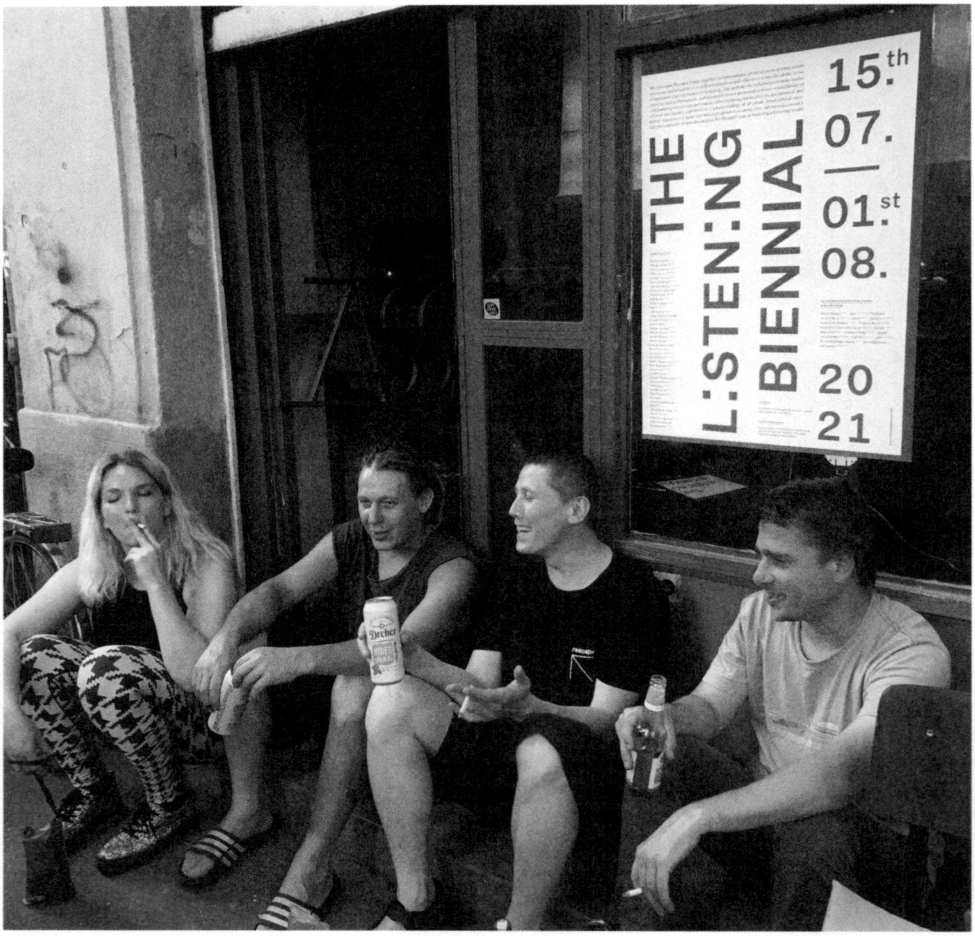
THE
L:STEN:NG
BIENNIAL
15.th
07.
—
01.st
08.
20
21

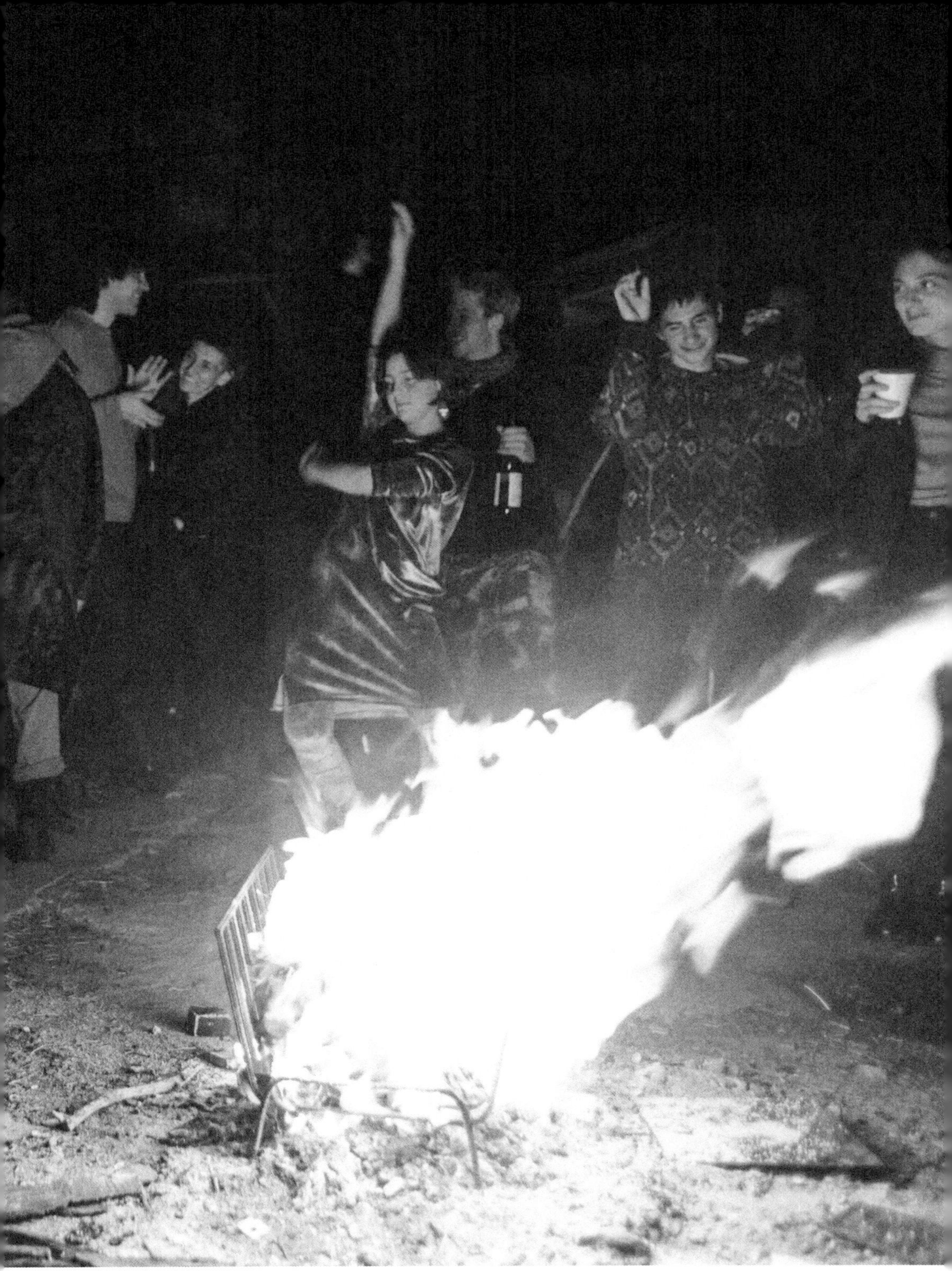

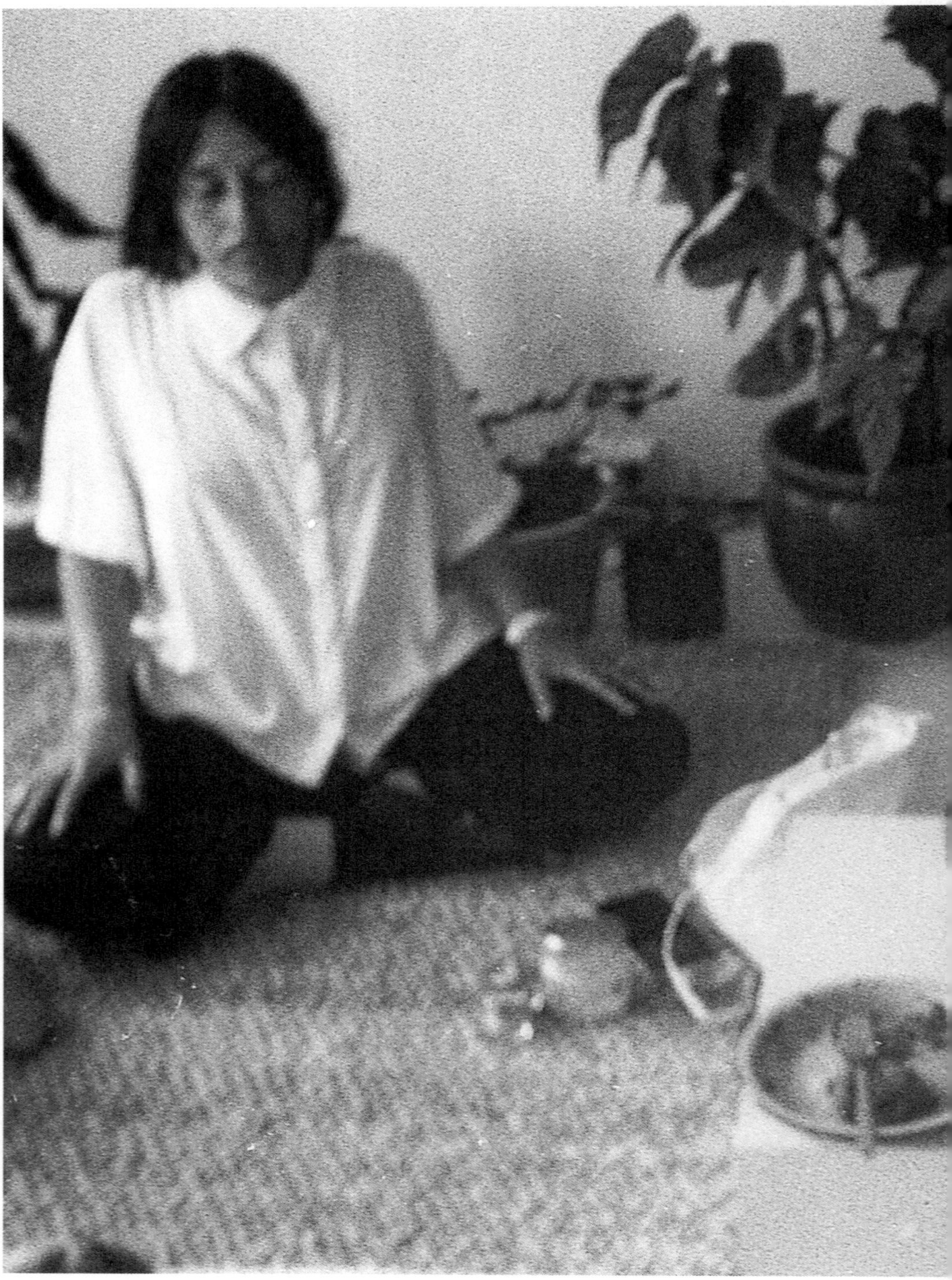

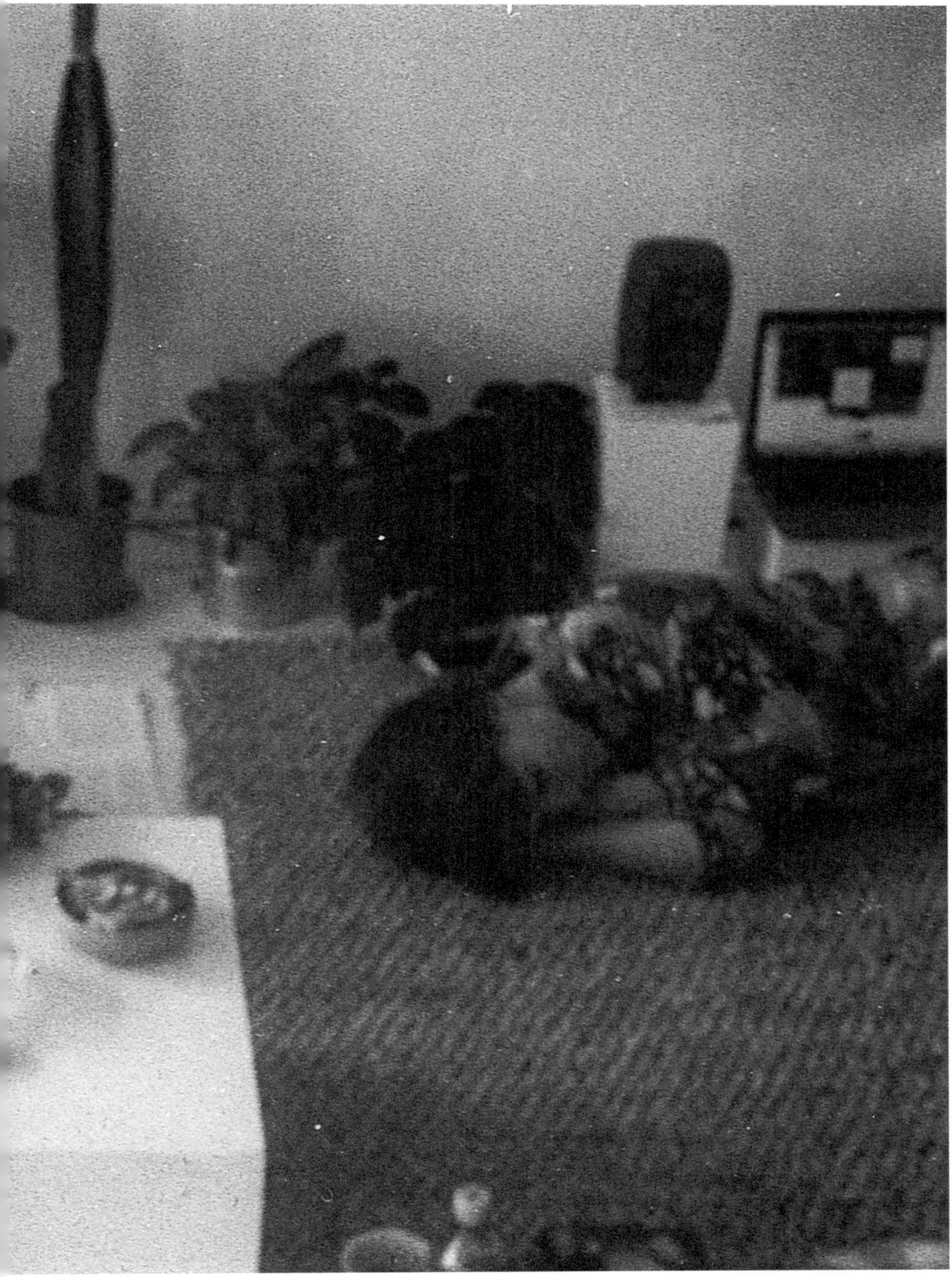

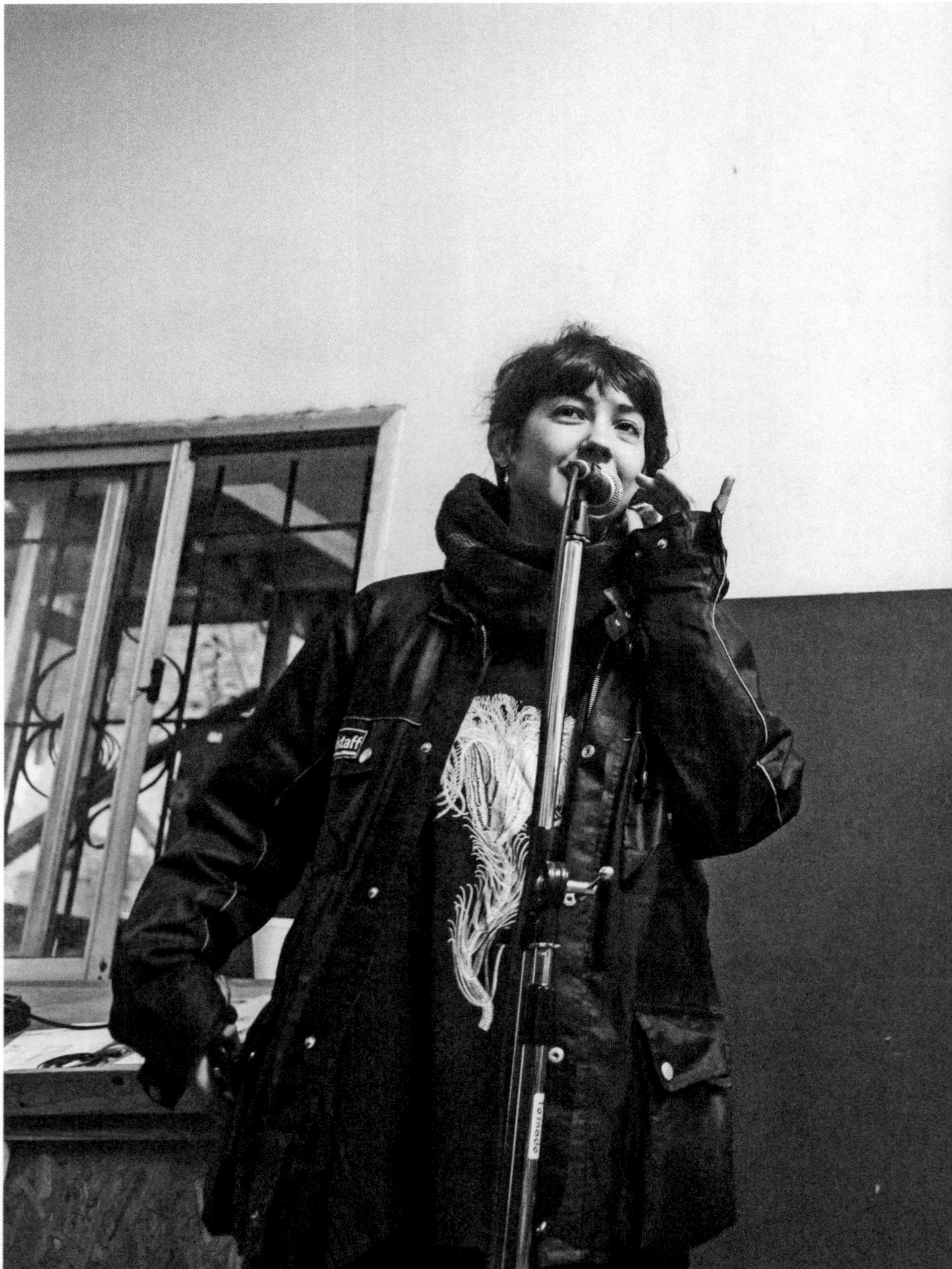
staff

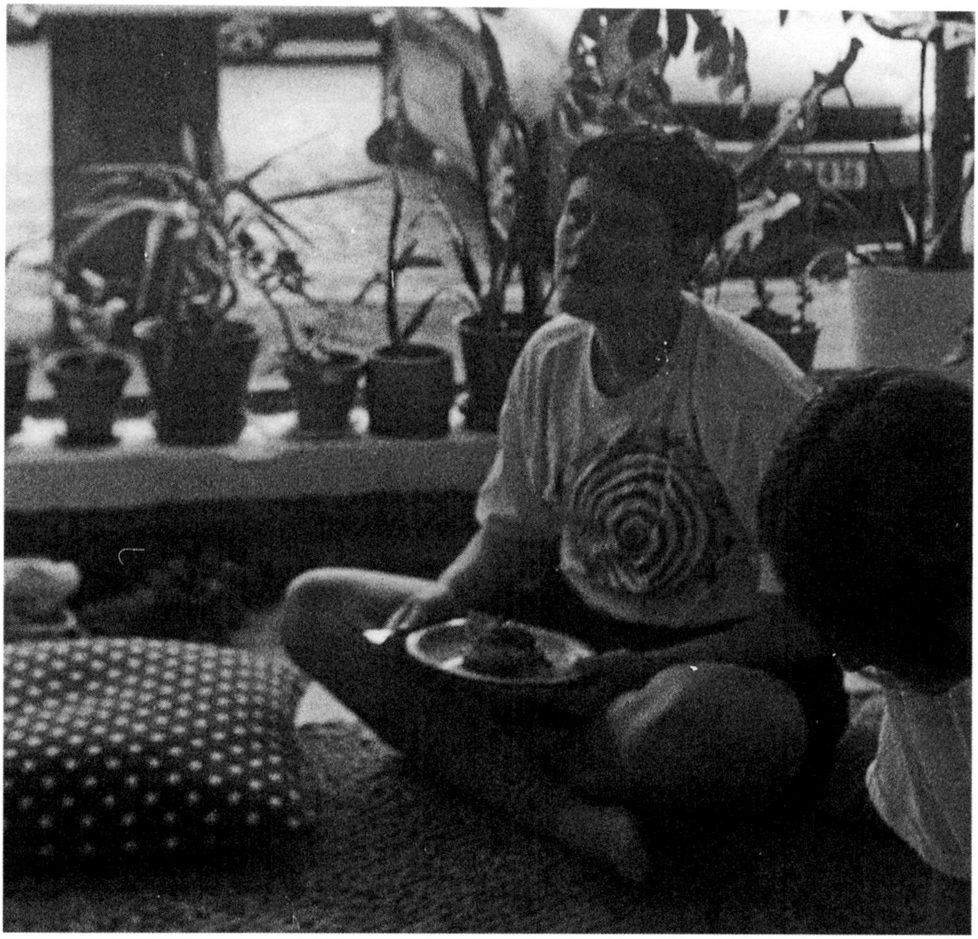

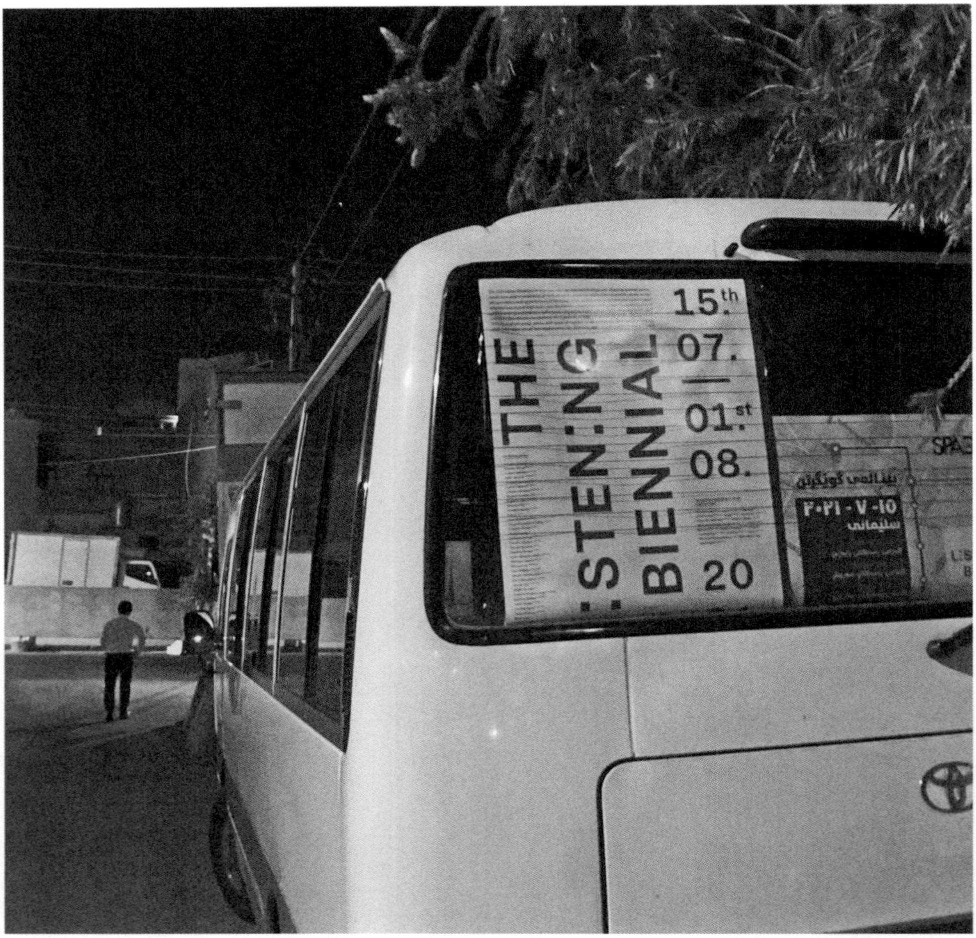
THE
:STEN:NG
BIENNIAL
15th.
07.
01st.
08.
20

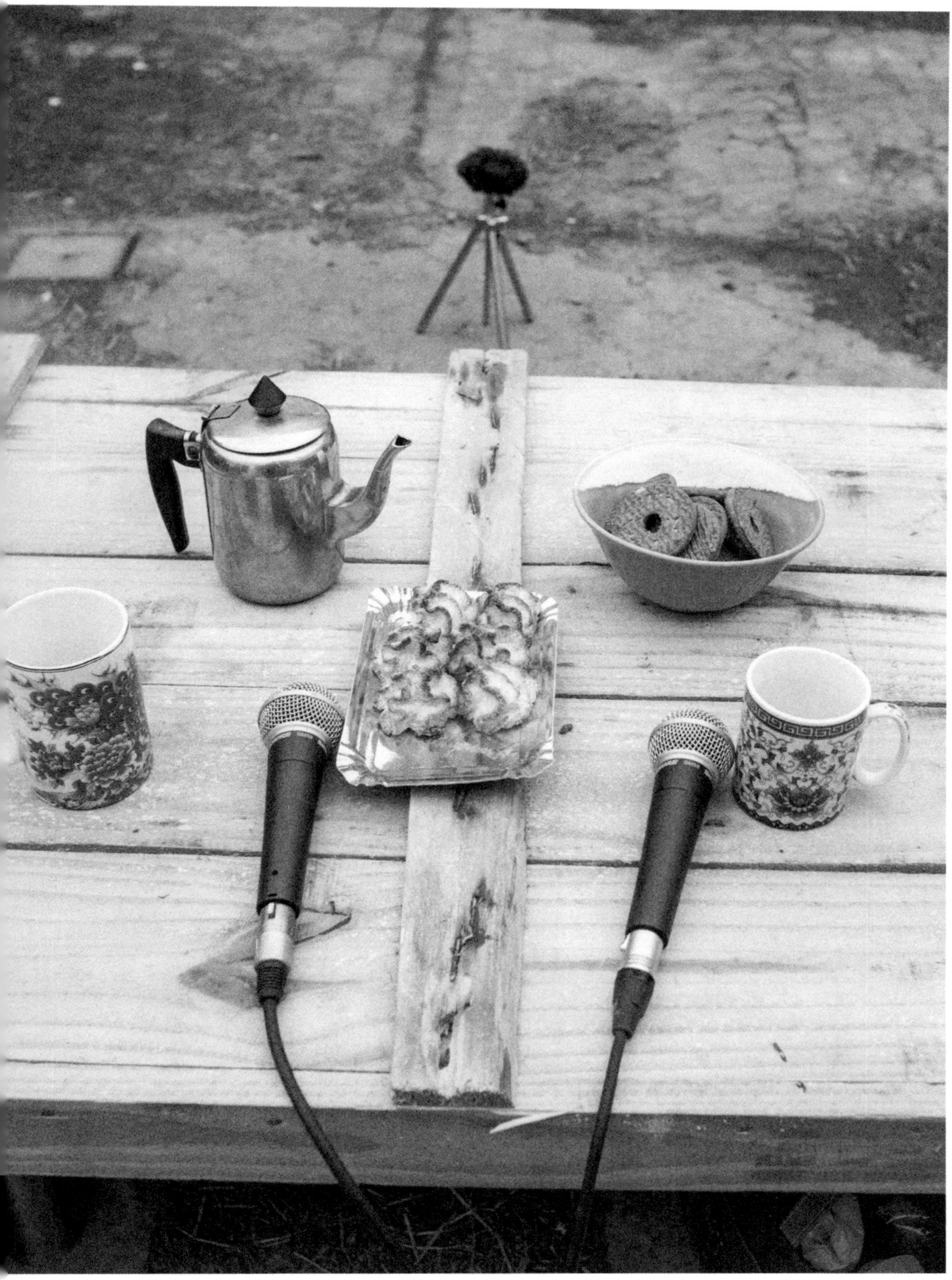

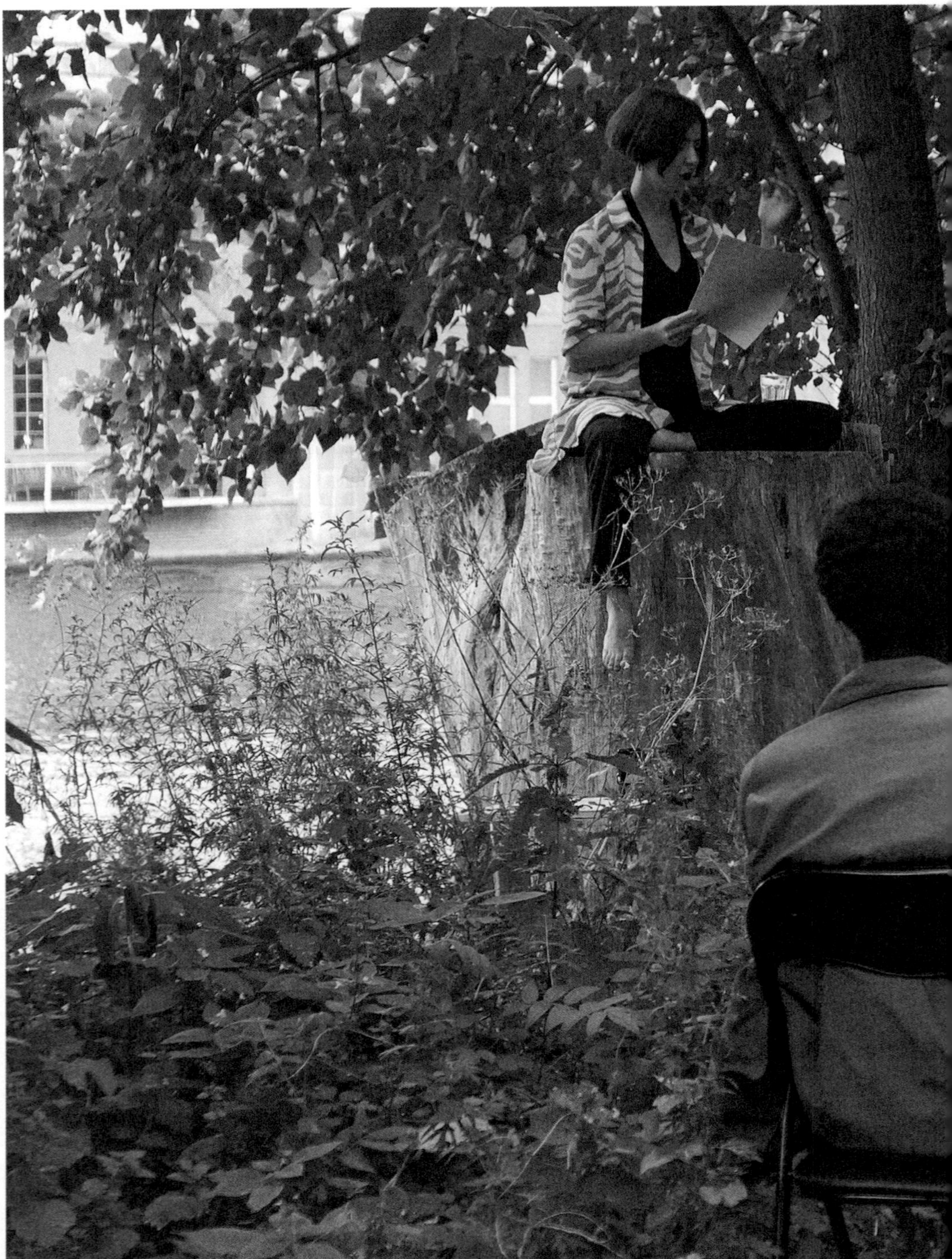

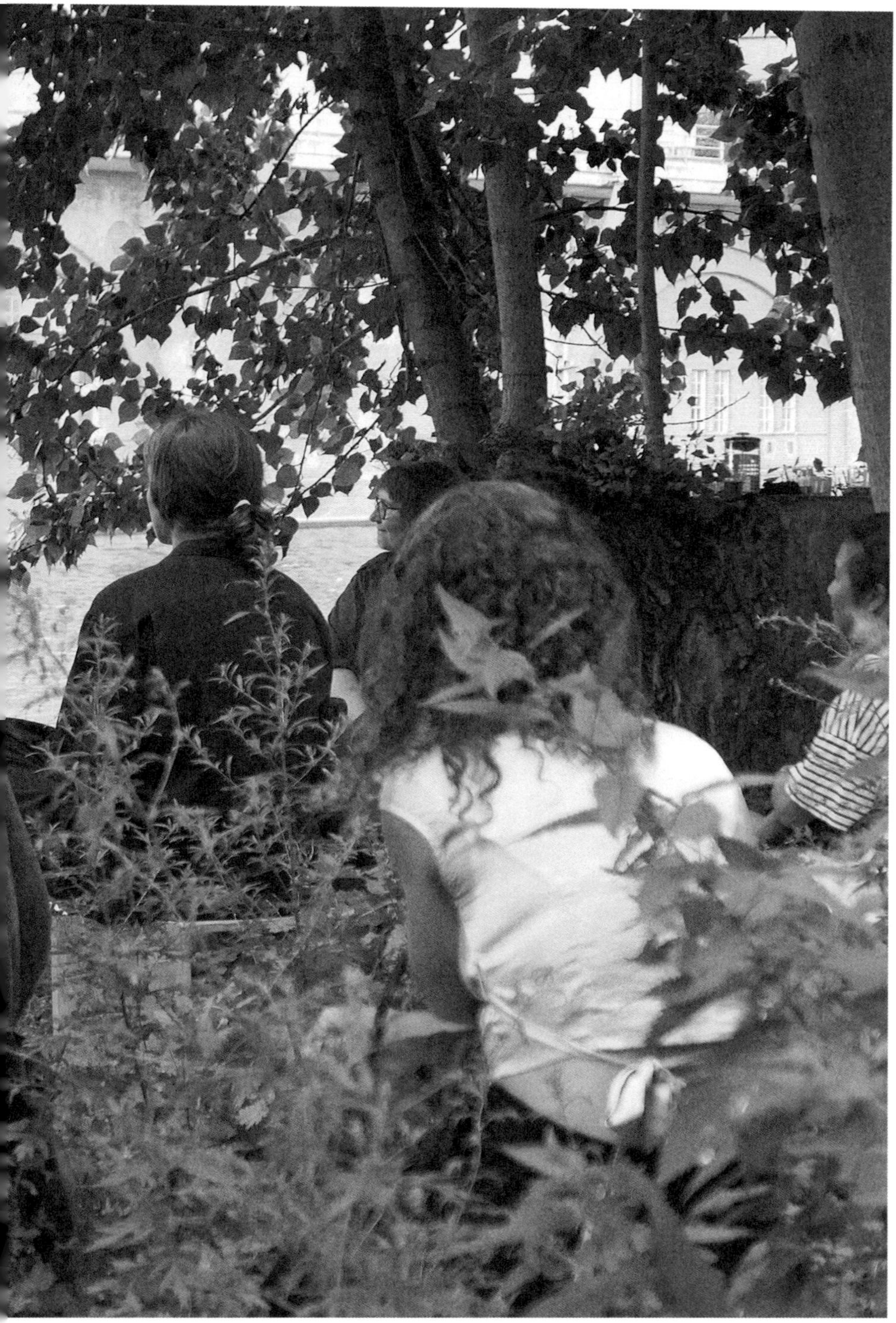

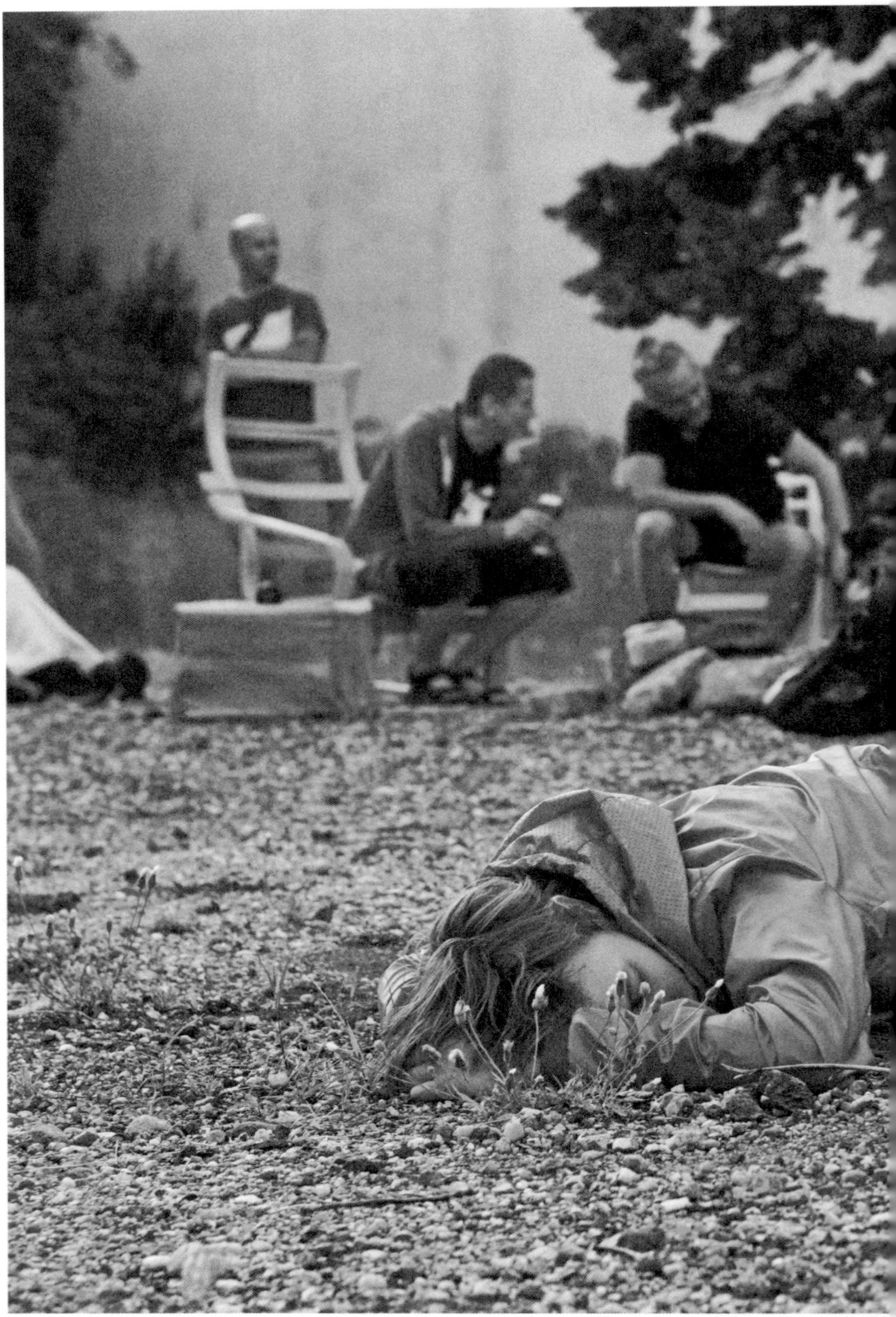

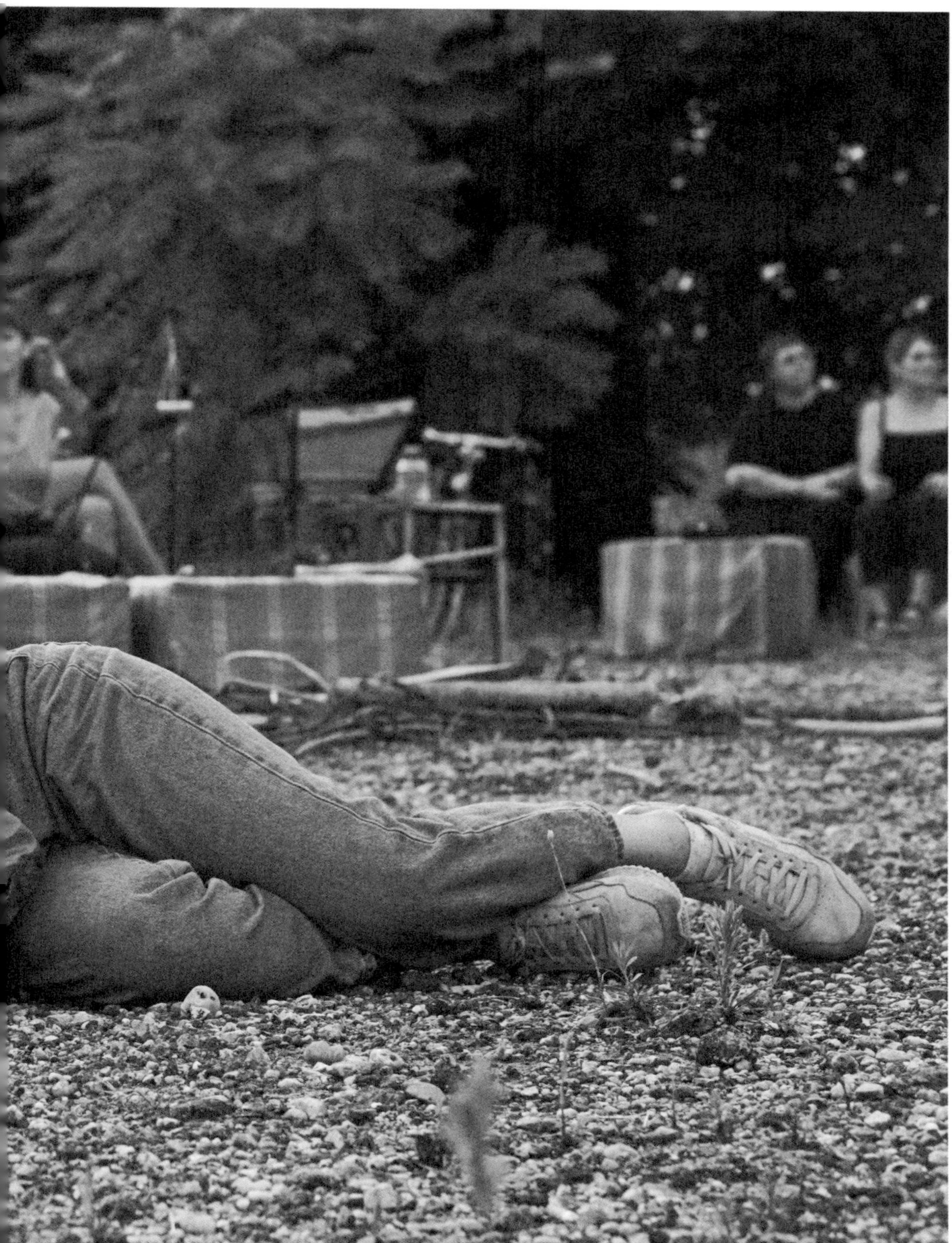

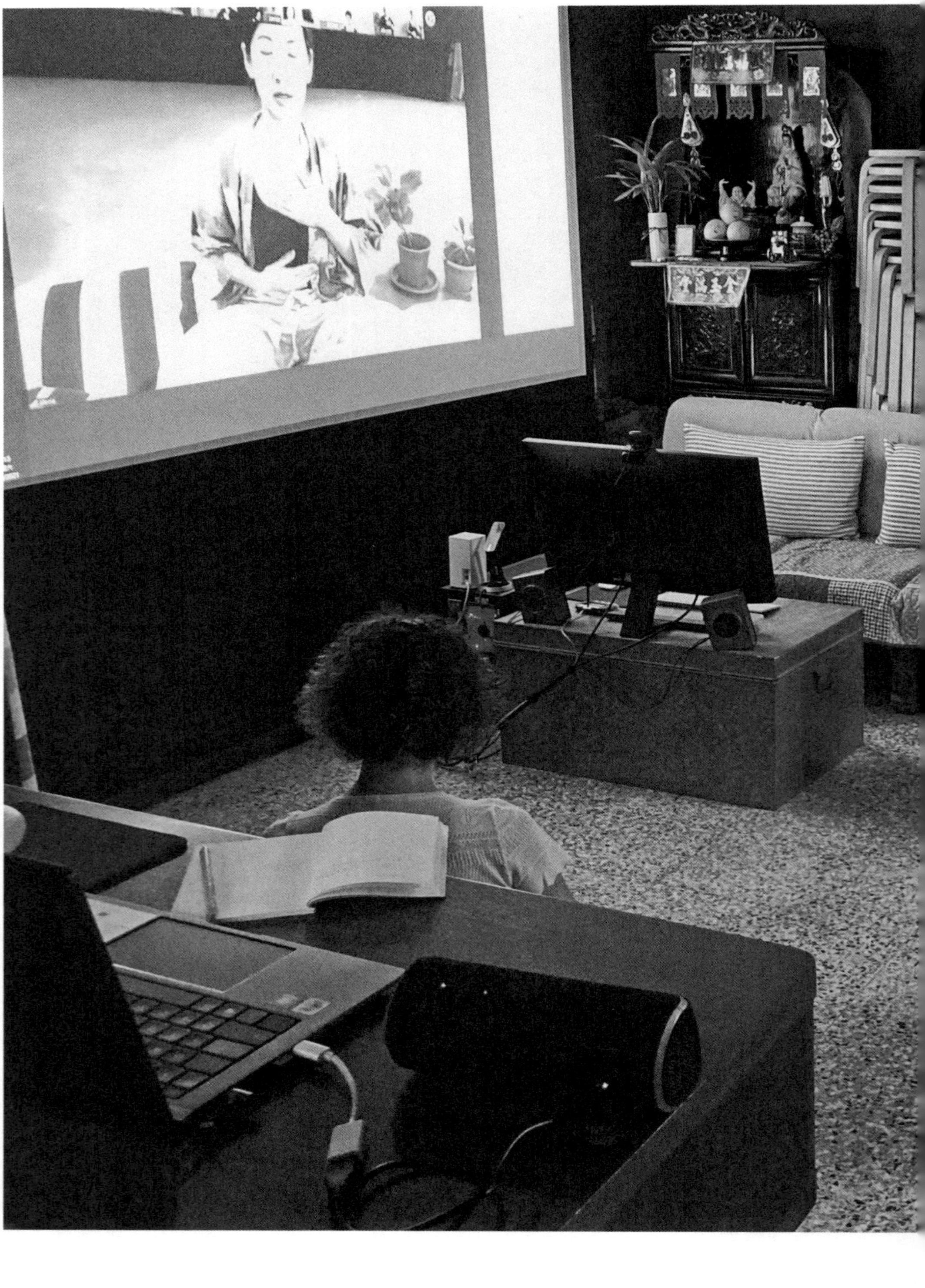

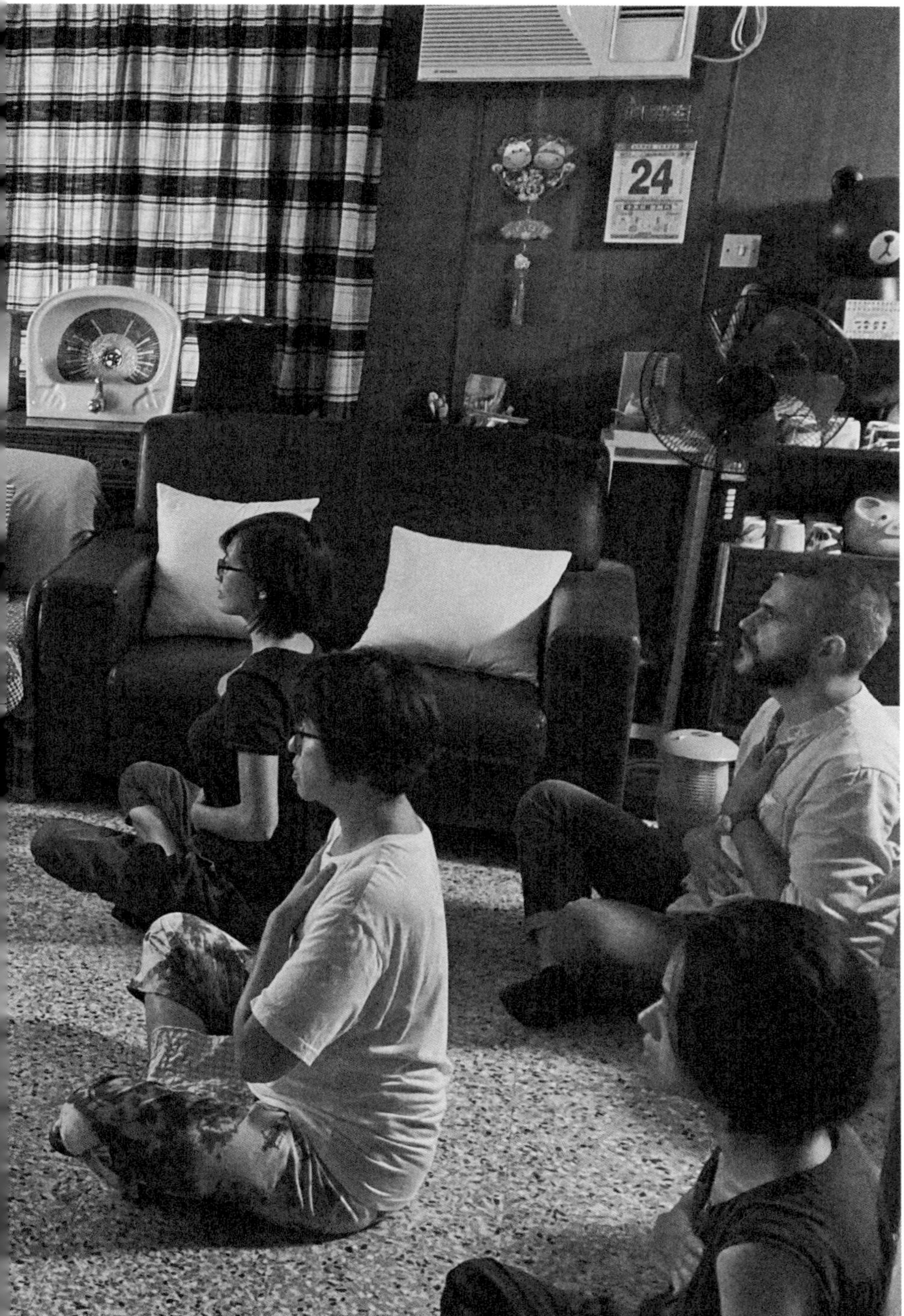

ALECIA NEO AND JILL J. TAN

Care Index: attuning to care infrastructures and movements

A formalized continuation to an ongoing conversation between Alecia Neo and Jill J. Tan, this dialogue reflects upon recent developments in Neo's work on her *Care Index* project, and where it might go next. Neo and Tan began as interlocutors on Neo's work with caregivers *Between Earth and Sky* starting in 2018, and are currently collaborating on a series of workshops for Neo's *Recipes for Wayfinding* project under the *Care Index*. Here, they chat about modes of listening and caring, as well as the complexities of attending to care gestures, infrastructures and systems amidst volatile and violent realities.

JILL: To start, shall we talk about how listening and attentiveness comes into your project in terms of making an index, and working with contributions that you receive via open calls? How do you receive, attend to, and be present with each work in and of themselves, and then collectively, as you're building this repository? And is there any particular way that you are mediating, curating, choreographing, arranging them as you present them to a wider audience?

ALECIA: The context of the Covid-19 pandemic lockdown in Singapore propelled this project into being. The first lockdown was when we had to put a stop to everything. Projects were disappearing and practitioners around the world were all finding different ways to connect in our isolation. That became a starting point for me to begin listening.

Listening, first of all, to my own body's internal murmurings and movements. At the same time, I felt a strong need to connect with others. I followed this desire to reach out to people across the globe via a simple open call with textual prompts. Anyone, whether they are an artist or not, can participate by submitting a video recording of their care practices. They were encouraged to express stories and experiences of care through gestures and movements. Beyond creating a public archive for the web, I was interested in people discovering their new relationships with themselves, other people and the environments they have to navigate through. These prompts become a resource that they can play with and return to over time. When I receive these videos, I like to think of these contributions as slices of time that have been offered to this collective portal. One that allows others to dwell in, and spend time with too.

The contributions to the first open call[1] were quite diverse and each one taught me different modes of listening and caring that people across cultures were practicing in their daily lives. Amongst art and dance films, I also received contributions of everyday gestures and activities which lifted people's spirits and brought pleasure, comfort, strength, or symbolic movements which reflected on time, loss, fatigue, recovery, maintenance and endurance. There were numerous interactions with human and non-human bodies, exploring a myriad of ways to come closer, set boundaries and co-exist. People also sent in care practices they observed, such as how locals were gathered together to provide food and aid to flood victims in Bintan, Indonesia and death rituals. It was important to me that each contribution lived with its own story and credits on the website, and that when their videos were exhibited they would be aware of it. While each video contribution is a world of its own, the process of inviting each contributor to index their movements with keywords unveiled a tightly interconnected web that bound everyone's experiences together. For some of my public *Care Index* workshops, I've also invited some open call contributors to read participants' stories, where I sense a connection between their experiences. I record their voices reading these incredible lines which are then used in parts of the workshop. So the participants hear their own stories read back to them by a stranger. It was a way of drawing the invisible connections between people.

I'm also in the process of annotating the movements from the public submissions[2] and drawing links between the keywords submitted by each contributor. I've also been collaborating with some contributors in public workshops, where they work with me to develop movement scores which are taught to the workshop participants, who engage in visual, aural, and aesthetic modes of listening to these scores.

JILL: I'm wondering whether you found a difference in working with the first initial open call on care gestures, versus systems and infrastructure? Are there any particular insights that move beyond the interpersonal to think about infrastructure and institutions and the way that the body moves within them? I'm also thinking about whether it surfaced anything about the potential limits of care and the limits of empathy because I think as you're seeing, with a focus on something like infrastructure and systems, a larger point can be made that sometimes there are systemic issues at that level that are beyond our immediate mediation. In that case, what do we do, how do we care?

ALECIA: Individual actions can be overpowered by dominant structures and systems, creating challenges for the practice of centering care in our govern-

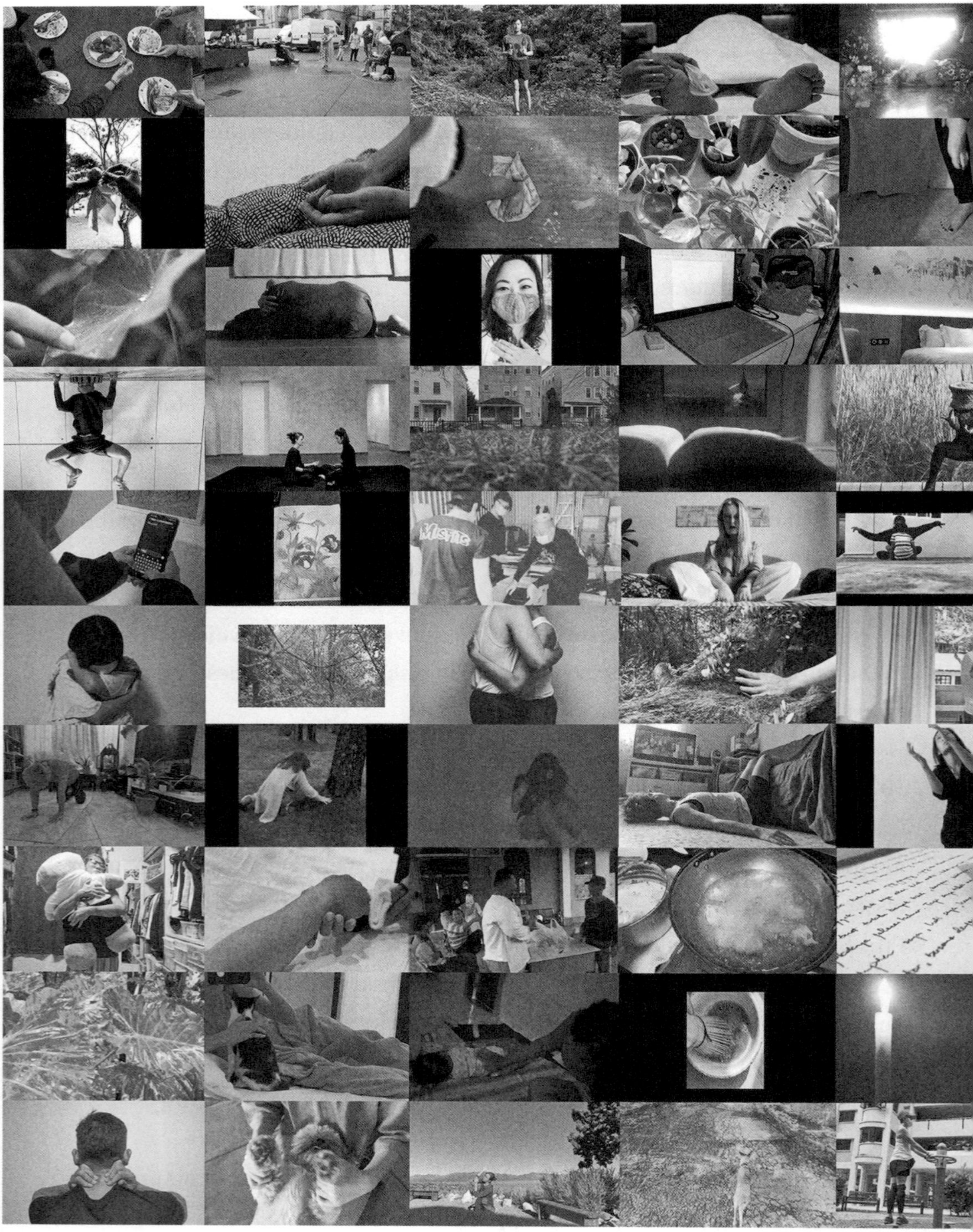

ments, institutions, organizations and communities. And unfortunately, a lot of the weight of caring falls on those who already bear the labor and cost of caring. I think one of the first places to start as individuals is to open up and advocate for access to resources for everyone, in particular groups who are disabled by our socio-political systems, so that they can grow in their capacities and thrive, instead of being treated as recipients of care. I'm also interested in your belief that social action should arise alongside our work, such as yours as an academic. This also reminds me of artist and facilitator, Kei Franklin's reflections on nurturing conscientization and acknowledging that "the power dynamics that sustain broad systems of injustice are reflected in our relational lives. Any meaningful change, therefore, must involve intervention in the inter- and intra-personal realm."

While working on the project *Between Earth and Sky* (2018)[3] with collaborating artist Sharda Harrison, Ajunta Anwari and a group of caregivers, who care for their loved ones living with mental illness, I learned how transformative the process of listening to and expressing one's own story through embodied movements could be. When you observed our process, you wrote about how the project connects the physicality of care work with personally choreographed forms of body movement. I became interested in whether these subjective experiences can be transmitted to a wider audience. What kinds of sensations and insights get transmitted? What changes in this process of teaching, learning and embodying another person's gestures and movements? These questions began to evolve with a focus on care infrastructures for the Listening Biennial in 2021.

During the workshop, I invited individuals who work within specific care systems to contribute a movement score. One of them is Meghna Bhardwaj, an academic and dancer from New Delhi, who has collaborated with me

Video stills from the public submissions to the *Care Index open call* in 2020, which are currently archived on careindex.net.

on different projects. She then roped in her dance students from Shiv Nadar University. She was concerned about the state of education during the lockdown and how that created barriers to rigorous learning and deep connection with and between students. What does it mean to teach an embodied art form like dance online, and how does an educator be empathetic to the unequal needs and circumstances of her students, while pushing for artistic excellence? Educators are often subjected to the overwhelming stresses of fulfilling care responsibilities in spite of the lack of resources and support for their own well-being. How does a teacher bring in her vulnerabilities into the classroom, which opens up room for connection and discourse about the students' own uncertainties and challenges? We also spoke about this bureaucratic posture one adopts in institutions to perform power or compliance; how does one adopt a kind of wilding of the body by taking on unsophisticated, animalistic positions challenge the bureaucratic body?

Another collaborator was a frontline worker whose job was to conduct swab tests for foreign workers at their dormitories. He expressed how the body becomes a potent site for resistance in a system that primarily values efficiency and compliance. The gestures that emerged from his story were about an insistence on slowing down. He was reframing the act of slowing down as serious work and responsibility, a person-centered choice that respects the person being swabbed, no matter the person's identity or status in society. Slowing down meant listening, allowing time for each person to ask questions, and to understand what was being done to their bodies. These are the lived realities and decisions that frontline workers make every day, which are often obscured from official data and reports in everyday news.

The last group was two women working in the professional caregiving space. Caregivers Carol and Alvyna were both involved in my previous project *Between Earth and Sky* (2018). I was interested in the transitions they experienced moving between positions of caring in their own private homes to performing care for others, in a professional capacity. What happens when care work becomes commodified, rated and left to market forces to determine its value, allocation and circulation? How are care workers perceived and treated

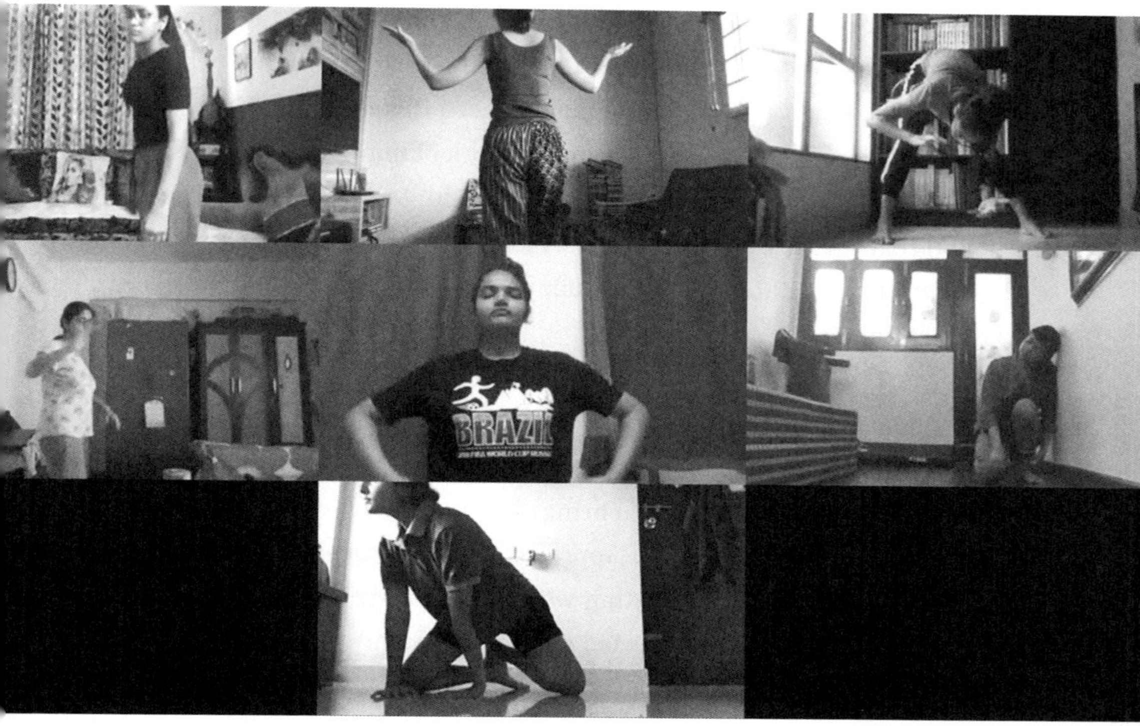

Documentation from preparatory digital workshops during Dance Nucleus Element Residency for *Care Index* with Alecia Neo, Meghna Bhardwaj and her dance students from Shiv Nadar University.

in our society that is used to low-wage care with limited rights and mobility? I'd love to know how you'd approach care in your work. What are the practical and imaginary tactics that one develops to survive and resist in an uncaring world?

JILL: I think one thing that feels really important is being able to acknowledge that caregiving can hold ambivalence. I'm thinking about Felicity Aulino's ethnography on care work in Northern Thailand, wherein she observes that contemporary usage of the English word "care" may contribute to the tendency to assume a correspondence between particular internal states, such as feeling affection or being concerned ("care about"), and the acts of best providing for another ("to care for"). Aulino cautions against such conflation which may lead to only placing value on emotional concern in acts of providing for others, and focuses on physical and pragmatic work of maintenance in her ethnographic work on caregiving practices. As you said, too, for many people it's a livelihood that is really part of a larger system where there are significant deficits in terms of being able to provide fair compensation to people for the care that they're giving.

ALECIA: Joan Tronto's work on wealth-care and how neoliberal societies organize their decisions for policies based on gaining wealth has been illuminating for me. She coined this term to bring clarity to how people in power make decisions important to our lives. Appreciating this concept requires a major shift from focusing on accumulating wealth, to redistributing wealth and resources to impoverished or neglected communities and spaces, which are fundamentally interconnected with everyone else. These ideas are also discussed and expanded upon in *The Care Manifesto* by the Care Collective, which highlights numerous pathways to centering care in our societies. Many of the caregivers I've met in support groups and through projects, wrestle with the contradictions and ambivalences of caregiving in their lives. Our current context in Singapore continues to place primary focus on care performed by family or outsourced low-wage foreign workers, leading to narratives of self-sacrifice and unsustainable, exploitative caring relationships. We need to fully acknowledge the competencies, time and resources involved in performing care work in order to allocate fair compensation for care workers. Again, we come back to the idea of circulating and redistributing care at all levels of society. People don't want to be dependent on others, nor do they want to feel that special concession has been provided for them. In my ongoing collaborative projects with disabled artists and persons, they taught me the importance of reimagining the care narrative. Disabled persons need to be given the ample resources which would allow them to build the capacities they need to live life with dignity, where they can exercise choice and autonomy.

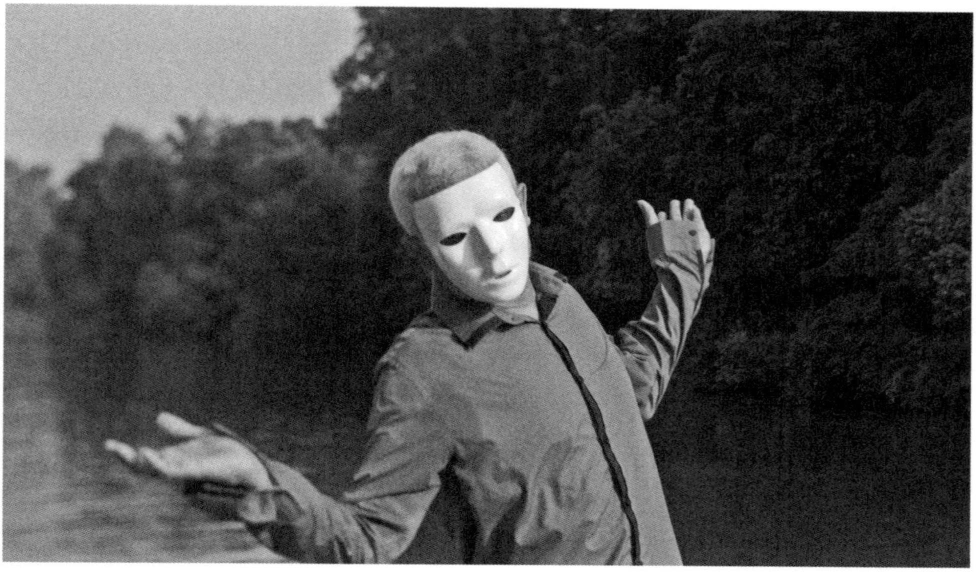

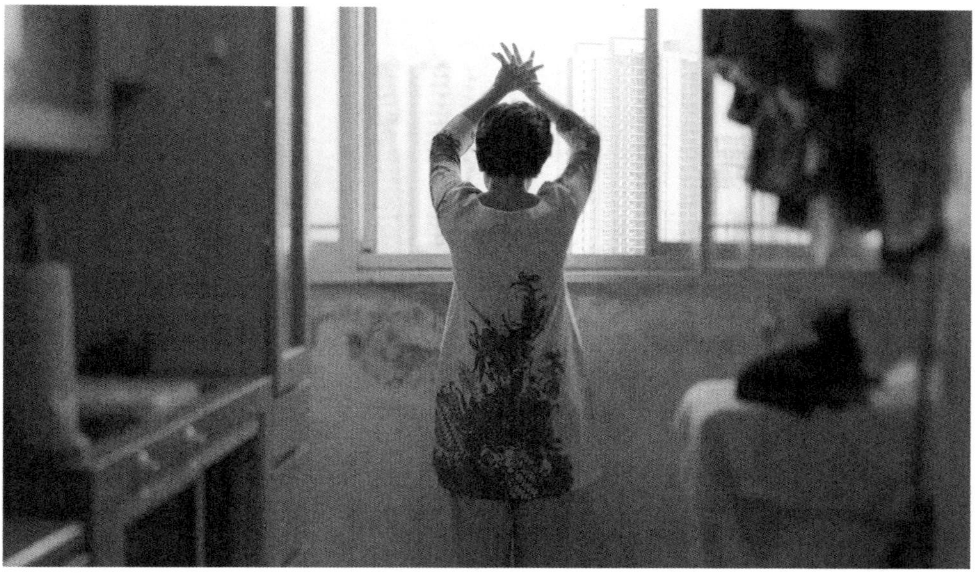

Video still from *Between Earth and Sky* (2018), Alecia Neo, performance by Frank M.

Video still from *Between Earth and Sky* (2018), Alecia Neo, performance by Nur Hidayah.

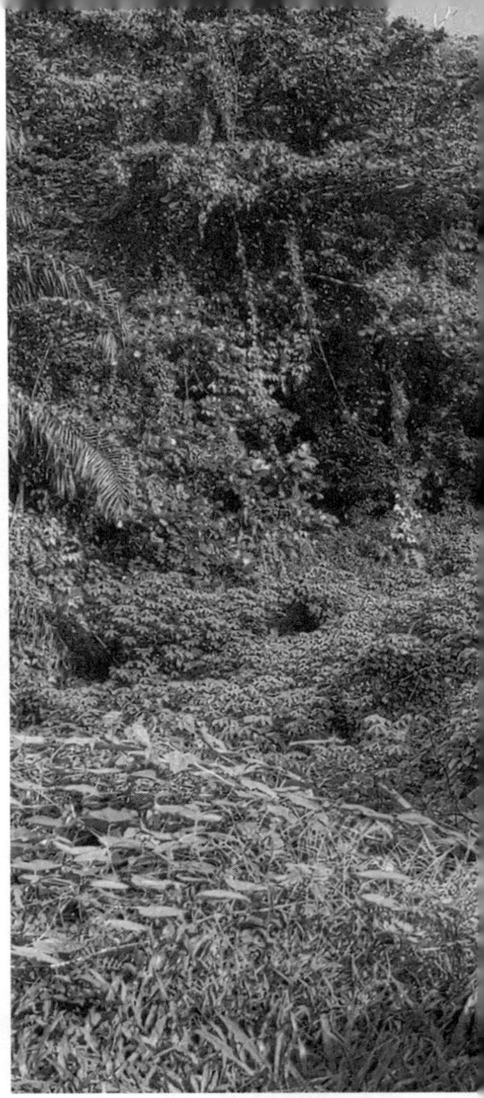

Video still from *On Being Asked for Words of Encouragement* (2020), by Ou Ning Fei, Singapore.

JILL: One thing I want to ask you about, when you were talking earlier about the frontline worker as well, in terms of slowness as resistance; generally when we're thinking about these ideas around care, there is a certain kind of aesthetic, or performative premising of the slow and the gentle. With the *Care Index*, that feels apparent as I'm watching and listening to most of the submissions in this repository. At the same time, I'm also curious about how you see the modalities of this project evolving, in content as well as in terms of holding space for different aesthetics possibilities. As it is, when you were mentioning in the

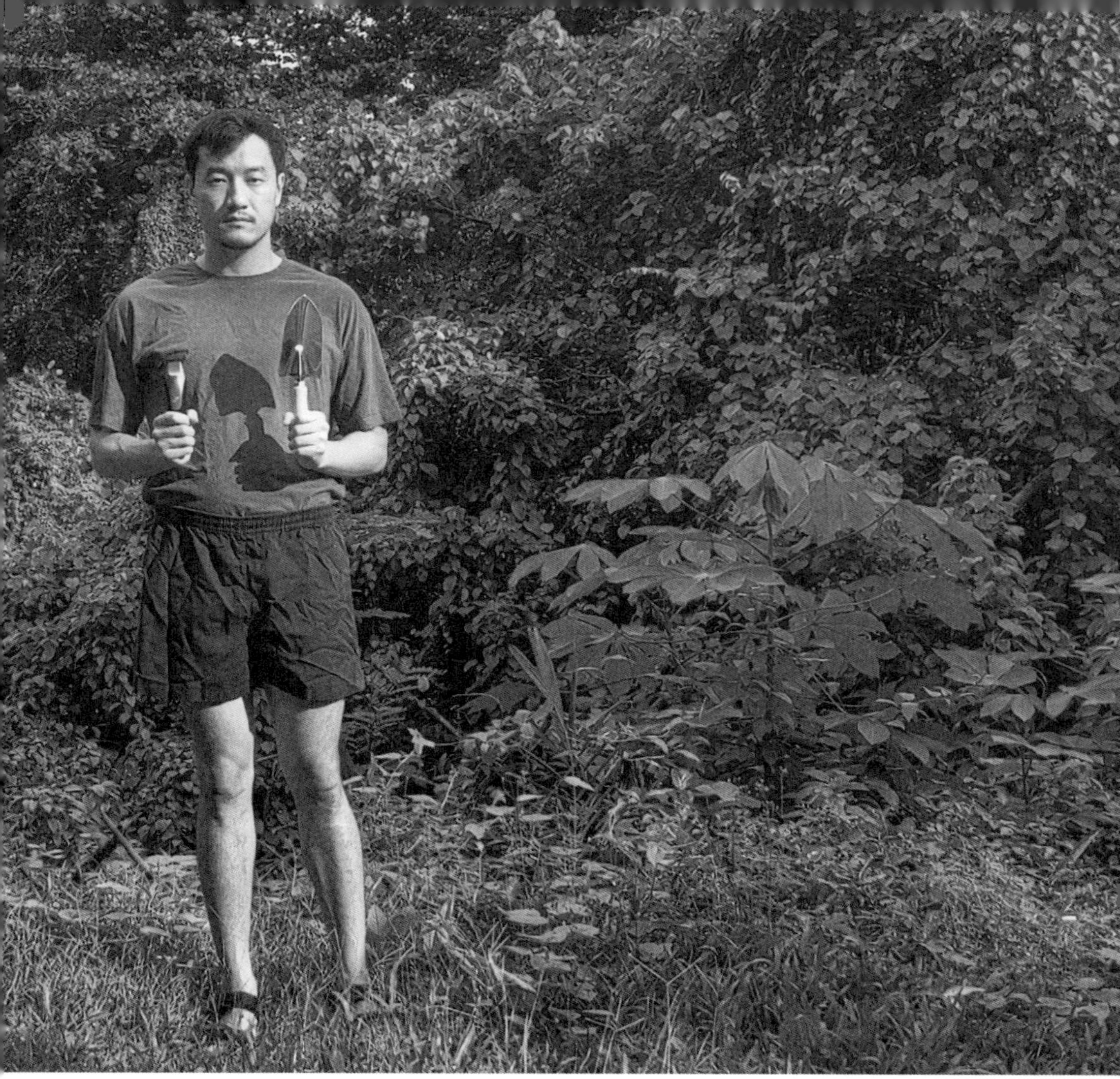

first open call that you had a mix of performative care gestures, while other submissions were featuring maybe more actionable notions of care such as a rescue mission. How do you see those kinds of things sitting alongside each other in terms of your index, and are there other directions the project is circulating beyond a slow, nourishing care?

ALECIA: I do feel that the various aesthetic iterations are driven by impulses that manifest differently with the different groups. The recent collaboration

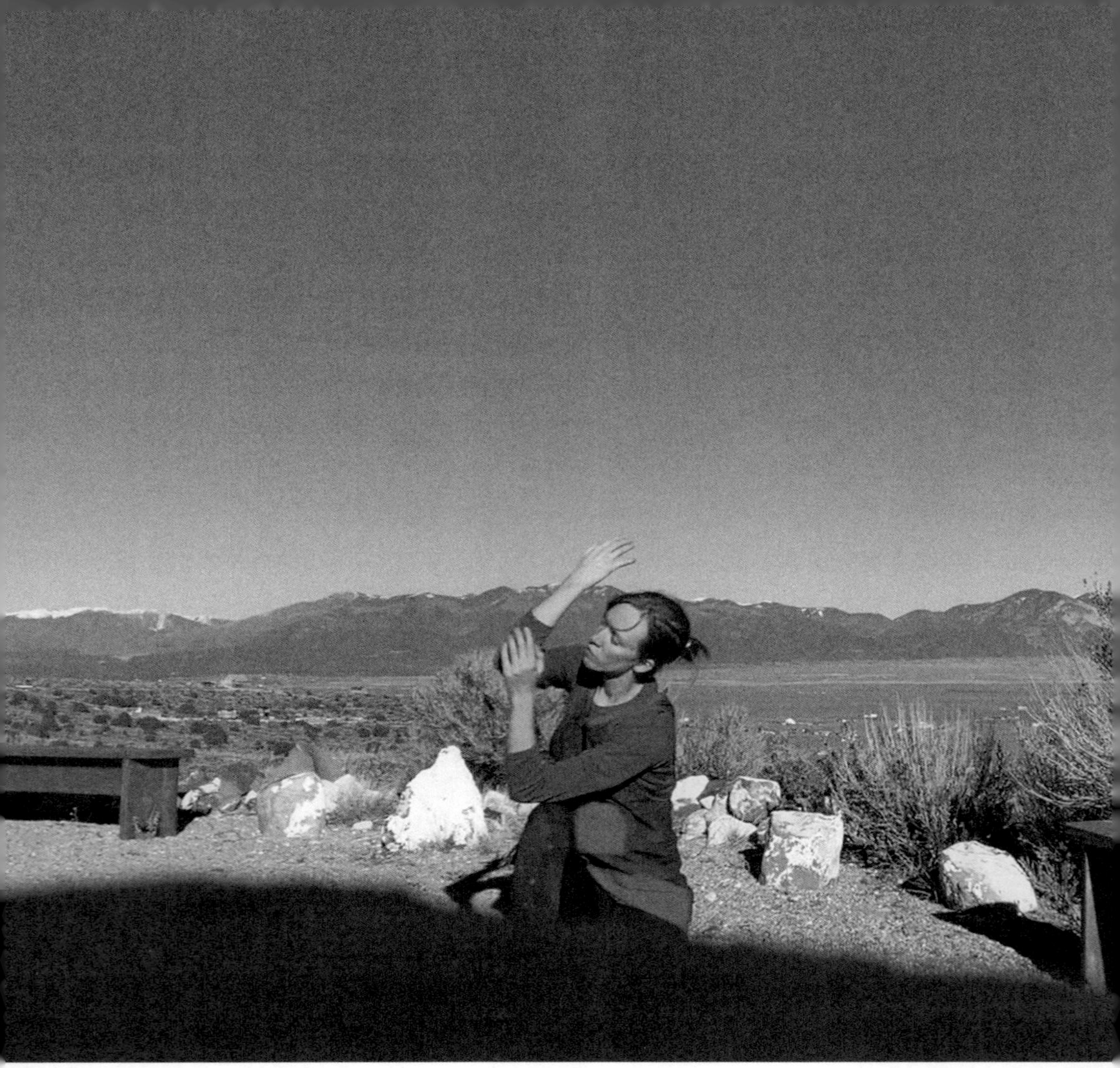

Presence of Mind,[4] a residency and exhibition project examining the intersection of mindfulness, Buddhism and the creative processes of artists, organized by curators Dr Kath Fries and Rachael Kiang of Gallery Lane Cove in Sydney, Australia, brought together Australian and Singaporean visual artists for a rich gathering. During our discussions about gestures of welcome from a Buddhist perspective, we could not avoid talking about the conditions of the ongoing refugee crisis going on in other parts of the world, distant from us. That was something that bothered a lot of us: how do you care from a

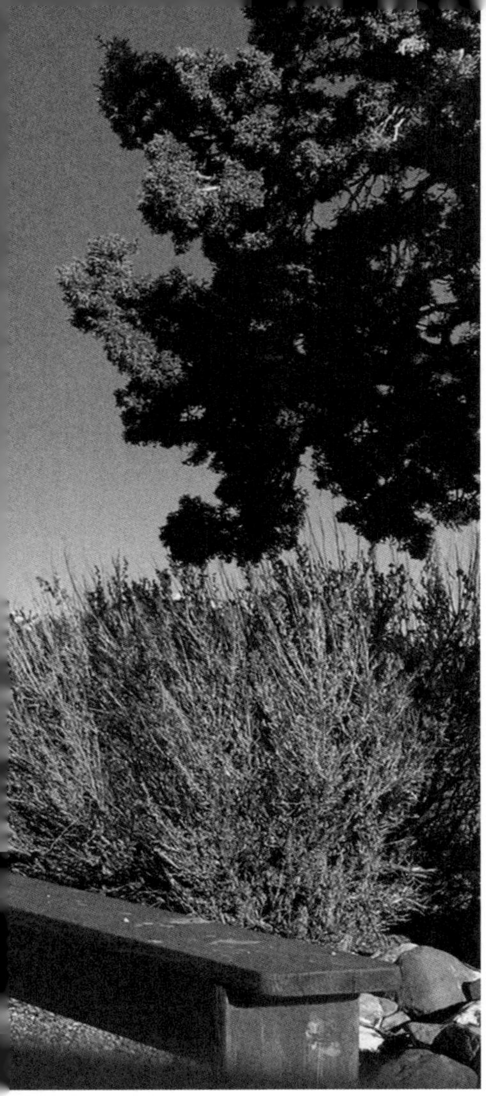

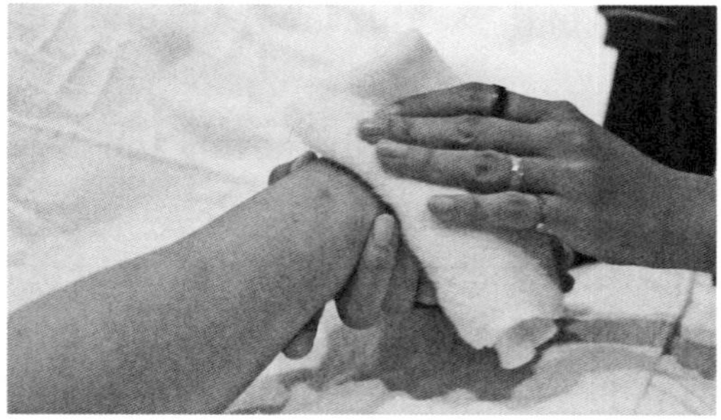

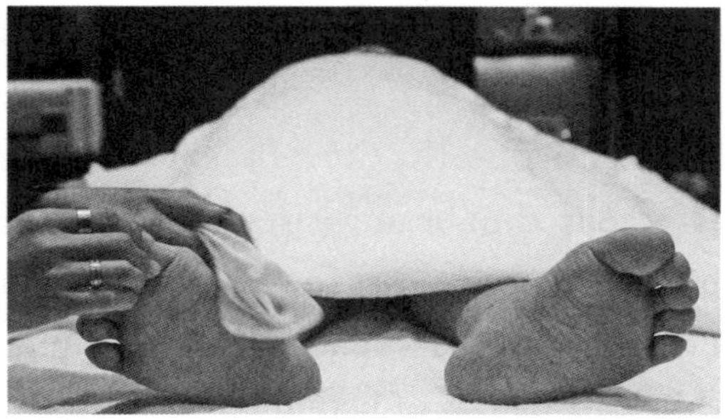

Video still from *Necessary Osmosis* by Kei Franklin, Tres Orejas Chöten, New Mexico (USA).

Video submission from *Showers Of Love Sanctuary* by Angjolie Mei, Founder of The Life Celebrant.

distance? Especially with the luxury of distance. In most Buddhist communities there's a lot of emphasis on peace, non-violence and a gentler kind of approach. We began to ask if there was room for more difficult kinds of discussions. To what extent was conflict, disagreement or even violence and aggression tolerated?

JILL: I am compelled by thinking about this from the Buddhist perspective, because it asks: what is the point of contemplative practice if it doesn't have implications in the world? I'm really interested in hearing, building on what you've already shared about your experience with this group of practitioners, how you see this project on care moving and developing. This feels like another mode of listening: listening to what the project is evolving into in response to the different groups that you're working with. I think it's a really porous way of being with the people that are coming into this work. Do you have a sense of what binds the work together, what contours are cohering it, or might you ever need another project or container to convey another valence. Or do you think this concept of a *Care Index* is capacious to hold all of it?

ALECIA: Honestly, *Care Index* is really at the start of its journey and I'm fully prepared to be surprised at the shapes and forms it adopts over time. It is important to me that the research and making process is done collaboratively. Primarily, this is a space for co-learning, and as you've described, for entering different modes of listening to and with others. This attempt at indexing care practices and transmitting them is a journey of making sense of all the discoveries, contradictions, failures and also grappling with *not knowing*, as you often mention in our conversations. What is interesting for me is how the journey of attuning to others creates space for diverse or even contradictory forms of aesthetics to develop. And also how might the research process offer new bodies of knowledge which can be applied to specific contexts.

In the long term, I'm curious and excited about how this collective process of developing an index of care from an embodied, relational perspective will contribute new knowledge to the current methods of researching health and well-being indices.

JILL: Still dwelling on proliferating ideas of care, and specifically honing in on the politics of this work, I want to talk about priming the audience for it as it evolves. "Care" as a topic can bring with it certain associations more easily aligned with wellness and mindfulness. As you're showing from the discussion amongst the group of Buddhist practitioners, however, even within some of these resonances that there are often really important political stakes in at-

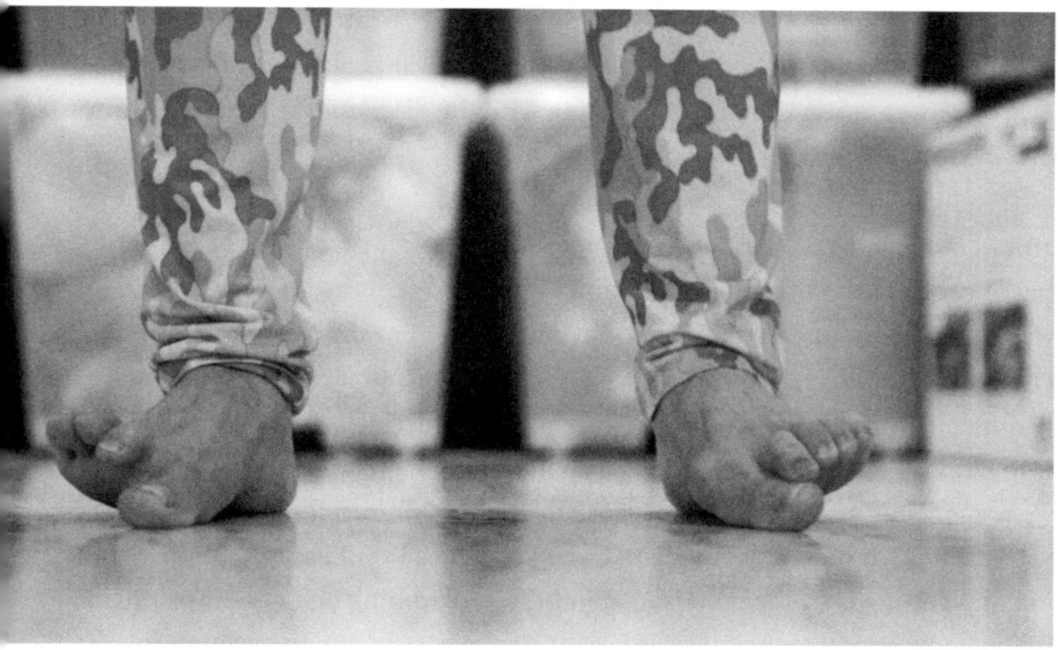

Video still from caregiver Carol Ee's movement score for the Listening Biennial 2021.

tending to some of these notions of care, labor, violence. So I'd like to push on this a little more.

ALECIA: There's a tendency towards short-term band-aids when planning policies addressing issues, such as the current climate crisis, economic and social inequalities, and the mental health epidemic. I've been thinking about how an audience can meaningfully engage with these socio-political stakes... priming the audience for a shift in human consciousness is the current challenge for this work as it develops. I've found some inspiration in theatre educator and dramaturg Charlene Rajendran's research on FaciliActing,[5] which "expands the potential of play-based embodied learning" in plural, complex societies through the facilitation of dialogue and drama processes. She talks about how the effective use of fiction and nuanced role-playing creates new spaces to collectively reimagine our futures, offer provocations, while being conscious of the social, political and economical structures that impede some of us more.

How are you thinking of working with the discomfort that arises from delving into the politics of care?

JILL: Looking at the *Recipes for Wayfinding*[6] project materials, in the framing of getting lost and found, something that I keep coming back to is how, as we're talking about trauma, the body remembers. From personal experience, sitting in meditative practice can be very grounding, but it can also be extremely difficult, and I think people can have a very romanticized notion of what it is to be sitting with ourselves, and our pain. Thinking relationally, too, how do we responsibly and accountably create the pre-conditions for sitting with ourselves and with others, listening to the body and the soul in pain? In wayfinding and getting lost, I wonder too about the programing and residing of pain in the body, and the possibility of forgetting. We're told staying present in our bodies is a good thing generally, but I would also like to attend to the aspect of letting go, dissolving points of coagulation after witnessing and confronting them, and thinking of the loss of certain bodily memory as necessary. For future consideration on working with scores, as in *Recipes to Wayfinding*, I'd love to explore non-didactic ways of helping people move through these flows – comfortably, or maybe with a generative discomfort.

ALECIA: I'm thinking about Urmimala Sarka Munsi's important work on reimagining the bodies of survivors of trafficking,[7] whose work I came to know about through Meghna Bhardwaj. In her writing, she quotes Roger Bechtel's work on trauma and traumatic memories: Traumatic memories do need to be "recovered" in order for the victim to mourn, but they are not holistic and intact, waiting anxiously for a probing therapeutic intervention to reveal them. In fact, what makes an event traumatic is one's inability to transform the lived experience into memory at the time of its occurrence. A traumatic memory, then, is not one that is hidden, but one that is not yet made. Instead, the traumatic experience becomes trapped in the body – "possesses" the body, as Cathy Caruth puts it – for the traumatized body cannot let down its guard, the lingering activation of its "fight or flight" response to the traumatic threat keeping it in a state of adrenalized hyperarousal.[8]

His insights into trauma are powerful when thinking about the act of forgetting and dismissing conflict as well. When we are able to acknowledge the wounds and vulnerabilities that are exposed during times of rupture and crisis, particularly at the time of occurrence, we can begin to pave the way for repair and dialogue.

JILL: I've been thinking about our previous conversations about preparing people for entry into a work, whether it's a workshop or simply encountering the repository or set of scores online. Could you talk about listening, and training modes of attention, and specifically about the use of scores to train people's modes of attention and attunement to some of these circuits, gestures, and complexities of care? I'm also curious about whether, for both audience and creators, there is a difference between textual and video scores; and further, if there is a difference between a kind of score that invites rest versus one that invites meditation on conflict.

ALECIA: The audience's commitment to spending time with the process is crucial. Experiencing a shared moment with others and staying with a certain movement or instruction, requires cutting out distractions. I usually begin with some grounding exercises to remind them of their breath and bring them back to their bodies. When running some of the workshops digitally, quite a bit of pre-workshop preparation had to be done to minimize technical hiccups once the session begins. Depending on the demographic of the groups I was working with, I also had to attune to digital gestures and modes of connecting and dialogue. Verbal dialogue was more embraced by some older participants, so I've also used other non-verbal channels such as the chatbox to encourage other meaningful responses from participants. I think a score offers a starting point, to begin. Without the presence of a score as a guiding map or list of instructions, it's like working in a large empty studio. It can be incredi-

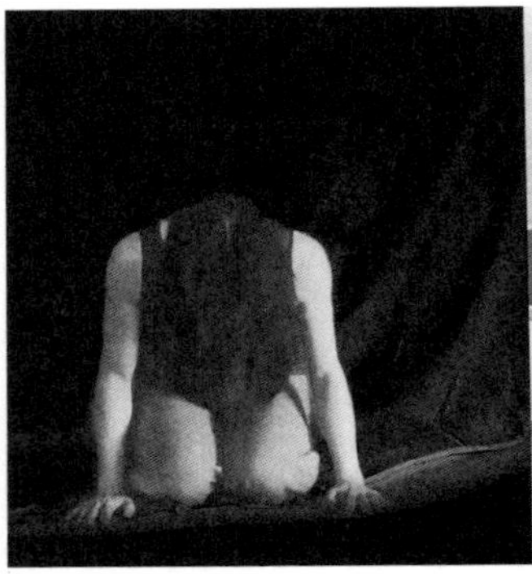

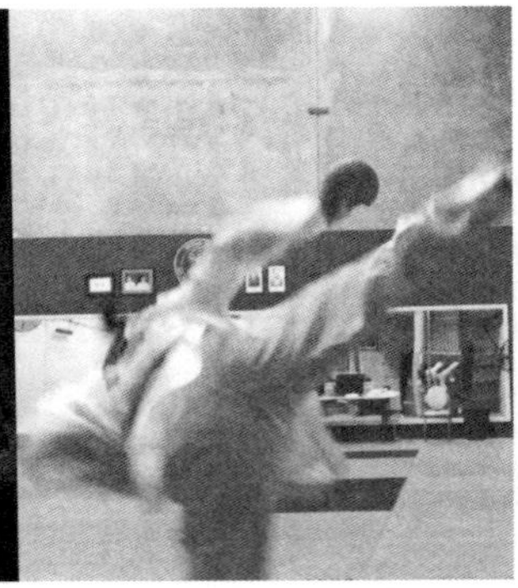

Video still from *Breath, Void, Tremble* (2021), video score contributed by Alecia Neo during the *Presence of Mind* Digital Residency.

Video still from *Kiai* (2021), video score contributed by Kristina Mah during the *Presence of Mind* Digital Residency.

bly challenging and intimidating for anyone. I think of the score as means for people to discover their own rhythms, methods and pathways. Engaging with a score, particularly one that has emerged from another person's lived realities, invites concentration, potentially the capacity to read a story differently. The use of video scores contributed by different collaborators is often accompanied by textual prompts and descriptions that facilitate the understanding of the videos.

For the *Presence of Mind* digital residency project, several contributions delved into our interdependence with nature, while others reflected upon

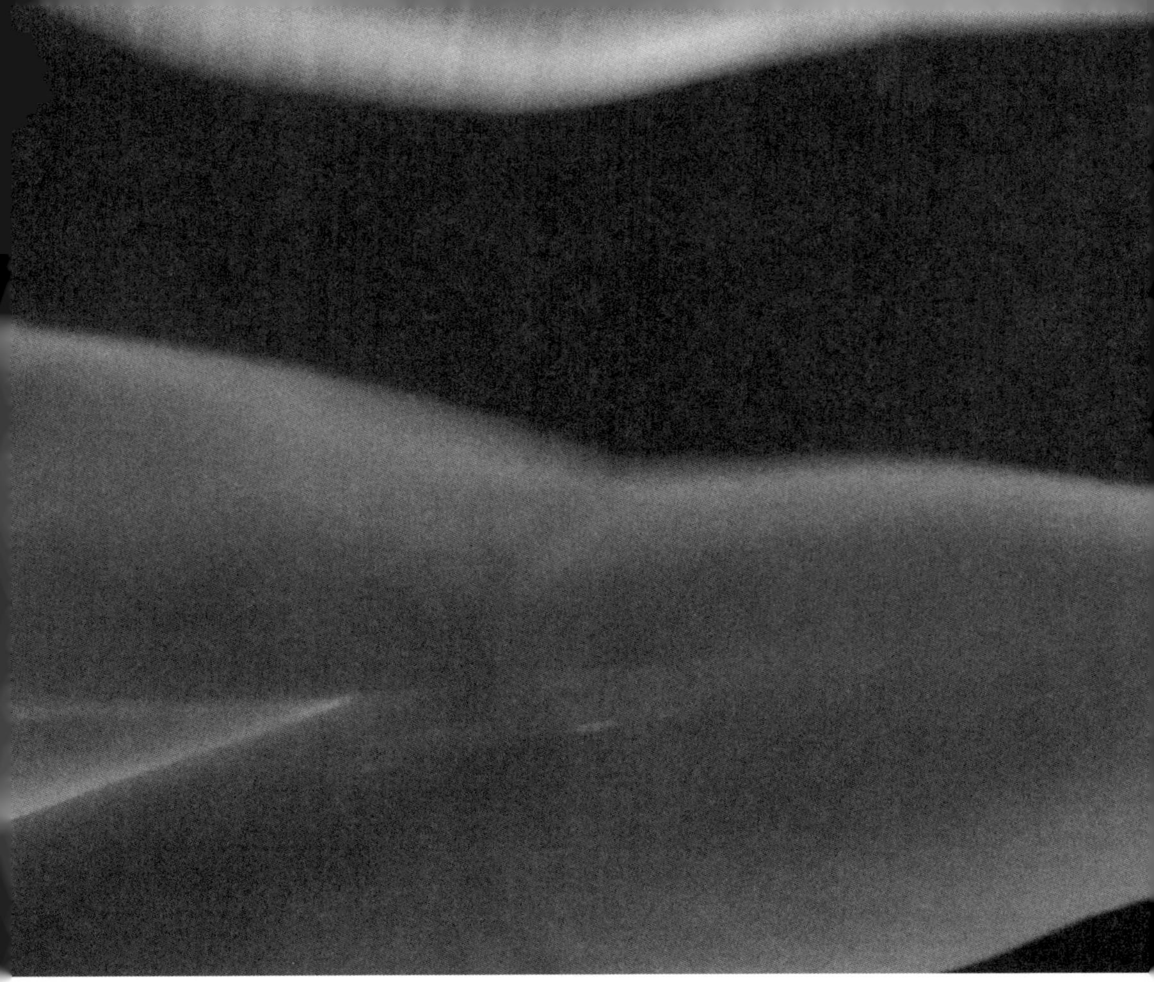

mortality, impermanence and grief. In one of the video scores titled *Kiai*, contributed by artist Kristina Mah, who is also a competitive karate athlete, she reflects on dwelling as a process of being in transition. This reflection emerged from the throes of deep preparation for the World Championships in Karate. She writes, "After the structure is established, we must develop our own sense of confidence in the practice that leads to courage and safety. This unfolds through nurturing, resting, yielding. But this 'softness' moves together with 'hardness', perseverance, striving, and difficulty. These are two aspects of one process." I think her score *Kiai* speaks to the non-linear journey of learning and developing maturity in a practice. It requires expanding one's capacities to hold space for conflicting but necessary needs ... to exceed, endure, maintain, fail and recover. She also created a second score *Shift*, which was a direct response to the process of confronting the pain and profound losses from a recent physical injury, which disrupted her participation in the World Championships. These two scores that emerged from the *Care Index* digital residency captured "scenes" from the same journey for Kristina.

My own contribution reflects upon anger's relationship with care, vulnerability and forgiveness. In classical Buddhist teachings, compassion is described as the heart that can tremble in the face of suffering, and I experimented with inviting proximity to trembling via movements of light and breath. During our discussions with the group, we talked about how to invite restfulness in anger. A process that involves acknowledging its presence, looking closely at it, and tracing its origins to uncover its true nature.

NOTES

1. Neo, Alecia. "Open Call." *Open Call*, 2020, https://www.careindex.net/open-call.
2. Neo, Alecia. "Public Archives." *Care Index*, 2020, https://www.careindex.net/public-archives.
3. Centre for Photography and Film, *Objectifs*. "Personally Speaking: Alecia Neo." OBJECTIFS, 9 Apr. 2019, https://www.objectifs.com.sg/ps_alecianeo/.
4. Fries, Kath, and Rachael Kiang. "Presence of Mind: 11 December 2021 – 26 February 2022." *Gallerylanecove*, Gallery Lane Cove + Creative Studios, 2021, https://www.gallerylanecove.com.au/presence-of-mind.
5. Rajendran, Charlene. "Becoming a Faciliactor: Playing at Fiction on the Borderlines of Culture." *Applied Theatre Research*, vol. 8, no. 2, 2020, pp. 245–257., https://doi.org/10.1386/atr_00041_1.
6. Neo, Alecia. "Wayfinding Scores." *Care Index*, 2022, https://www.careindex.net/scores/wayfinding-scores.
7. Munsi, Urmimala Sarkar. "Urmimala Sarkar Munsi, 'Mediations around an Alternative Concept of 'Work': Re-Imagining the Bodies of Survivors of Trafficking.'" *Lateral*, Cultural Studies Association, 9 July 2021, https://csalateral.org/issue/5–2/mediations-work-bodies-survivors-trafficking-sarkar-munsi/.
8. Bechtel, Roger. "The Body of Trauma: Empathy, Mourning, and Media in Troika Ranch's Loopdiver." *Theatre Journal*, vol. 65, no. 1, 2013, pp. 77–93. JSTOR, http://www.jstor.org/stable/41819823. Accessed 8 Jun. 2022.

KATE LACEY

Slow Radio, Easy Listening and the Ethics of Care

Circling around the idea of "slow radio," this essay offers a critical reflection on how listening is presented as a form of care in the media. The discourse of "sonic self-care" has become increasingly familiar with the promotion of noise-cancelling technologies, digitized sound therapies, personalized track lists and other forms of what Mark Hagood calls "orphic mediation." As orphic media "foreground a deep desire for control as freedom," it is perhaps not surprising that they seemed to become more prominent through the pandemic and its privations.[1] But listening as a care for self, and as a care for others, has long been entangled in the history and infrastructure of radio and other audio media. It can be found most explicitly in relation to the business – whether mainstream or marginal – of producing sounds and music mixes with a focus on contemplation, relaxation and slowing down.

The BBC is just one major broadcaster that has begun playing with the idea of "slow radio" in recent years, most notably with a series of broadcasts-turned-podcasts on BBC Radio 3, its station for classical music, arts and cultural programing. The BBC website promotes *Slow Radio* as "an antidote to today's frenzied world," a chance "to step back from the busy hurly-burly of life."[2] Suggesting that slow radio allows you to "take time out to recharge and understand the world and all its crazy ways in a new light" Radio 3 Controller, Alan Davey, has said that Radio 3 is the "natural home for slow radio because we are the place where things have always taken the time they take."[3] The BBC extended its offer of slow programing during the pandemic, with the launch of Radio 1 Relax, a streaming service of soundscapes, calming noises, and advice on mindfulness aimed to support young people dealing with the stresses of lockdown.[4]

The *Slow Radio* series is, slowly, building up an archive of immersive sound walks, nature recordings and audio close-ups of nostalgic, meditative or restorative sounds. Examples include the sounds of slow sheep in southern Spain, a mountain climb in the Lake District, and the sounds of a Norwegian forest that involves, among other things, the sound of tadpoles hibernating in the snow. An early contribution included a "late night duet between a shakuhachi player and a nightingale."[5] For anyone interested in the history of British radio, this last example will ring a bell, as it immediately – and self-consciously – conjures up inherited memories of the famous Nightingale broadcasts with the cellist Beatrice Harrison.[6]

In May 1924, the BBC's very first experiment with outside broadcasting had featured Harrison playing a "duet" with a nightingale in her Surrey woodland garden.[7] It clearly resonated with listeners, attracting some 50,000 fan letters, and turning Harrison's garden into something of a tourist destination. Its success saw the duet repeated annually for the next 12 years, relayed by international broadcasters like CBS, and recordings released by HMV. From 1936, ten minutes of nightingale song was also broadcast before midnight every night, to "bring solace" to the listeners.[8] Commenting on the surprise success of this experiment, the famously dour Director General, John Reith, remarked that "something closely akin to emotionalism" was sweeping the country. While he might not have entirely approved, he did acknowledge the "glamour of romance" that had "flashed across the prosaic round of many a life."[9] It brought the sound of nature to urban listeners and a brief shelter from the shadows of war and human turmoil. The cello and the nightingale programs somehow continue to resonate in the national imaginary, and people petitioned the BBC to record a new version on the 90th anniversary in 2014.[10]

In his extensive essay on the making and meanings of this early media event, Iain Logie Baird reflected on the affective responses to these broadcasts in highlighting the "bluesy emotionality" of the Nightingale duets. He speculates about their function in relation to managing the encounter with what, in 1924, was still a strange new medium:

> By expressing or experiencing intense emotions [...] creatively through a new auditory medium, perhaps it seemed easier to come to terms with the uncertain emotions that radio itself stirred up – to regain a feeling of control – by its "taming" a natural environment that was familiar, and presenting it as content to console the listener.[11]

Antidote, solace, consolation: a century of broadcasting framed by a common vocabulary of care and compensation – and control. It is this striking parallel, expressed through broadcasts more than 90 years apart, that motivates this attempt to think through the ethics of care in broadcast communication, by examining in historical context the discourses circulating around such experiments.

It may be overstating the case to speak of a slow radio "movement," but recent experiments in slow radio can be seen as part of the wider slow movement that is usually traced back to the slow food manifesto of 1989.[12] Connected to the eco-activism and self-reliance movements of the 1970s, the manifesto emerged out of an Italian protest against McDonald's as the epitome of fast food and throwaway culture.[13] The movement set itself up in resistance to the temporal logics of industry and the machine, which activists argued were insistently colonizing and enslaving private space. It was a resistance of the local against the global, of craftsmanship against mass production, and of good taste against bad. It was also, significantly for the discussion to follow, a resistance politics based in the demand for "guaranteed sensual pleasure," a demand rooted in a politics of self-care.

Gradually, the slow movement moved into other areas of life, by now taking in slow travel, slow cities, slow schools, slow books, slow living and slow money.[14] There are many books on the subject, both popular and academic, and any number of calls to slow things down, such as slow business, slow journalism, slow art, slow fashion, slow beauty and, appealingly, slow scholarship.[15] Unsurprisingly, there are also calls for "slow media."[16] One expression of this is the "slow media manifesto" declared in 2010 which, like the slow food manifesto, envisages a consumer-led resistance to the commercial logic of the mainstream.[17] It focuses on the quality of communication, the sociability of the social, the mindfulness of mediation and the acknowledgement of the act of listening as equal to the act of speaking up. In this more critical iteration, it is a rejection of the acceleration and proliferation of data and information flows under capitalism, and a promise of a return to reflective and deliberate public engagement.[18] A similar manifesto for the digital age has been declared under the rubric "Slowcial Media," dedicated to "unhurried and meaningful" human to human communications, and highlighting apps, platforms and other initiatives with similar aims.[19] Slow media, in short, continue to be proffered as an antidote to a wide range of social and political ills of the digital age.

It is no surprise that the slow movement took to the air, alongside other media, to spread the word. In fact, Carlo Petrini, the leading figure of the slow food movement, had run one of the first stations of the Italian free radio movement in the 1970s, Radio Bra Onde Rosse, that decades later came to inspire projects like the slow food podcast network, Heritage Radio.[20] Slow Living Radio, one of many such online channels, carries the tagline, "Tune in. Slow down. Live well," describing its intention to "create a strong sense of place, a better balance and an appreciation of the simpler experiences life has to offer."[21] But as well as media evangelizing the slow movement, there have also been plenty of aesthetic and commercial experiments in slow media.

"Slow cinema," with its aesthetics of duration, stillness and even boredom, has many antecedents, particularly in counter-cultural and art cinema, but began to be recognized as a distinct genre in anglophone film criticism in the last two decades.[22] Meanwhile, "Slow Television" launched in Norway in 2009. These marathon broadcasts, usually a live feed from a single static camera, included continuous footage from a seven hour rail journey along the entire length of the Bergen line, eighteen hours of live salmon fishing, and the twelve-hour long broadcast on National Wood Night in 2013 that attracted a fifth of the population to tune in to programs about chopping, drying and stacking wood, culminating in the live transmission of eight hours of an open fireplace.[23] Thomas Hellum, the producer of these pioneering shows, said the secret of slow media is "that there is no producer who has decided what is exciting and what is not. Everything is there, and the viewer himself [sic] must find out what is interesting and what is boring."[24] It was a statement that not only obscures the production choices and broader institutional infrastructures of broadcasting but seeks to offer a populist defence of a quite esoteric experiment. In doing so, it encapsulates a perennial tension in thinking about the audience of slow media, revealing as it does a curious mix of crediting the audience with the ability to produce meaning for themselves, while implying that in every other media encounter the audience has surrendered this capacity more or less passively to the whim of the producer.

At root, though, it is a description that wants to demonstrate slow media's care for the audience.

When these programs first launched, the broadcasting of such non-events was, paradoxically, "event television." They were later promoted as "the next big thing" by on-demand services like Netflix,[25] and are certainly now commonplace on most streaming services, albeit listed under adjectives like "meditative," "wellbeing" or "calming," rather than specifically "slow."[26] Social media platforms like YouTube, Reddit and Vimeo provide a convenient location for more local or amateur production of longform and ambient video, including livestreaming.[27] Livestreams from zoos and aquariums became especially popular during the enforced isolation of lockdown.[28]

Amazon was a relatively early adopter of slow content, with its "Window Channel Network" offering "immersive and rejuvenating" scenic films that unfolded to soothing real-time field recordings of ambient sound.[29] In 2018, WCN was acquired by a digital health company, *Sharecare*, to expand its business in the multi-billion dollar mediation and relaxation industry. Alongside providing longform relaxation videos for healthcare and spa settings, the acquisition was driven by the recognition that engagement with slow media via data-gathering apps could be personalized, quantified, gamified, and monetized.[30] Users' engagement with *Sharecare*'s content produces personalized data sets where meeting certain "health indicators" earns them rewards and unlocks access to premium services.[31] It is just one example of the exponential marketization of technologies of the self in an era where the desire for individual autonomy and self-knowledge meet consumer culture and digitized forms of networked individualism.[32] Self-care (as self-tracking, self-improvement, self-disciplining) through digitized slow communication, quietude and silence has, in this way, been thoroughly appropriated by the accelerated consumer culture from which it promises its users an escape.

Some of this slow video material is decidedly nostalgic, particularly for analogue forms of media. A lot of it is also pitted decidedly against the insistent pull of screen culture, not least the pestering temptations of the mobile phone, albeit that many of these videos will be accessed via phones and their apps. There is much to say about this, but for the purposes of this essay the key thing is how much these efforts seem to be about making screen culture function more like the classical idea of radio: there is a constant or at least very extended stream of output; it works as a secondary medium, providing distraction and accompaniment while doing other things; and it is precisely the audio track that provides the unbroken engagement with the text. Sounds of birdsong and water tend to dominate. Many slow videos are almost motionless, bringing their soundtrack to the fore, and claiming this makes them perfect background material to accompany "sleep, study, work, or relaxation." One aficionado of slow TV on Netflix is quoted as saying: "I've been putting it on when I'm doing other things, like painting, going through bills, folding laundry [...] Slow TV is good for making the room feel more alive, while at the same time not competing for my attention."[33] *Sharecare Windows* on Amazon Prime even offers "black screen" videos, like "9 hour Rainstorm for Sleep."[34]

Perhaps this is one of the reasons that among all the experiments with and discussions about the varieties of slow media, there is actually rather little about slow radio. Google "slow radio" and you're more likely to come up with various easy listening stations than anything else.[35] This is interesting because it might suggest that there is, from the perspective of the listener at least, a very long history of "slow radio," and the pleasures and distractions it offers, but that it has simply gone by other names. The second is that the term "slow radio" is otherwise used to denote radio that precisely eschews or at least minimizes the staples of what is clearly taken to be "normal speed" radio, namely music and speech.

In his archaeology of the term in the context of American radio, Keir Keightley finds "easy listening" used from the late 1930s (but dominant 1946–66) to describe a radio-friendly style of presentation, that didn't go "hammer and tongs," but was "restrained, less emotional."[36] Here is another paradox. "Easy listening" is used as a shorthand not only for a particular kind of music, but for a particular kind of auditory experience that was one expression of "care" for the listener – a promise not to disturb, but to accommodate to the domestic conditions of reception, offering soothing companionship and respite for the ears. On the one hand, "easy" became part of the promotional vocabulary of advertisers who sought to sell their products with the promise of freedom from labor (while disguising the labor embodied in the products and the labor required to earn the means to consume such projects). On the other hand, it became a dismissive, even disdainful, shorthand for a kind of attention that is precisely undemanding and easily available to all.[37]

Meanwhile, the more critical tradition of slow radio often requires its audience to invest in the labor of listening, to work at listening more deeply. It is often explicitly interventionist in aiming to disrupt broadcasting conventions and convenient listener experiences. One such activist attempt at subversion was Radio Boredcast, 744 hours of eclectic slow content broadcast as part of the 2012 International Festival of Art, Technology, Music and Film.[38] Despite being described as freeform radio, there was a good deal of unrushed curation that aimed to fill the available time over the four week festival with an eclectic mix of "engaging, entertaining and unpredictable" content. To this extent, it bears a striking resemblance to the vernacular modernism of the early public radio schedules in the years before broadcast genres and conventions had become established, when the new medium offered up a premonition of empty time to be filled.[39] And yet, from the perspective of those caught up in contemporary commercial media logics, the idea of "freeform" radio can be posited as an alternative participatory ethic of care, not only in relation to listeners, but also in relation to fellow creative practitioners, with the promise of liberation from the shackles of the schedule.

A radically different approach to filling time is represented by the slow radio produced by the Wetland Project. Each year on April 22, Earth Day, a single day-long soundscape of the Saturna Island marsh in Canada is streamed worldwide.[40] These recordings, by Brady Marks and Mark Timmings, are made in the spirit of acoustic ecology, and specifically Bruce Davis' 1975 call for "wilderness radio" as a kind of radio that "listens in," rather than "broadcasts out."[41] For Brady, American commercial radio's stylistic and acoustic template was all about "tending towards smoothness and speed to maximise domestic listeners' receptiveness to advertising messages."[42] In contrast, the slow, jarring and unpredictable sounds of the wilderness, overlain on the urban soundscape would, he claimed, disrupt listeners' expectations and recalibrate their relationship to mediated sound, time and the environment.[43]

SLOW RADIO AND HIERARCHIES OF ATTENTION

Throughout radio's history (and beyond), these different modes of attention – the distracted and the concentrated, the indiscriminate and the discerning – have been used as markers of distinction, mapped, as often as not, onto prevailing class distinctions. And certainly, it is possible to see this at play in the way in which "slow radio" is actively distinguished from "easy listening radio," in terms of content and the spaces in which it operates. Its heritage lies more squarely in the traditions of sound art, soundscapes and acoustic ecology than broadcast radio. But the rhetoric about care for the listener, and about providing an acoustic balm for the trials of modern living, is remarkably similar, and crosses otherwise persistent borderlines.

In this respect, the popularization of slow radio in its more mainstream forms as "easy listening" contrasts with those forms of slow media where the purpose of slowing down is precisely to demand or facilitate greater concentration, deeper attention. Slow cinema, for example, is difficult, challenging cinema, a rejection of the fast editing rhythms of mainstream film, and an invitation to contemplate the "image of the duration of things" (Bazin in Mulvey, p.103). It can be demanding on the body, too, spending hours or days on end in darkened auditoria. In some instances, this challenge is pushed to impossible limits. There have been attempts to scale up slowness;

for example, a "very slow movie player" has been mooted that would slow a movie down so much it would take a year to view.[44] There are many instances of stretched audio, too, of course. A neat example that encapsulates the interplay of the corporate and the experimental is a super-slowed version of the Microsoft 95 sound, a 7 second sonic corporate logo originally composed by Brian Eno, champion of ambient music.[45] But in terms of sheer continuous duration, even the most mainstream radio schedule in its endless flow has always already exceeded comprehension by an individual listener. Individual radio shows and dramas can run for years and decades. Slow radio is rarely as physically demanding as some forms of slow cinema, though it can also be about challenging auditory norms and about encouraging heightened awareness – of duration, certainly, but also of space and the environment. However, the broader terrain of slow radio output does seem designed less to challenge the senses than to soothe them.

There are, then, two contradictory tactics at work here – distanciation and immersion (tactics that might crudely be associated separately with the eye and ear). The first is about creating a critical distance by drawing attention to the absence of conventional forms of editing and presentation. This is perhaps particularly evident where "slow radio" is embedded in the normal flow of broadcasting (like the slow radio segments on Radio 3's "Late Junction" or Radio 4's "Broadcasting House"). Here it acts as an extended pause button, a putting on of brakes. Paradoxically, its more contemplative mode serves as an interruption, a formally discomforting break from the norm, however comforting the content. The second is about encouraging the listener to experience sounds "in the moment," as they unfold as if in real time. Here is where we see the connection to current discourses about "mindfulness" as a response to the distractions and permanent receptivity of modern mediated experience, the irony of doing so through another form of mediation, notwithstanding.

Occasionally, these two tactics overlap, as in the example of "Radio Lento," a slow radio podcast that made waves during the Covid-19 lockdowns. The podcast consists of "unedited" 3D field recordings of the British countryside made as a hobby during family walks. The couple who makes them, Hugh

Huddy and Madeleine Sugden, contrast their work with the formalism and artistry of Radio 3's "Slow Radio" which for them is embedded in the traditions and interventions of soundscape craft. They eschew the "overly designed overly edited speeded-up view of the world,"[46] claiming it is the very "concept of time" that they want to "preserve."[47] However, the key ambition is to offer up their recordings as therapeutic access to nature, and as a shield against noise, distraction and the travails of modern life.[48]

SLOW RADIO AND THE ETHICS OF CARE

In this way, slow radio, in line with the broader slow media movement and the whole "mindfulness industry," is commonly framed in terms of an ethics of care for the self, as a defensive and privatized response to the "malign velocities" of contemporary life.[49] It is a trope that was at work a century ago at the dawn of broadcasting, but that has in recent years become ubiquitous as it is so easily aligned with the interests of neoliberal economics and the politics of individualism.

There is a lucrative market for slow media genres that either incongruously or cynically exploit the apparently widespread desire to escape media logics. To this extent, these forms of slow media (together with many apps and podcasts offering varieties of "healing sounds") are connected to familiar strategies like "digital detox," "unplugging," or "monotasking" promoted to help consumers with what is variously called the "barrage," "bombardment," or simple "addictiveness" of media. But using slow media as a salve, or as a temporary respite, seems only to shore up those dynamics, to serve the interests of what Evgeny Morozov already nearly a decade ago called "the mindfulness racket."[50] From this perspective, slow media can only offer the semblance of escape, rather than working for change; in fact they work to accommodate the user more effectively to the prevailing conditions from which they seek to escape. It is a paradox that pervades such programing, even when it is offered by public service broadcaster like the BBC.

Similarly, for all its promise of resistance, the slow media manifesto is caught up in these wider logics. Article 11 declares that "Slow Media are auratic [...] They generate a feeling that the particular medium belongs to just that moment of the user's life" (David et al., 2010, n.p.). This is a discourse of control, but also of retreat to interiority. In terms of slow radio, it is arguably a denial of the open-ended collectivity inherent in the classic broadcast address. In the rise of the discourse of "mindfulness" and "self-care," there is a real sense in which the iniquities and stresses of life under neo-liberalism or "fast capitalism" can no longer be resisted or contested, let alone overturned; we simply have to work on ourselves to feel better – and work more efficiently – within the system.

This aspect is mirrored in the mainstream in the way radio channels increasingly produce schedules, shows and mixes designed explicitly to create a certain mood, whether designed to help focus more on the secondary task at hand, to gear up for a new day's work, or to recover and relax from the exertions and stresses of the day. There are mixes to pick you up, but there seem to be even more to calm you and to wind you down. There are even programs to help you sleep, once the last escape from the media world.[51] Away from slow radio per se, there are any number of podcasts that offer slow stories, slow news, and variations on the internet sensation (literally) that is ASMR, with its slow, hypnotic whispering, tapping and other audio triggers.[52] Listeners are addressed and interpellated as private individuals, entire unto themselves rather than as members of a public.

So, there is certainly a risk that self-care draws people away from a more political or proactive response to the situation they find themselves in. But from another perspective, self-care is ethical, in the Foucauldian sense of ethics as the self's relationship to the self. Foucault delineated an ethical framework for "living a beautiful life" in which caring for the self becomes "a matter of pleasure, autonomy, and self-mastery in the present," a self which is created and regulated through daily choices and practices.[53] Switching off, and tuning out of the normal flow of media messages – or immersing oneself in the *longue duree*, rather than floating along amid the flotsam and jetson of the data flow – might be one example of such a practice. Indeed, there can be a radical dimension to such an ethic of self-care. The American civil rights activist, Audre Lorde, famously argued that in some contexts self-care is not about self-indulgence, but rather self-preservation. Self-care, she argued, could become an act of warfare, a way "to exist in a world that is diminishing."[54] Not all forms of self-care are about accommodation to the system, but about surviving to fight another day.

But, as ever, context is all. There is a pervasive sense in which the vocabulary of self-care has been appropriated by the very neo-liberal system from which it ostensibly offers some respite. Self-care all too often is literally sold to us, available only in pre-packaged and commodified forms, requiring new forms of labor and more calls on our time. There are powerful images in circulation of what a cared-for self should look like, the norms to which the cared-for body should conform. These hollowed out forms of self-care are then put on display and recirculated as what might be called "selfie-care."[55] Thus the cycle is ratcheted up, producing new forms of exclusion for those who can afford neither the time nor the money for the extravagant forms of self-care demanded by the logics of neo-liberalism. Whatever form it takes, an ethics of care that is focussed only on the self could never be sufficient. Feminist and radical care ethics highlight the need for interdependency, the need to care for both self and others and to do so as part of everyday relations and practices.

The paradoxes and contradictions around the experiments with slow radio and its various counterparts in the end suggest that the ethics of care are neither predicated nor constrained by what kinds of sounds are played, nor for what duration. Speed is relative, after all, and the care we need comes in different forms. But the discourses that circulate around slow radio might matter, sitting as they do along a series of familiar fault lines – between image and sound, the mainstream and the margins, invocations of good taste and bad, the individual and the collective. How these discourses are embedded in structures of care is also important, and in this context, that includes the institutional structures and infrastructures where slow radio is presented and how it interpellates its listeners. Slow radio in the end treads the shifting line between discourses of public service media and media that are merely self-serving.

NOTES

1. See Hagood, M. (2019). *Hush: Media and Sonic Self-Control. Durham,* NC: Duke University Press. Also: "Everybody Hertz: These Artists Heal with the Profound Power of Sound," *Elephant*, no.40, 29 January 2020: https://elephant.art/healing-sound-art-gong-meditation-pauline-oliveros-29-01-2020/
2. This programming began with a short series in 2017, becoming a permanent feature from 2018. BBC Radio 3 Slow Radio: http://www.bbc.co.uk/programmes/p05k5bq0; BBC Radio 3: A Slow Radio Soundscape: Birdsong and Vapour Trails http://www.bbc.co.uk/programmes/b08rg41l. There is also a regular weekly "slow radio" item on Radio 4's *Broadcasting House* show, where listeners send in their own soundscape recordings.
3. Mark Brown (2017), "Raft of new BBC Radio 3 programmes will take 'slow radio' to the next level," *The Guardian*, August 30.
4. Anita Singh (2020) "BBC's cure for pandemic stress: the streaming sound of rustling paper," *The Telegraph*, April 22.
5. https://www.bbc.co.uk/programmes/p0689tgk#play. This isn't an isolated case of musicians duetting with nightingales. David Rothenburg has made several recordings with nightingales in Berlin. See: https://www.nightingalesinberlin.com
6. Robert Seatter (2016) "The cello and the nightingale", *BBC News*, 25 March, https://www.bbc.co.uk/news/magazine-35861899. To listen to a recording, visit: https://www.bbc.com/historyofthebbc/anniversaries/may/cello-and-nightingale-duet.
7. For a detailed account, including the technical aspects, see Iain Logie Baird (2015) "Capturing the song of the nightingale," *Science Museum Group Journal* 19 October, Issue 4 T DOI: http://dx.doi.org/10.15180/150402; The BBC has recently revealed that this first broadcast was a "fake" as the sound engineers had frightened the nightingales away, and so they resorted to a "siffleuse," a whistling artist, to stand in for the bird. See Dalya Alberge (2022) "The cello and the nightingale: 1924 duet was faked, BBC admits," *The Guardian*, April 8.
8. Michael Guida (2015) "Britain's sonic therapy: listening to birdsong during and after the First World War," *Remedia* June 2015. https://remedianetwork.net/2015/06/16/britains-sonic-therapy-listening-to-birdsong-during-and-after-the-first-world-war/ See also: Guida, Michael (2021) *Listening to British Nature: Wartime, Radio, and Modern Life, 1914–1945.* Oxford University Press.
9. John Reith (1924) 'The broadcasting of silence' Radio Times 3:37, pp. 437–8.
10. Hannah Furness (2014) "BBC relives first wildlife broadcast 90 years on," *The Daily Telegraph*, May 11.
11. Logie Baird (2015) op cit.
12. "Slow Food Manifesto: International movement for the defense of and the right to pleasure." See: http://slowfood.com/filemanager/Convivium%20Leader%20Area/Manifesto_ENG.pdf. Also: Sabria David (2015) "The Slow Media Manifesto and its impact on different countries, cultures, and disciplines." In: *Of slowness in the age of speed.* Acta Universitatis Sapientiae, Social Analyses, 5, 1 107–112.
13. Kate Willink (2019) "Food culture, relationality and the Slow Food Movement," *Journal of European Popular Culture* 10, no.1, 61–73.
14. See: https://www.slowmovement.com. See also: Carl Honoré (2005) In *Praise of Slowness.* New York: HarperOne.

15. Ann Gallagher (2018) Slow ethics and the art of care. Emerald Group Publishing, 2020; Chambers, Jonathan, and Stephannie S. Gearhart, eds. (2018) *Reversing the cult of speed in higher education: the slow movement in the arts and humanities*. London: Routledge.
16. Jennifer Rauch (2011). "The origin of slow media: Early diffusion of a cultural innovation through popular and press discourse, 2002–2010," *Transformations* 20.
17. Sabria David, Jorg Blumtritt and Benedikt Kohler (2010). "Slow Media Manifesto," January 2. https://en.slow-media.net/manifesto. The manifesto led to the founding of the online "Slow Media Institute": http://slow-media-institut.net/. See also http://slow-media.org// Also Jennifer Rauch (2018) *Slow media: Why slow is satisfying, sustainable, and smart*. Oxford University Press.
18. See Christian Fuchs, "Slow media: how to renew debate in the age of digital authoritarianism," *The Conversation*, 23.4.19. Republished in *Digital Fascism*, 2022.
19. https://slowcialmedia.com
20. Gibson, Allison (2015) 'Welcome to the golden age of food radio: How a 1970s Italian pirate radio station is still shaping the conversation about how we eat. Eater https://www.eater.com/2015/7/15/8962823/food-radio-evan-kleiman-heritage-radio. See also: https://heritageradionetwork.org.
21. http://www.slowlivingradio.com
22. Bordwell and Thompson, 2011, cited in De Luca, Tiago and Nuno Barradas Jorge, eds (2015) *Slow Cinema*. Edinburgh University Press, 2015, p.2.
23. Roel Puijk (2015) "Slow television," *Nordicom Review* 36, no. 1, 95. There were earlier versions, like the German "Bahn TV," a specialist channel of Deutsche Bahn, the German rail company. See Sarah Lyall (2013) "Bark up or down: Firewood splits Norwegians," *New York Times*, February 20.
24. See Daniel Bukszpan (2016) "Slow TV: Netflix's chill, mesmerizing antidote fot he madness of 2016," *Daily Beast*, April 13. https://www.thedailybeast.com/slow-tv-netflixs-chill-mesmerizing-antidote-to-the-madness-of-2016. For an account of watching a 17 hour train journey across Australia, and the different kind of perception that evolves, see Naaman Zhou (2018) "I watched a 17-hour broadcast of a train crossing Australia. It didn't disappoint," *The Guardian*, January 14.
25. Bukszpan (2016) op cit.
26. An interactive map identifying slow television broadcasts from around the world is available at https://slowtvmap.com.
27. Some sites are available as apps, too, e.g. EarthCam TV.
28. Emma Gill (2020) "Zoos are livestreaming animals so isolated families can watch them play," *Manchester Evening News*, April 17.
29. https://thewindowchannel.wordpress.com/about/
30. https://about.sharecare.com/press-releases/sharecare-acquires-window-channel-network-closes-investment-from-wells-fargo-strategic-capital/
31. In 2020, Amazon's Alexa voice assistant service linked up with Sharecare to provide health information to users. Separately, though interestingly in this context, Amazon has recently been promoting Wi-Fi-enabled "Echo Frames" (audio glasses with microspeakers and a microphone in the arms of the frame) that allow users to take Alexa with them and engage with Amazon content hands-free and on the move. Unlike earphones, their selling point is allowing the user to "stay in the moment" as they allow ears to stay "open." See: https://www.amazon.com/All-new-Echo-Frames/dp/B083C58VDP

32. See, for example, Karakayali, N., Kostem, B. and Galip, I. (2018) "Recommendation systems as technologies of the self: Algorithmic control and the formation of music taste," *Theory, Culture & Society*, 35(2), pp.3–24; Ajana, Btihaj. "Digital health and the biopolitics of the Quantified Self," *Digital Health* 3 (2017): 2055207616689509.; Castells, M. (2007) "Communication, power and counter-power in the network society," *International journal of communication*, 1(1).
33. Bukszpan (2016), op cit.
34. https://www.amazon.com/Sharecare-Windows-Prime-Video-Movies-TV/s?k=Sharecare+Windows&rh=n%3A2858778011
35. One portal at the time of writing (2022) lists167 slow radio stations with names like Mello FM, Slow Jamz and Love Radio. See https://streema.com/radios/genre/Slow.
36. Keir Keightley (2008) "Music for Middlebrows: defining the easy listening era, 1946-1966," *American Music* 26, no.3: 309–335, p.312.
37. Keightley, op cit. p.313.
38. People Like Us: Radio Boredcast Schedule: http://peoplelikeus.org/2012/radio-bored-cast-schedule/. The whole event, together with its tagline, "As Slow as Possible" countered the 2012 Olympic motto,"Faster, Higher Stronger." See Geeta Dayal (2012) "Got a moment? Listen to a 744 hour radio show," *Wired*, March 9, https://www.wired.com/2012/03/slow-radio/. See also Elena Razlagova (2013) "The past and future of music listening: Between freeform DJs and recommendation algorithms," in Jason Loviglio and Michele Hilmes, eds. *Radio's New Wave: Global Sound in the Digital Era*, New York and London: Routledge, pp.70–71.
39. Kate Lacey (2018) "Radio's vernacular modernism: The schedule as modernist text," *Media History* 24, no. 2: 166–179.
40. "Slow Radio Broadcast" http://www.wetlandproject.com/ra-more.php. This page contextualises the broadcasts and reproduces the listener feedback received about the 2020 Earth Day broadcast (i.e. during the pandemic).
41. Bruce Davis (1975) "FM radio as observational access to wilderness environments," *Alternatives* 21–27. See also: World Forum for Acoustic Ecology, https://www.wfae.net
42. Davis (1975), ibid, p.22.
43. For an interesting discussion of slow TV in relation to temporalities on an ecological scale, see Julia Leyda and Sara Brinch (2020) "Anthropocene slow TV: Temporalities of extinction in Svalbard," *Journal of Scandinavian Cinema* 10, no. 3: 297–309.
44. Bryan Boyer, "Creating a Very Slow Movie Player," *Medium*, 22 December 2018, https://medium.com/s/story/very-slow-movie-player-499f76c48b62
    This is part of a longer and evolving history of how media users (as audiences and producers), can speed up or slow down media content. See, for example, Jonathan Sterne and Mara Mills, "Second Rate: Tempo Regulation, Helium Speech, and 'Information Overload,'" Triple Canopy #26 (2020): https://www.canopycanopycanopy.com/issues/26/contents/second-rate
45. Brian Eno – Windows 95 Sound x23 https://www.youtube.com/watch?v=fNIfbdi41ho&t=2s
46. https://radiolento.podbean.com. Cited in the description for Podcast 112, Suffolk Wood, part 12, 26.3.22.
47. Cited in Carrie O'Grady, "Next – a hedgehog snuffling! The lockdown lifeline capturing the sounds of Britain," *The Guardian*, 1.12.20. https://www.theguardian.com/culture/2020/dec/01/radio-lento-lockdown-lifeline-sounds-britain-hedgehog
48. https://madlinblog.wordpress.com/2020/09/18/digital-experiences-of-nature/
49. Noys, B. (2014) *Malign velocities: Accelerationism and capitalism*, John Hunt Publishing.

50. Evegeny Mozorov, “The Mindfulness Racket,” *The New Republic*, February 24, 2014. See also, Chandler D and Reid J (2016) *The Neoliberal Subject: Resilience, Adaptation and Vulnerability.* London: Rowman & Littlefield.

51. Sounds of nature and gentle music are common in sleep apps; slow “sleep stories” are also becoming very popular, where soothing tones and unexciting content are designed not to be listened to the end. Siobhan Norton (2020), “Can’t sleep? Millions are using the Calm app to hear a soothing bedtime story for grown-ups,” *inews*, October 10. There is also a growing market in radio sets and white noise machines designed for sound and sleep therapy. See also Jonathan Crary (2013) *24/7: Late capitalism and the ends of sleep*, London: Verso Books.

52. There is an extensive literature on ASMR, but for an interesting discussion that focuses on its sonic, aesthetic and material qualities see Joanna Łapińska (2020) “Vibrations of worldly matter. ASMR as contemporary musique concrète,” *Estetyka i Krytyka* 57, no. 2: 21–35.

53. Laurie Ouellette and Jacquelyn Arcy (2015) “‘Live through this’: Feminist care of the self 2.0.” *Frame* 28, no. 1 95–114, p.100.

54. Audre Lorde (1988) *A burst of light: Essays*, London: Sheba Feminist Publishers.

55. Sarah Sharma, Lynx Sainte-Marie and Lauren Fournier (2017) “Antinomies of self-care,” *The Blackwood* 1, 14–15.

BRANDON LABELLE

Toward Acoustic Justice

In what ways does the urgency around *being heard* suggest or demand a deeper engagement with the dynamics of listening? And if being heard forms the basis for justice and recognition, as well as relational processes of emotional support, how might greater attention be given to fostering the conditions needed for such hearing to occur?

It is my concern to bring into focus the issue of acoustics and the ways in which it can be mobilized in working through such lines of questioning. While acoustic design is mostly understood as a professional practice contributing to urban planning, and the construction of specific architectures, such as concert halls or recording studios, I focus on capturing acoustics by way of the acts or practices whereby people modify and retune their environments or situations in order to support the movement of particular sounds. In doing so, such enactments contend with a given order of hearing, or what Roshanak Kheshti terms "regimes of aurality" (Kheshti 2015: XIX).

In considering such a perspective, I'm led to pose acoustics as a political question. If we consider acoustics as a range of material and social practices that condition or enable the movement of sound, and often in support of the articulation of particular views or desires, it can be appreciated how it impacts onto experiences of participation and emplacement, defining who or what is heard – whose voice may gain traction within particular places and in what way. In this sense, I highlight acoustics as *the distribution of the heard* extending from Jacques Rancière's political theories, and how "politics revolves around what is seen and what can be said about it, around who has the ability to see and the talent to speak, around the properties of spaces and the possibilities of time" (Rancière 2013: 8). As the distribution of the heard, acoustics contributes to what or who one hears, to the ways in which such hearing impacts onto processes of self-orientation, and how orientation gains definition according to the particularities of environments, institutional systems, and ideological leanings.

Following such perspectives, sound is emphasized as a deeply relational medium, one that enables social connection, processes of synchronization and desynchronization, attunement as well as interruption, and that moves across hearing and feeling, listening and touch; from the consonant to the dissonant, the harmonic to the cacophonous, sound provides a compelling framework for probing questions of relational experience as well as social equality.

Acoustics, in this sense, is positioned as a critical framework for engaging a politics of listening and the differing imaginaries and ideologies that work upon listening habits. As Kheshti highlights, regimes of aurality call upon particular ways of listening, establishing or reinforcing certain meanings and understandings of "the ideal listener" and how we take pleasure and support from what we hear. Yet, aurality is never so fixed, as one may equally find unexpected routes, or ways of hearing differently, tracing over or disturbing the acoustic lines placed before us.

What kinds of material, spatial or social arrangements are made to facilitate the movement of a given sound? To support the articulation or reverberation of certain voices and meanings, and the profound need to be heard? In what sense does acoustics function to host shared desires, or to hinder their circulation? What acoustic forces or forms exist that enable one's own voice to resound within particular rooms or institutions, and that aid in struggles over recognition? And further, how is one situated within the acoustic economies and histories at play within specific contexts?

In probing such questions, I argue for acoustics as the basis for considering approaches toward social equality and the making of collective worlds; acoustics as a path for reflecting upon the different forces at work in shaping the movements of people, particularly in struggles over recognition. In this context, the concept of acoustic justice is posited, one that can help in framing the critical work of being heard. This extends across micropolitical and macropolitical levels, from the immediate ways in which questions of access, fairness, and ethical regard play out within street-level encounters, and further, to how acoustics participates on the level of law and governmentality, for instance in the courtroom or the classroom, by contributing to the rules of audibility and the norms that impact on how bodies and voices are made to matter. Acoustic justice moves across issues of architecture and affect, social equality and recognition, and is posed in order to engage how hearing and being heard are vital to a political ecology of mutual concern and civility.

ORIENTATIONS: THE PSYCHOACOUSTIC TO THE SOCIAL ACOUSTIC

Understanding acoustics as a political question is based foremost on recognizing it as both a material and social issue. On one hand, acoustics is understood as the physical conditions, the architectures and spatial arrangements, that facilitate and shape the reflections and reverberations of sound: acoustics as a question of the physics of sound, the material properties of space, and the physiology of hearing, and how these are applied to strategies of design (Grueneisen 2003; Blesser / Salter 2015).

Following this perspective, acoustics dramatically contributes to a sense of personal orientation as well as social participation, lending to how one navigates through spaces and environments in capturing a sense of place or belonging. This includes appreciating how one synchronizes, attunes, and aligns with others by way of what one hears and feels, and how bodily or affective experiences support forms of participation. From such a material and social base, acoustics is understood to affect experiences of hearing as well as that of sociality, to influence the relationships one may form and within which listening becomes more operative. This leads to considering acoustics as having an impact onto the politics of recognition and location, and subsequent articulations of forms of life: acoustics as a politics through which struggles over recognition and rights, movement and access, belonging and participation are drawn out.

From a street-level perspective, acoustics may be considered less as a professional skill or science, and more through the everyday practices or gestures that work at securing paths of orientation. For instance, the spatial arrangements and social scenes, the vocal articulations and verbal arguments, the technological systems and cultural expressions communities make in support of particular forms of life, come to position acoustics within the arenas of everyday experience. Here, acoustics can be underscored as a *performativity*.

Such a view may be further unpacked to recognize a series of levels or modes by which acoustics is operative. This includes engaging with the psychoacoustic, and the physiological and neurological experiences or conditions of hearing that greatly inform not only what one is able to hear, but additionally how those experiences nurture a form of auditory cognition and imagination, and that are also shaped by way of the cultural particularities of one's listening positionality. Following the psychoacoustic, and the more personal status of hearing, we may consider the social acoustic and the dynamics of life with others; how acoustics, and the circulation of acoustic information, influences all types of social relationships – social acoustics as the exchanges afforded by way of sound and listening within given environments. An acoustic model or framework further integrates the electroacoustic, as the mediations of distributed sound and the technological apparatuses that enable sonic diffusion, that "point" sound in particular directions and around which social identities often gravitate, for instance in musical cultures. Finally, acoustic ecologies of human and more-than-human life allow for greater appreciation of acoustics as a critical ecological framework, which can assist in practices of care and sustainability. Through such an ecological perspective, a notion of the bioacoustic may be put forward to also speak toward the ways in which conceptualizations of *life by way of hearing* become politically operative, for example by the positioning or othering of the Deaf as being "unable" to hear and therefore less-than-human (Bauman 2004; Ladd 2003).

These levels or modes are suggestive for elaborating how acoustics can be thought in terms of regimes of aurality, and how the establishment of sonic and acoustic norms become sites of contestation – to contend with the social or bioacoustic framing of what counts as "good" or "acceptable" sound for example, or with the technological constructs that distribute sounds in particular ways to figure listening positionalities and behavior. In addition, identifying acoustics across a range of perspectives provides a base for querying how individuals and communities construct paths of resistance, togetherness, and social consciousness by way of sound and listening. This may be found in a range of instances where people rise up to demonstrate against systems of oppression or injustice. Throughout the uprisings in Beirut starting in October 2019 for example, there appeared a constant reference to "feeling unheard" on the part of ordinary people. Dubbed "the open-mic revolution" (Battah 2019), the protests and subsequent assemblies organized in Beirut were consistently based upon upsetting a given distribution of the heard (as dominated by the political elite and related media channels), and can be appreciated as an attempt to reorient the acoustic or sonic norms that often define not only what one hears, but equally how such auditory experiences can meaningfully resonate to impact systems of governance.

Rather than a strict concentration on sound, acoustics brings focus to the material, technical, and social conditions that surround and that affect embodied and collective life. In this regard, focusing on acoustics – from sonic imaginaries to electroacoustic mediations – enables a range of inquiries, which have at their center a concern for the ways in which one navigates and negotiates systems and discourses that impact onto defining a sense of place and participation. While expressions of sonic agency find articulation by way of the punctuated sounds one may make, acoustic justice is figured by considering the arrangements and configurations that allow for different types of orientation, from social and political to bodily and communal.

QUEER ACOUSTICS

Following this critical framework, I'm concerned to mobilize acoustics as the basis for contending with a politics of orientation; from the experience of hearing a specific event to the processes by which communities develop specific forms of being together – how some find their way by drawing support from the materialities and affordances of sonic experience, which include communicational, organizational, and affective capacities of acoustic acts, from the silences and noises, rhythms and vibrations that shape and inflect a sense of place and possibility. Acoustics may come to define a range of processes around which bodily orientation and recuperation, cultural expressivity and negotiation, social navigation and construction are worked at. To listen therefore is not only to hear, but to also attune and detune, balance and rebalance the forms and forces by which one is figured as well as participates in the figuring of others.

In her book *Queer Phenomenology*, Sara Ahmed challenges the ways in which traditions of phenomenology may bypass the more socialized, racialized, sexualized and gendered shape and impress of the phenomenal; the objects and things, the architectures and rooms that surround are never neutral, never only there for us, but rather, are made available through a range of highly situated, historical, and social processes that work to establish the normative shape of what we may associate with and how (Ahmed 2006). For Ahmed, one's figuring in the world is thus always already defined by a set of dominant constructs that are deeply material and spatial, coded and regulated, and that enable or constrain the particular grasp specific bodies may have onto the world around. One gains entry or not according to the availability of passages and pathways, and how they open for some more than others. In short, bodies are never only just bodies, but are already shaped by social, political, and identity norms, which act to limit the phenomenal availability of things according to the social, racial, sexual and gendered specificity bodies and spaces carry.

> The lines that allow us to find our way, those that are "in front" of us, also make certain things, and not others, available. What is available is what might reside as a point on this line. When we follow specific lines, some things become reachable and others remain, or even become, out of reach. Such exclusions – the constitution of a field of unreachable objects – are the indirect consequences of following lines that are before us: we do not have to consciously exclude those things that are not "on line". The direction we take excludes things for us, before we even get there (Ahmed 2006: 14–15).

Ahmed opens an important view onto how orientation is never freely found, but rather, is shaped by established patterns that bring one into certain alignments, or that make particular misalignments dangerous. One is equally oriented by the world as one makes orientation for oneself. Orientation is performative, whereby one may seek support through the material world while contending with the lack of availability of access or things. One therefore practices orientation, which shifts as bodies shift, as one aligns or misaligns, attunes or disturbs, is welcomed or pushed out. This includes the ways in which some bodies are racialized, positioned by way of a dominant white world that defines how people of color experience a relation to things and spaces, and what it means to be at home in the world. As Ahmed poses: "If the world is made white, then the body at home is one that can inhabit that whiteness" (Ahmed 111). Being at home in the world, feeling as if things and spaces of that world are made available, is deeply influenced by a racialized ordering, for example, and its social and political orientations.

Situatedness extends beyond the question of racial appearance as well, and the physical reading of the body; sexual orientation is equally made to matter within dominant heterosexual society, placing emphasis on the straight life that comes to cast other sexual behaviors and orientations as "deviant." "To become straight means that we not only have to turn toward the objects that are given to us by heterosexual culture, but also that we must 'turn away' from objects that take us off this line. The queer subject within straight culture hence deviates and is made socially present as a deviant" (Ahmed 21).

Following these perspectives, Ahmed poses the concept of "queer phenomenology" to challenge the seemingly neutral matters of worldly contact and how ideas of "free movement" are defined (or assumed) by way of a white, heteronormative imaginary and ideology. In contrast, Ahmed captures how orientation is a question of "lining up" – a "falling in line" often derived by way of heteronormative ordering, where "being straight" is often to "straighten up." In response, Ahmed mobilizes a critical phenomenology, which can support the making of other alignments and movements. "Queer orientations are those that put within reach bodies that have been made unreachable by the lines of conventional genealogy. Queer orientations might be those that don't line up, which by seeing the world 'slantwise' allow other objects to come into view" (Ahmed 107).

I'm interested in following Ahmed, and what she emphasizes as "the work of reorientation," in order to consider how enactments of non-normative worlding queer the acoustic, giving accent to the ways in which acoustic practices assist in processes of (re)orientation that upset the dominant tonality or pitch of a given place. Voices find resonance within certain environments according to the availability of particular acoustic matters – those who listen, or those things that invite one to speak or not, that acoustically welcome or support certain bodies and their sounds. The rhythms by which one moves are enabled or enhanced by material and social supports, while such rhythms may also work to demand entry, seeking to bend or break the shape of a given situation so as to move differently, to give expression to an altogether different pattern. Acoustic orientation is thus never only about the material supports that enable the movement of a specific sound, rather it contributes to the establishment of particular acoustic norms, setting definition to what counts as "good" or "fitting" sound – fidelity here must be underscored as political, forcing the question: fidelity to whom or what, and for what end?

Writer and scholar Nina Dragičević offers similar lines of thinking through her research into the culture of queer community life (Dragičević 2019, 2017). Focusing on the social environments of bars in the city of Ljubljana, and the formation of the lesbian disco, she highlights how sound and music, listening and an overall acoustic dynamic, contribute greatly to supporting queer togetherness, particularly when speaking out loud may put one in danger. Rather, the articulation of lesbian desire partly turns upon a sonic axis, a queer acoustics, finding facilitation through the playback of particular music.

Historically, Dragičević considers how the making of lesbian scenes within heterosexual bars (in the US for example) were greatly strained by an environment dominated by homophobia, which impacted on ways of socializing together. The playback of songs on a jukebox, for instance, came to assist in narrating otherwise unspoken communications, where potential partners may stand in or identify with singers, or those being sung to. Songs, in this sense, provided an acoustic affordance enabling the expression of lesbian desire, and importantly, for the construction and maintenance of a culture of queer life.

Extending her research into more contemporary situations, Dragičević moves from the jukebox, and the strict territorialization of heterosexual bars, to the live DJ and the lesbian disco. Within such spaces and scenes, lesbian desire finds greater traction by way of outright collective volume, a loudness that can "act against oppression" (Dragičević 2017). From the jukebox, and the undercover flirtations enabling an articulation of desire, to the DJ, and the collective volume of the lesbian disco, Dragičević captures a sense for the particular power of sonority in struggles and celebrations of shared identity. Finding orientation by way of such sonorities and expressions greatly affords world-making activity, that is, the making of a space and time that does not need to continually differentiate itself against heteronormative society. Rather, as Dragičević poses, the lesbian scene celebrates itself and each other by way of volume, and the making of a particular acoustic norm, allowing for a deeply emancipatory and affirming sense of togetherness.

Following Dragičević's work, a queer acoustics as I'm suggesting poses an interruption or distortion onto the heteronormative tonal shape of a place to allow for other resonant flows or vibrational constructs, other communal worlds and volumes; queering the acoustic may enable the retuning of a sonic horizon, surprising a given auditory arena with the rarely heard or with an altogether different reverberation. A queer acoustic may give support by upsetting the acoustic training and positionality informing how one hears or listens, to critically agitate or color the particular leanings and learnings that affect what one is able to hear, and how this comes to figure a sonic imaginary. In this sense, a queer acoustic might strain phenomenology with the noise of social conflict, the rhythms of particular identity struggles and desires, and the configuration of marginalized spaces and their histories, tensing given regimes of aurality so as to allow for the articulation of accommodations as well as resistances to emerge: to pose the work of acoustic justice.

ACOUSTIC JUSTICE

The notion of acoustic justice aims at highlighting practices or actions that rework the distribution of the heard, detuning or retuning the tonality of a place, and a given acoustic norm, so as to support the movements of bodies and voices, especially those put at risk by appearing or sounding otherwise. Central is a concern to frame the deeply human necessity *to be heard* and how this comes to be enacted across a range of settings; whether within local scenes of discussion and debate to greater institutional arenas where having a say and being heard support processes of justice and recognition, the imperative of being heard calls out for a particular critical framework.

Acoustic justice is thus posed as such a framework, one that can help in engaging how material, social conditions of particular places lend to establishing ways of listening, as well as how individually one may seek out and construct paths of (re)orientation, which is always related to struggles over belonging, of negotiating the performative figuring of oneself and others. The acoustic modalities of such acts, from the rhythmic to the vibrational, the loud to the hushed, often work to support the movements of a shared collectivity, emboldening the energetic force of communal determination by way of the unifying or sympathetic potentiality of the auditory. Such movements and experiences are often the socio-material basis from which communities or collectives acquire a sense for the possibilities of what one may compose within given environments or situations, extending from sonic warfare to acoustic welfare – from sonic force to acoustic care. And through which understandings of justice are played out in the everyday in terms of working at social equality, not to mention safety and protection.

Acoustic justice is also about expanding upon listening as an extremely dynamic expression of bodily power, as a sensual and deeply transformative capacity by which to express individual and collective understanding and cooperation. Listening as a broader capacity to attune and attend, to hold and nurture, defend and debate, and which supports reflection and sympathy, compassion and care, for oneself and for others, and that greatly assists in contending with dominant and prevailing systems that make and unmake bodies. As Silvia Federici poses in her argument on the need to reappropriate the body: "Our bodies have reasons that we need to learn, rediscover, reinvent. We need to listen to their language as the path to our health and healing, as we need to listen to the language and rhythms of the natural world as the path to the health and healing of the earth" (Federici 2020: 124).

Listening is underscored here as the means by which to learn the languages of the body, to attune to its inherent rhythms as paths of power and knowing, as well as healing. Against the colonial legacies of modernity, and conflicts over forms of life and the biodiversity expressive of a pluralistic world, listening is wielded as a capacity to contend with genealogies of capture and exploitative enclosure by explicitly forging an agential, restorative path – an acoustic frame by which to cultivate more considered approaches for being on the planet, which further entails a commitment to decolonization (Vázquez 2012; Mendes 2022).

Such an egalitarian, planetary view finds a compelling articulation in what Cormac Cullinan terms "wild law" (Cullinan 2011). For Cullinan, it is imperative that existing modes of Western governance are radically adjusted – modes that are grounded in legacies of what Rolando Vázquez highlights as the modern/colonial order (Vázquez 2012) – so as to work at greater ecological sustainability and flourishing. By way of wild law, Cullinan makes the argument for Earth governance, in which understandings of the legal status of the human subject be extended towards the Earth community as a whole, shifting the human-centric basis of law and rights in order to support a bolder planetary order. Such a view finds support by referencing Indigenous understandings and cosmologies, especially the concept of *buen vivir*. *Buen vivir* (or *sumak kawsay*) argues for an expanded understanding of "the good life" or "well-being" beyond the individual (and the concept of individual rights); rather, *buen vivir,* from an Andean cosmological view, understands well-being as a collective and planetary question and concern that exceeds the human. Increasingly taken on in a range of constitutional reforms, for instance in Ecuador in 2008, the "rights of nature" come to appropriate liberal concepts of rights in the making of new constitutional and legal structures. As Vázquez poses, "*buen vivir* signals the borders [of the modern / colonial order] and it gives voice to the outside of modernity" (Vázquez 1).

Cullinan's "wild law" takes guidance from the concept of *buen vivir* and aims to elaborate upon the rights of nature, as what may productively guide Western systems of law in crafting more ecologically attuned policies. Importantly, Cullinan approaches attending to the rhythms and qualities of the natural world by way of listening. As he envisions: "If we want to participate fully in the dance of the Earth community we need to listen carefully for the beat and adjust our rhythm and timing accordingly" (Cullinan 2011: 137).

In this respect, returning to Federici's call for "listening to the body" as a path toward health and healing, it is important to question in what way listening to the body takes place, or is given place, and how it may truly reorient larger systems and structures that situate oneself, or that impact onto the well-being of a greater social or planetary body. How do I listen to my body? If I understand my body as an acoustic chamber, as something that resounds, how does it give way to such listening, accommodating or resisting it? And in what ways is such listening challenged or undermined by understandings of listening, by one's own cultural background, or the regimes of aurality that shape or direct one's listening – that inscribe onto one's listening ability a set of ordering (and straightening) lines? Or by way of technology, and the electroacoustic systems embedded within environments, that we carry with us, and which participate in defining listening's reach and abilities? Further, what might such listening generate or engender – how to carry this listening into the world and our communities, into the rhythms of planetary ecologies and the project of decolonization?

Struggles over recognition and participation often find traction by intervening upon the conditions that define hearing and being heard, voicing and being responsive, sounding and listening, which regulate or inform one's attention and orientation with respect to oneself and others. It is these conditions that are of concern, and which leads me to understand acoustics, or more specifically, acoustic justice, as those things one does in order to make listening to the body and each other possible, and that one may carry further, to underscore the importance of hearing a diversity of views and life-stories within institutional and public settings as well as bringing attention to the voices and rhythms beyond human sociality.

In this regard, it is important to articulate a *critical acoustics*, which can bring forward an interrogative view onto acoustics and its specificities. From my perspective, this includes arguing for an understanding of acoustic rights or principles in order to open pathways for elaborating how listening may be nurtured. Such a concern requires a consideration of the right to free speech, or the right of reply, as human and civil rights, and which dramatically entail acoustic understanding, or an *acoustic literacy*. In this regard, it becomes essential to address the importance not only of the freedom of speech, but equally that of setting the (acoustic) conditions in support of such freedom. This includes arguing for a deeper engagement with listening as what often fulfills the power and possibility of speech.

Is not the freedom of speech equally a question of the freedom of listening (Lacey 2013)? As Vázquez argues, listening performs a "critique" of the modern/colonial order by specifically supporting a relationality denied by modernity in which the arrogance of a universal Western voice forcefully silences others (Vázquez 2012). In what ways is listening constrained and undermined within institutional and public environments, and how might "listening as critique," as relational opening or accountability, be enabled?

Fostering greater concern for listening from different perspectives, and from different cultural positions, can be articulated along a number of lines, such as the right to listen to each other, as the sharing and circulation of life-stories (King 2008), and which can help in attending not only to the said and the articulated, but equally to facilitating concern for that which is missing, where listening acts as a creative "holding environment" (Griffin 2016): listening as giving room for what needs to be said and heard, especially that which tenses a given regime of aurality. Emphasizing greater engagement with listening in this way can also help move from nurturing human relationships, and elaborating a diverse public discourse, to acknowledging ecologies of human and more-than-human life in a sustainable manner: to support greater attunement with a biodiverse planet by acknowledging the "polyphony" of its voices (Tsing 2015).

Approaching acoustics as a question of rights or responsibility along these lines can also allow for greater concern for education, where listening as a practice, a skill, a history, may be enriched, for listening profoundly supports the capacity for understanding, affection, responsiveness, as well as critical and creative inquiry, and is essential within learning environments. This explicitly gives way to engaging a politics of recognition, and questions of cultural identity, social mobility, and institutional access, which includes contending with racialized or gendered acoustic norms and the affective economies at play within contemporary biocapitalism which, as Federici suggests, are always instrumentalizing the vitality of oneself as a situated body. How to attend to the ways in which bodies – some more than others – are stressed and strained by forces of exclusion and discrimination? In what ways can such attention be sustained, made forceful within greater economies that fully capitalize on attention itself?

Acoustic justice further works at considering the technological or medical approaches to "hearing ability," and that draw out a bioacoustic politics – a politics contending with dominant conceptualizations of life by way of sound and hearing, and thus to further address the issue of recognition by expanding understandings of language and voice to include the diversely abled, issues of translation and interpretation, and that attends to verbal and nonverbal, spoken and signed expression (Bauman 2008; Mills 2011): a bioacoustic politics that may work at diversifying what counts as voice as well as hearing.

Finally, a focus on acoustic rights or principles works on behalf of an acoustic commons, as the commoning that may position sound and listening as social resources in manifesting a radical ethics of openness. Such a commons may ultimately contribute to honoring, as well as protecting, the right to be heard so necessary for nurturing a life of dignity.

From the micropolitical to the macropolitical, from questions of subjectivity, positionality, and the complex experiences of listening and social orientation, to issues of institutional access, structural and systemic exclusions, and what might be gained from bringing acoustic knowledges into the framework of education and ecology, law and government, acoustic justice works across a diversity of issues and sites. The right to listen, as a counterpoint to the right to free speech, captures the necessity for turning toward what must be heard: the expressions often occurring outside or beyond the acoustic norm of distributed sound. In this sense, acoustic justice lends to the forming of gestures and practices – listening practices, wild practices, decolonial practices – that attempt to reshape the arrangements enabling such rights and principles, and in doing so, modulate the norms by which we may encounter and enrich each other. This includes bringing a critical view onto the issue of rights in general, and the importance of challenging state sanctioned recognition; rather, acoustics, and the arguments I'm making here, may support enactments of poetic world making that do not so much redistribute the heard, in attempts at having a voice, but lead to another form of the sensible entirely.

* An earlier version of this essay originally appeared in "Acoustics of Justice", James Parker, Sara Ramshaw, Mehera San Roque (eds.), *Law Text Culture*, Vol 24 (2020): 550–572.

BIBLIOGRAPHY

Ahmed, S. *Queer Phenomenology: Orientations, Objects, Others*. Durham: Duke University Press, 2006.

Battah, H. "An Open Mic Revolution in Lebanon". *Al Jazeera*. October 25, 2019. https://www.aljazeera.com/indepth/opinion/open-mic-revolution-lebanon-191025150455130.html. Accessed March 10, 2021.

Bauman, H-Dirksen L. "Audism: Exploring the Metaphysics of Oppression" in *Journal of Deaf Studies and Deaf Education*, Vol. 9, No. 2 (Spring 2004): 239–46.

Bauman, H-Dirksen L. "On the Disconstruction of (Sign) Language in the Western Tradition: A Deaf Reading of Plato's Cratylus". In Bauman, H-Dirksen L. (ed.)*Open Your Eyes: Deaf Studies Talking*. Minneapolis: University of Minnesota Press, 2008: 83–99.

Blesser, B. and Salter, L – R. *Spaces Speak, Are You Listening? Experiencing Aural Architecture*. Cambridge, MA: The MIT Press, 2006.

Cullinan, C. *Wild Law: A Manifesto for Earth Justice*. Cambridge, Green Books,, 2011.

Dragičević, N. from a lecture given at Sounds, Songs, and Politics, International Ethnomusicological symposium, Institute of Ethnomusicology, University of Ljubljana, 2019. Author in attendance.

Dragičević, N. *Med njima je glasba: Glasba v konstrukciji lezbične scene*. Ljubljana: Društvo Parada ponosa, 2017.

Eidsheim, N. *The Race of Sound: Listening, Timbre and Vocality in African American Music*. Durham: Duke University Press, 2019.

Farinati, L. and Firth, C. *The Force of Listening*. Berlin: Errant Bodies Press, 2017.

Federici, S. *Beyond the Periphery of the Skin: Rethinking, Remaking, and Reclaiming the Body in Contemporary Capitalism*. Oakland: PM Press, 2020.

Goodman, S. *Sonic Warfare: Sound, Affect, and the Ecology of Fear*. Cambridge, MA: The MIT Press, 2010.

Griffin, Fred L. *Creative Listening and the Psychoanalytic Process: Sensibility, Engagement and Envisioning*. New York: Routledge, 2016.

Grueneisen, P. *Soundspace: Architecture for Sound and Vision*. Basel: Birkhäuser, 2003.

Kheshti, R. *Modernity's Ear: Listening to Race and Gender in World Music*. New York: New York University Press, 2015.

King, T. *The Truth About Stories: A Native Narrative*. Minneapolis: University of Minnesota Press, 2008.

Lacey, K. *Listening Publics: The Politics and Experience of Listening in the Media Age*. Cambridge: Polity Press, 2013.

Ladd, P. *Understanding Deaf Culture: In Search of Deafhood*. Clevedon: Multilingual Matters, 2003.

Mendes, Margarida. "Sounding the Mississippi". In B. LaBelle (ed.) *Radical Sympathy*. Berlin: Errant Bodies Press, 2022: 49–70.

Mills, M. "Do Signals Have Politics? Inscribing Abilities in Cochlear Implants". In T. Pinch and K. Bijsterveld (eds.) *The Oxford Handbook of Sound Studies*. Oxford: Oxford University Press, 2011: 320–46

Parker, J. "The Soundscape of Justice." In *Griffith Law Review* 20/4, 2011: 962–93.

Parker, J. E. K. *Acoustic Jurisprudence: Listening to the Trial of Simon Bikindi*. Oxford: Oxford University Press, 2015.

Rancière, J. *The Politics of Aesthetics*. New York: Bloomsbury, 2013.

Stoever, J. L. *The Sonic Color Line: Race and the Cultural Politics of Listening*. New York: New York University Press, 2016.

Tsing, A. L. *The Mushroom at the End of the World: On the Possibility of Life in Capitalist Ruins*. Princeton: Princeton University Press, 2015.

Vázquéz, R. "Towards a Decolonial Critique of Modernity: Buen Vivir, Relatinoality and the Task of Listening". In Fornet-Betancourt, R. *Capital, Poverty, Development, Denktraditionen im Dialog: Studien zur Befreiung und interkulturalität*, Vol. 33, Mainz Aachen: Wissenschafts-verlag, 2012: 241–252.

BUDHADITYA CHATTOPADHYAY

Co — listening: theory and practice

What I listen to and what you listen to differ from each other. My listening pleasure might be a traumatic experience for your ears: we often encounter older inhabitants of an apartment building complaining about loud party nights at the younger occupants' clumsy flats. Listening as an act is often very private and context-dependent. There are subjective positions taken at each moment when there is a mysterious process of sensing and cognition unfolding. Philosopher Jean-Luc Nancy suggests that listening suspends between sensing and understanding (2007).[1] What I understand and what you sense, can be different based on our cognitive universes, economic-socio-cultural contexts, personalities, sensibilities, and the unique auditory situation of the self in a particular moment. Perhaps a sound will generate a good memory in you, and distress in me given in which private moment I am listening to that sound. There is little of an objective reality – much of what we make sense of upon listening, seeing, touching, or through other sensory modalities, are born out of our inner conditions.

Does this typically modern human condition mean that there is no way we can listen together? Biologist Christopher N. Templeton showed that "A variety of animals eavesdrop and learn to use other species' alarm calls to avoid predators" (2018). In the non-human worlds, such collective listening for survival is quite common. Why is the modern human condition such that listening divides subjects into individuals? Or are there exceptions? I often used to share earphones with my first girlfriend. We used to sit in a park stretching our legs, listening to alternative or Gothic Rock bands: The Cure or Anathema. The left earplug in her left ear, and the right earplug in my right ear, we used to share the same music but each getting only the half of the stereo mix. We could listen together, and the underscoring was on this sense of togetherness, not on what we were listening to individually. Perhaps our listening and sense-making were different. But we used to listen holding hands with a spirit of sharing sounds.

As we, humans, grow up and go through a modernization and culturalization process, our cognitive universes harden to become insular, and we cannot co-listen anymore like the experience I just shared. We do, occasionally, listen together. We go to the movies or concerts, where we tend to listen collectively in a social situation. But more and more this social experience gravitates towards individualization of the experience by consuming sounds through headgears, earplugs and silent disco headphones. Often our reactions to different sonic moments are diverging. But sometimes one strong sound cue may generate a consensual hush as a communal reaction, sparking our memory of a fragmented collective consciousness and a decaying sense of togetherness. This mode of socially decentered listening helps to build communities. During covid restrictions in Italy and India, neighbors in a locality used to hit utensils together to make sounds from their balconies or terraces, windows and street corners, to resurrect this lost sense of sonic community-hood, reciprocity and social cohesion through acoustic means. I coin this practical instance of sounding and listening together as "co-listening." This term, however, needs to be further unpacked.

In some online portals,[2] co-listening is understood as having equal time limits for talking and listening between conversational partners in organizational communication. Co-listening can, however, be expanded from this narrower definition towards a social and community driven listening mode. While equity between and respect for the listenting partners are important, the non-judgmental and compassionate approach in co-listening is central, and therefore cannot be restricted within professional instructions. What happens when there is a fertile pause in speaking, thinking, looking out the window, and coming back to the conversation with a new perspective? The immeasurable and ineffable moments in listening are as important as making meaning by following a steady pattern. The focus of co-listening should be on this sense of unpredictability, emergence, and flux in listening together, often without making sense, but with a compassionate engagement even in silence, holding hands without talking, without navigational cues, or orientation signals. Co-listening needs a lot of loving and caring between humans, and non-humans. When a cat answers back with a purr after a pat on its head, no meaning-making is necessary. In these moments of resonant togetherness, any ontological and epistemological constraints suspend in favor of affective reciprocity, loving, sharing and caring. When we try to listen together with another person or non-human fellow, we celebrate the acoustic space we share, and the common *auditory setting* (Chattopadhyay 2021).

To offer a conceptual interpretation of the term co-listening, I refer to critical studies in sound and phenomenology to explain how I position the idea within a larger discourse around listening, thinking, and sociality. Philosopher Don Ihde asks "What is that listening that occurs within my self-presence and that accompanies the presence of the things and of others in the perceived World?" (Ihde 2007, p.118). Co-listening tends to answer this question. The term opens up a listening space between the self and the other(s), and thereby engages with the process of a social formation.

As philosopher Gemma Corradi Fiumara underscores: a propensity to listen to others without making immediate judgments is crucial (1990).[3] This non-judgmental listening may potentially lead to bridge the troubled water of difference, be it racial, social or political. On a personal level, listening in a certain place and time requires me to be there and learn the historical trajectory of the place and its inhabitants, both human and non-human. Once I listen to this history, I can start engaging with the place. I find the listening becomes problematic when the listener's position is colonial: to extract sounds as much as possible from the place. On the contrary, I advocate for developing an inter-subjective relationship with a place through the medium of sound. Rather than phonography, in terms of recorded sound, in my work I prefer co-listening, in which a reciprocal and inter-subjective approach to situated listening is vital.[4] In this practice, the psychogeographic exploration of a site is considered a ground for phenomenological engagement, much like a poetic unpacking of a lived and felt reality. Often, I don't record at all in a place, though I might spend months in that place exploring nooks and crannies of its sonorous body, and listen in-depth by making the place respond to my intervention in a shared resonance. This sonic reciprocity and being open to self-attunement is central to this idea of *co-listening*.

Is there something novel in this listening mode? Michel Chion, in his seminal work *Audio-Vision* (1994), delineated three primary listening modes, drawing on the phenomenological perspectives of composer Pierre Schaeffer (Schaeffer, 1966/2017). These are: causal listening, semantic listening, and reduced listening, respectively. Causal listening consists of listening to a sound in order to gather information about its cause or source, or (sounding) object. When the cause is located, sound can provide supplementary information about it, such as its spatial position. Causal listening is based on this epistemic knowledge about things that vibrate and reach a listener through the passage of sound, and the listener recognizes the thing to learn about it. Semantic listening refers to an interpretation of messages from speech and other vocal sounds through a spoken language or a predetermined code (for example, Morse code or spoken words). This mode of listening acts through a complex and layered unfolding of meaning-making that follows a process of linguistic decoding and a semantic chain of understanding that has been widely studied. Reduced listening, on the other hand, focuses on the volume, pitch, tone, textures and other characteristics of the sound itself, independent of the cause or the source, or the sounding object, and also of its meaning. According to Chion, "Reduced listening takes the sound—verbal, played on an instrument, noises, or whatever—as itself the object to be observed instead of as a vehicle for something else" (1994, p.29). In musical practice, reduced listening is useful for composing and performing sounds based on their character.

Challenging the epistemic object of sound embedded in the causal listening mode, and taking a clear departure from reduced listening approach of concentrating on the sound itself for ontological and compositional exploration, co-listening instead meditates on the convivial resonances a listener feels when listening at a social setting shared with other human and non-human inhabitants/occupants. What distinguishes this mode of co-listening from Chion's three modes of listening? The term suggests a way of going beyond reduced and causal listening modes to involve the context of the listening act and nurturing its social and communal potential. For example, I hear the laptop fan as a sound-producing object, but an act of co-listening will make me contemplate the auditory associations with the object and my attachment to it, and the memories this may trigger to develop a due course of inter-subjectivity in sound perception through a process of self-attunement to the laptop fan. My work *Indecent Whispers* (2021) is derived from attentive listening to the intimate surroundings and various everyday objects in conversation with the self during a long self-quarantine.[5] As I mentioned earlier, in co-listening this reciprocal and inter-subjective approach to listening is central. Co-listening as social practice in my workshops[6] enables interspersing daily life and community art within a social and collective rubric that is interchangeable. Co-listening supports and advances acoustic ecology by helping move it further from its Anthropogenic tendencies, and proposes a new context in which ecology is understood as co-dependence and interconnectivity between all human and non-human participants of collective living.

In experiences of listening, many sounds are considered noise if they fall outside a socially accepted network of cognitive signification. But due to their ontological ambivalence, these noises affect listeners on a level deeper than they might be usually aware of. In co-listening mode, noise is listened to through an adaptive perception. A co-listener does not undermine noise as it is done from the Schaferian soundscape approach (Schafer 1994). I personally don't like the term *noise*; I consider that all noises are *sounds*. I rarely get annoyed with so-called "noise" in public and private spaces, because often such a concern is socially constructed. I am fascinated by the materiality of noise, its many splendors, many textures and multiple layers. I am not a "noise artist" the way it is defined. I work with listening, and I advocate for sensitizing the listening faculty to noises that have socio-political connotations. For a typical co-listener like me, noise is a polyphony of sounds – and this polyphony is born out of an act of co-listening with the environment, and the others who inhabit the environment. My motivation, or the drive to work with sound is to develop a kind of inclusive, contemplative relationship with the lived environment and its co-habitants, human and non-human. For a co-listener, noise at a material level is fascinating, and on a philosophical level can engage a number of issues around subjectivity. It is also an artistic strategy – think of the many vociferous, extrovert and expressive artists in the Global South for example – their embracing of noise is political, much like taking a parasitical social position of polemical intervention. Such an approach to noise lends to an expansion of Michel Serres' work *The Parasite*,[7] in which he argues that a parasite uses noise to hide itself. The noise artists' sole instrument to reach the political establishment is harsh noise; it's an anti-establishment stance, an activists' challenge to the status quo. Indeed, their artistic position conceals the individual artist but accumulates a collective activism against colonial models of exploitation and extraction of local resources. If as an artist and co-listener I don't engage with noise, I fail to take an activist role. From this perspective, co-listening is an act of resistance.

How can one become more aware of the effects that noise has on a sensitive co-listener on a subconscious level? Is noise a connecting energy between co-listeners like the untapped *whispers* demonstrators used to communicate with each other in Istanbul, Beirut, Hong Kong and Delhi? Noise is the song of the oppressed. Any sound that is ontologically unrecognizable to humans is generally termed noise by the humans given that their capacity to hear is limited to 20 Hz to 20 kHz; hence noise is essentially a social construct. On a subconscious level, the ontological ambiguity of noise rests on a poetic rupture and an evocative and highly galvanizing audio leakage. This is a crack in the body of understanding, and through this crack, sensing may take different poetic forms conducive to self-attunement against the Western colonial mode of othering prevalent in the sonic gentrification. Joanna Kusiak, in her contribution "Acoustic Gentrification" for *The Acoustic City* project describes how "sound and silence have been historically used as forces of political class struggle" in which "aversion to noise, and in particular to the sound of people loitering in public space" (2014) manifest in the gentrification policy-making at major cities in Europe and America, such as Warsaw and Berlin. Florence Feiereisen and Erin Sassin show that this approach of social noise abatement symbolizes in the context of Berlin "the erasure of the voices and culture of Berlin's long-term residents and argue that contestations over sound, brought on by West German migrants in what can be considered a 'hostile takeover' of parts of East Berlin, are a key driver of gentrification" (2021). In such gentrification policies deployed on fringe urban environments, European classical music appears as an epitome of cleanliness. No need to go further; from many instances we know how classical music is used to push immigrants and homeless people away inside night-time subways and metro stations.[8]

If we take a broader view, this sanitary approach of gentrification already existed in European classical music history, the way it is recorded inside closed studios, and performed in similarly insular auditoriums in order to isolate these privileged spaces from outdoor noises. The boundaries of noise, however, shape a sense of epistemic presence. As a co-listener taking noise as an entry point, I contend that it is often difficult to stay away from noise of any kind. Noise is powerful because it is omnipresent. Noise can infiltrate from any side of a tightly closed room and proliferate viscerally. Noise can buzz around the ear until one tends to recognize it, and interpret a meaning. Noise has its own aesthetics that can mobilize the public sphere. Likewise, noise can be understood as a composite sound, just as the color black consists of all the colors in a composite manner. Like the Black Lives Matter movement, Farmers' movement in India, anti-Establishment demonstrations in Beirut, freedom movement in Rojava and Hong Kong, and other community driven, ground up and participatory movements around the globe at this moment, a *Noise Movement* can be envisaged to connect various segments of societies against injustice of all kinds. Including noise within a sonic palette is something marginalized artists continue to practice as a way to secure a more dignified form of survival. For them, co-listening with socially marginalized humans and non-humans alike and their noises is crucial. This sense of adaptive perception and self-attunement is found in indigenous listening and thinking traditions – it's a step toward contributing to an acoustic community. The poetic, contemplative, relational, and emancipatory perspective of co-listening to connect to form a community, in my opinion, is at the core of Global South artists' work, or to any artist who feels marginalized in contemporary societies. Co-listening here is a shared promise of equity and inclusion.

There are many interesting Global South artists whose methodologies open up discourses previously unheard. Take for example, artists from South Asia or North Africa such as Khaled Kaddal or Isuru Kumarasinghe who question the complex link between the sound of politics and the politics of listening. Kaddal uses sounds of police sirens in the context of Egypt amongst other urban noise elements to expose audiences to an immersive sonic experience associated with the ominous feelings of "alert" and "alarm." In his work, urban noise is positioned politically by carrying information and impressions about the notoriously noisy Mediterranean cities of Alexandria and Cairo, to affectively engage listeners. Artists such as Khyam Allami challenge the Eurocentric biases embedded in modern technologies by offering a decolonial application platform such as Apotome.[9] In addition, Surabhi Saraf questions the forced immigration and surveillance mechanisms dominant in the Western world based on its racial profiling against immigrants and people of color, while Ish Sherawat hacks Western musical instruments to produce unconventional sounds.[10] I co-listen with this community of artists in my own work developing a sense of togetherness on the basis of reflecting on the present moment marked by issues of decoloniality, provincializing Europe, migration, social inequality and inclusion. This sense of acoustic togetherness allows us to engage in solidarity.

Often it's observed that artists outside of the West (Europe and North America) don't appear at the forefront of curatorial activities in Europe where cultural capital has been accummulated since and through the colonial times of plunder and extractive capitalism. Though lots of support is made available, they are only accessible to local artists who are registered residents of Europe. In this European fortress, migrating and diaspora artists are often marginalized and obscured. Contemporary Global South artists continue to be critical of Eurocentric listening habits they have been made to endure, as they engage with issues linked to their regions' turbulent and fraught history of colonialism and social division, along with acts of decolonization. These conflict-ridden experiences make their work interesting and thought-provoking. However, in Europe or in the greater Western world, where most of the funded curatorial activities take place, an unfair social divide is upheld in contemporary curation of sound and listening driven arts, as well as in the writing of its history. In the last decade there has been a profusion of scholarly, curatorial, and artistic works around sound and listening, including numerous publications, conferences, major exhibitions and projects. In this expanding body of activities in the West, predominantly, there is an astounding absence of sound thinkers and makers from the Global South. Let's measure how many Global South scholars participate in the major canonized texts in sound studies alone (2018, 2012, 2013): 1, that's just 2%! This flux of scholarly and artistic works have basically been Euro-American. Sounds in South Asia, Africa and the Middle East (broadly termed the Global South) have largely remained underexplored, although they contribute significantly to global outputs in audiovisual media. This divide is practiced often by a lack of critical engagement with the artists and thinkers from the Global South, and through ignoring, under-referencing, pigeonholing, or appropriation of "non-Western" scholarly perspectives, methodologies and sonic epistemologies. If the act of co-listening intervenes into contemporary curating, theorizing, and historicizing of sound arts, it may bridge this gap by creating an equitable environment of recognition and inter-cultural confluence, contributing to a more inclusive re-writing of sound and media art history.

From the scholarly interest of a co-listener, I would like to create a fertile entry point into the field of sound practice and listening modes found in the Global South in order to understand the unique sonic sensibility and media aesthetics of these regions. Such new knowledge may fundamentally shift the field of sound studies (as well as a global media art history), integrating a decolonial approach and how this may further allow for re-examining notions of temporality, spatiality and subjectivity. The research may additionally help engage the issues of media cultural encounters and technological transmissions between Global North and South as a two-way process of postcolonial confluence. This already ongoing research may benefit the pool of practitioners active in the Global South, particularly the media artists, audiovisual practitioners and makers, whose arts and crafts have often been neglected and ignored in the Eurocentric field of sound curation as well as in sound and media art histories. In this socially divided auditory situation, acts of co-listening across the Global North and South may introduce new modes of inter-sonic encounters and confluences; and a much-needed sense of equity and solidarity may be found through such practices.

NOTES

1. Nancy, Jean-Luc (2007). *Listening*. Trans. Charlotte Mandell. New York: Fordham University Press.
2. This term "co-listening" has only been used once previously on this website about organizational communication training: https://www.dinaglouberman.com/approach/co-listening/
3. Fiumara, Gemma Corradi (1990). *The Other Side of Language: A Philosophy of Listening*. London: Routledge.
4. For example, in my augmented book project *The Nomadic Listener* (2020) I have explored situated listening as a mode of inter-subjective interaction with the city.
5. Listen to the work released on the New Chronologies of Sound compilation on CD, LP and digital platforms: https://lifeisavicnic.bandcamp.com/track/indecent-whispers
6. Workshop series "Hyper-listening: Praxis": https://budhaditya.org/projects/doors-of-nothingness/hyper-listening-praxis/
7. Serres, Michel (2013). *The Parasite*. Minneapolis, Minnesota: University of Minnesota Press.

8. See one of these reports: https://www.washingtonpost.com/lifestyle/style/blasting-mozart-to-drive-criminals-away/2011/10/11/gIQAgDqPEQ_story.html
9. See the CTM festival featuring Apotome: https://www.ctm-festival.de/festival-2021/programme/exhibition/ctm-cyberia/apotome-by-khyam-allami-x-counterpoint
10. The works of the above-mentioned artists are featured in the first edition of The Listening Biennial (2021): For more information visit: https://listeningbiennial.net/
11. Connecting Resonances: https://budhaditya.org/projects/connecting-resonances/

BIBLIOGRAPHY

Bull, Michael (2018). *The Routledge Companion to Sound Studies*. London: Routledge.

Chattopadhyay, B. (forthcoming). *Sonic Perspectives from the Global South: Connecting Resonances*. New York: Bloomsbury Academic.

Chattopadhyay, B. (2022). *Sound Practices in the Global South: Co-listening to Resounding Plurilogues*. London: Palgrave Macmillan (in press).

Chattopadhyay, B. (2022). "Hyper-listening and Co-listening: Reflections on Sound, Selfhood, and Solidarity", in Woodland, Sarah and Vachon, Wolfgang (eds.), *Sonic Engagement: The ethics and aesthetics of community engaged audio practice*. London: Routledge (in press).

Chattopadhyay, B. (2020). *The Nomadic Listener*. Berlin: Errant Bodies Press.

Chattopadhyay, B. (2021). *The Auditory Setting: Environmental Sounds in Film and Media Arts*. Edinburgh: Edinburgh University Press.

Chattopadhyay, B. (2017). "Hyper-listening: Praxis", in Mateus-Berr, R., and Reitstätter, L. (eds.). *Art & Design Education in Times of Change* (pp. 171–5). Conversations Across Cultures, Vienna: de Gruyter.

Chion, M. (1994) *Audio-vision: Sound on screen*. Gorbman, C. (ed.). New York: Columbia University Press.

Feiereisen, Florence, and Sassin, Erin (2021). "Sounding Out the Symptoms of Gentrification in Berlin". *Resonance* 2 (1): 27–51.

Fiumara, Gemma Corradi (1990). *The Other Side of Language: A Philosophy of Listening*. London: Routledge.

Ihde, Don (2007) *Listening and voice: Phenomenologies of sound*. New York: Sunny Press.

Kusiak, Joanna (2014). "Acoustic gentrification: the silence of Warsaw's sonic warfare", in Gandy, Matthew and Nilsen, BJ (eds.). *The Acoustic City*. Berlin: Jovis.

Nancy, Jean-Luc (2007). *Listening*. Trans. Charlotte Mandell. New York: Fordham University Press.

Pinch, Trevor and Bijsterveld, Karin (2013). *The Oxford Handbook of Sound Studies*. New York: Oxford University Press.

Schaeffer, P. (2017). *Treatise on Musical Objects: An Essay Across Disciplines*. Oakland, California: University of California Press.

Schafer, R. M. (1994) *The soundscape: Our sonic environment and the tuning of the world*. Rochester: Destiny Books.

Serres, Michel (2013). *The Parasite*. Minneapolis, Minnesota: University of Minnesota Press.

Sterne, Jonathan (ed.) (2012). *The Routledge Sound Studies Reader*. London: Routledge.

Templeton, Christopher N. (2018). "Animal Communication: Learning by Listening about Danger". *Current Biology* 28 (16): R892–R894.

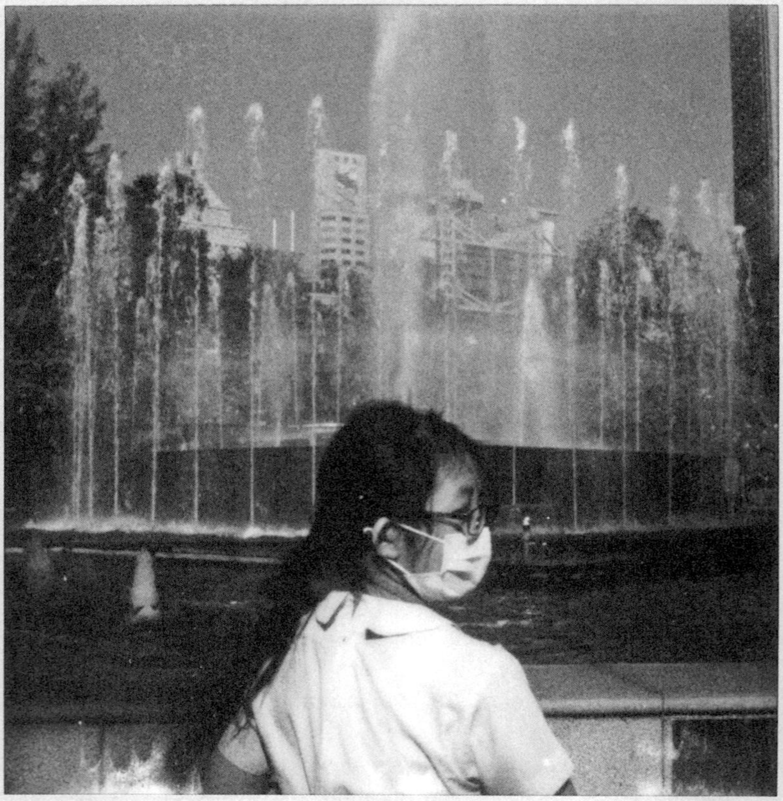

Sharon Lee, *Still Wish You Well*, 2020.

YANG YEUNG

to make of peace and listening as kin

It took me longer than expected to be confident enough to write about what The Listening Biennial had meant. One challenge might have been my inability to imagine how the Biennial was as a whole. I contributed my co-curation as a resident in Hong Kong, just as my co-curators did from their worlds. We had not had the chance to meet in person. I had not been to any of the Biennial events outside Hong Kong. To miss them was to miss the spontaneity that listening bodies would have drawn out of themselves, singularly and together. Another more enduring challenge was that the Biennial took place at a time when my thoughts on the relation between personal memories and historical memories had become contentious, at times confusing. I witnessed history fabricated into gigantic soundbites that came to occupy public space, to cleanse it of dissent and personal memories. The tension between the gigantic and the miniature as Susan Stewart discusses it is also a tension within the sentiment of longing. The obstinate and unresolved question about what art can do, however feeble its voice might be within distorted structures of memory, lingers.

Transformation came one day, when I had a conversation about peace with friends. They had been reflecting on how to advocate for peace as a discourse of public well-being. In hindsight, I realize the activities of making peace and of listening in the ways I encountered them in their work and mine share some qualities. We have kept these activities understated, but assertive. We sometimes move with them, are moved by them, but also stay still in them. In the face of them, we are never idle. We have regulated ourselves against being presumptuous about them. They don't need our consecration. The activities of making peace and of listening are challenged in similar ways, too. They are not points to be pinned down or crystallized. They don't have a face. They don't have a voice that routine speech could sound out. For this, these activities seem parasitic to and less urgent than projects by more forceful names like justice and liberation.

What to make of peace and of listening then? I propose their shared strength lies in their capacity to preserve the spontaneity of the individual. Without spontaneity, we repeat the same habits. We stop learning and evolving. Our world is foreclosed to others and to the future. With spontaneity "called into life," as Hannah Arendt suggests, our capacity to act becomes possible. It is subtle, but persistent. It is something with which I keep akin what I do not have first-hand experience of but can think with.

The following is a reflection on how listening and peace might have converged through the ways artists were acting in Hong Kong for the Biennial. It is but a fragment of the Biennial, but each fragment is perhaps always "a non-event between events/ holding a secret and a sense."[1]

0

Our stroll began on a warm winter morning. Brandon LaBelle initiated it. Co-curators of The Listening Biennial Israel Martínez and Budhaditya Chattopadhyay were there. We met online, but it felt like I joined hands with them. We shared a joke when the Listening Biennial website was about ready to launch: "What if it was declared open and we left everything online without doing anything else? Would people find out?" A shared laugh made the remoteness of our zoom calls kind.

1

An evening with Wantanee Siripattananuntakul.

We had a plan: to watch her video work *She Who Sings A Voiceless Song* together. We were to talk about the state of monarchy in Thailand, the complexities in identifying what's popular and what's propaganda, how to name a lone body mouthing a song, and more. We ended up being drawn to spontaneity. We shared similar scenes of oppression on the streets of Hong Kong and Bangkok. We shared how residents in both cities pondered about leaving, how the incompetence of governments during the pandemic had been depressing. And so it was. We sang the voiceless song, holding onto the spontaneity state power kept trying to snuff out.

A friend once told me that her son was born in a cold place. She was to take him into summer which would teach his body to sweat.

2

Sunset was near. Michele Chu had set up as a rectangular divider with plastic wrap in a plaza outside the train station. 100 meters away was a sales "station." A woman was promoting deals for solar panels. The Chinese characters she had on the table cloth said it all. She could keep fingering her phone without speaking. Michele's open call was different: "Come sit down and let's get to know each other." Mutuality and openness. Both were inviting. Both called for listening bodies. One such that profit may come. The other such that vulnerability would be welcome.

I sat down on one side of the plastic wrap. Michele was on the other. I was free to finger the plastic wrap in any way and Michele was to follow my touch. My eyes started to swell at some point. Was it when our index fingers or something else touched? The plastic wrap changed from being a barrier to a support: it held my hand; it held my curiosity and spirit up. Michele said she had a fear of intimacy. She made the work to challenge herself.

If, for George Steiner, "Vermeer's treatments of fabric have schooled our fingertips,"[2] Michele showed us our fingers could reach way farther than we routinely do.

3

Our night was dawn for Minoosh Zomorodinia. From San Francisco, online, Minoosh briefed us on a walk we were to take in our neighborhood.

"The first thing to come to your mind," Minoosh's prompted. I wrote "fight," "smell," "SIU MEI" (Cantonese for roast meat). I also scribbled, "FAI CHUN" (Cantonese for auspicious couplets and calligraphy made for the Lunar New Year), "drunk," "full moon lost and found."

"Pay attention to your surroundings" was the second prompt. Non-places, or between use and non-use, entrance and exits. "What's the sound like?" I took some notes on what came through my mind and my imagination:

1. Basketball: sneakers screeching; remembering a high school friend who was a particularly agile player. Miss Anna Wong, my high school PE teacher, wrote in my autograph book, "You are the builder of your own confidence."
2. A cart was pulled – remembering film reels in metallic cases my father kept. Sharp smell of acid.
3. Crickets calling – remembering cicadas in Amino. Akio Suzuki's drawings.
4. Dogs.

Minoosh shared Pujol's thought: "Silence is like water."

It was time to set out. To come close to the electric signals spilling out of tall street lamps, footsteps of "KAI FONG" (Cantonese for neighbors sharing the same street) going home, and cicadas hiding in the branches ... was to let sonic imprints of human voices fade away.

4

Months ago, Sharon Lee and I met by a fountain in Mid-levels, Hong Kong. She picked a sunny afternoon because that's usually when a rainbow would form. She had been collecting the silent wishes of watchers of the rainbow. She gave the wishes multiple layers – a whisper by heart, an image on a polaroid, a sentiment made and hidden in public, and a secret between pages of books she would have the Biennial show and make shelter for in a reading room in Berlin. She shared and extended the strength of wishful thinking to all.

The day turned out to be her birthday. We shared a small cake: dark chocolate topped with a bloodred cherry. Unmasking was not allowed in public places unless it was for eating. We ate slow.

5

Yannick Dauby and Au Wah-yan are passionately mindful of living beings sharing Planet Ocean with humans. Corals, mosquitoes, whales, frogs and toads...

Wah-yan read stories from her book *Dreams of a Toad*. I put together strands of eccentricities and read them out loud:

Wah-yan Wah-yan
How you turn dots into bolts.
Bolts.
Some thick, some light, some rusty and spiky, too.
Bolt. A word that forms a circle around itself.
Does lightning form circles around itself?
There, a bolt strikes where thunder drops.

Generous are her wings.
Misplaced talents of our doing.
Between your hands, she is freed from our prosaic
concerns.
Buzzing, ringing, humming...together, they orchestrate.
Alone, a ka-lei-DO-SCOpic mind
strains to be kind.

Can I give you a halfway hug,
if that's only so far I could reach
swimming over?
Inverted, you are sheltered;
between earth and sky, you are my shelter.

To be in your weather.

Yannick made music for the radio with our voices.

6

I was alone in 1983, an artist-home-turned-art-space in Hong Kong, waiting for Alecia Neo and the *Care Index* workshop participants to arrive. Tycho Brahe came to mind. I am not sure why. It could be that his counting of stars was for me a form of care. It could also be the tenderness of something a student once said about her dream. She wanted to become a pilot but was unable because she found out about the physical deficiencies of her eyes. She went into aeronautic engineering instead, "turning scars into stars."

Alecia guided us into relaxed, deep breathing. We then enacted gestures of care she learnt from care-givers and those cared-for. We collected weeds, felt weight between our hands, bent over to get closer to the earth. Inhale. We straightened our bodies. Exhale. We touched the ground. To weed is to say goodbye to it and to say sorry we have to say goodbye. Each gesture was individuated. We found our own expression.

We also worked together. In the room physically and via zoom, we traced the lines of others' hands and arms as they moved. I stole time to imagine tracing my father's palm from 40 years ago. There was no line, only a sense of thickness and warmth.

We heard from a carer's narrative about caring for someone with dementia. "Remove the danger."

Another carer found strength in the sky: look up and bring sunlight down her shoulders. Moveable arms, wearable sunlight. "Flow" – Alecia showed us how one memory flowed into others'.

"Trust" and "intimacy" were words most frequently used to describe the quality of relation between us. "Release" was a welcoming action.

Connect with others. Return to oneself. Repeat.

7

These days where I am, being-with as a way of life can not be taken for granted.

Spiritual – Nov 6, 2021 (Facebook post)

> Before sunset, I was at Mount Zero, hoping to find an artist's drawing of two souls walking into the light. Instead, I found around 50 patient, attentive, resonating bodies, heartbeat to heartbeat, listening to investigative journalists speaking about the state of the "us."
>
> She, the investigative journalist, encouraged us to pay heed to the histories of human suffering, and re-evaluate, with a sense of humility and reality, where we are, how we might still move.
>
> He, the investigative journalist, gave current investigative journalism in our home an adjective: "spiritual." Vehemently true, everywhere possible, despite or perhaps because of all that which makes us now.
>
> "Broken realities," "time lag," "aesthetics of decay," "situatedness"... ideas arising between artists, the project curator, and myself, ideas that bound us to the morning of San Francisco one Earth rotation before. It's about time we said goodbye to the "borrowed time" paradigm. We live our time.

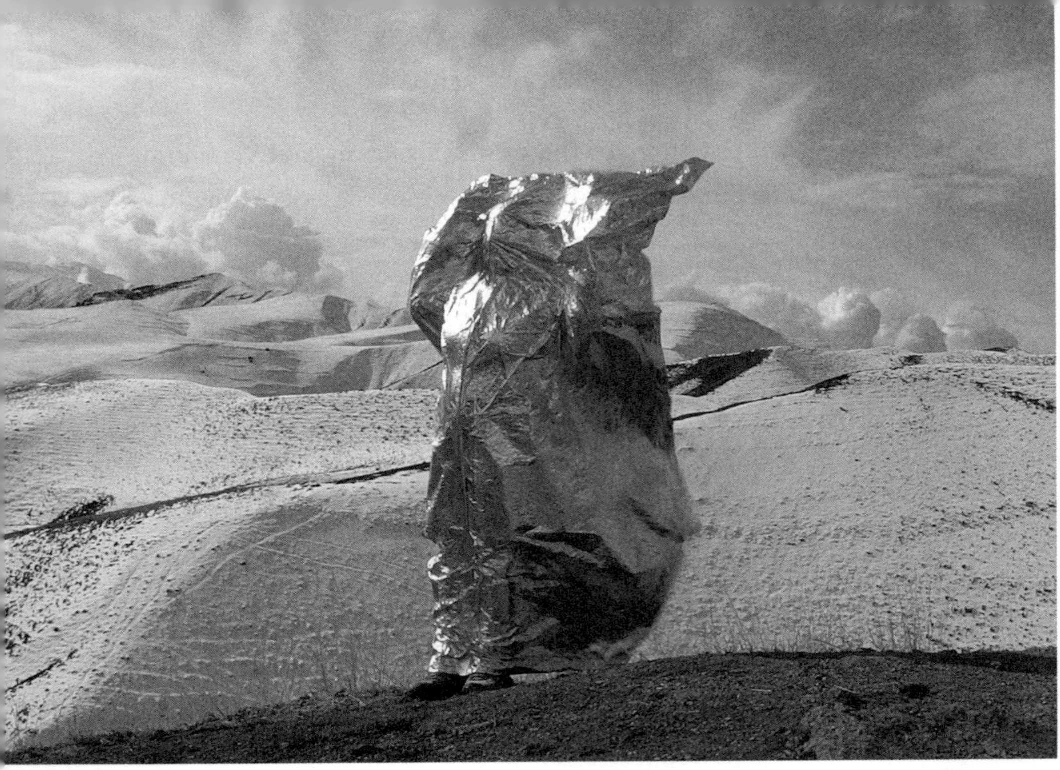

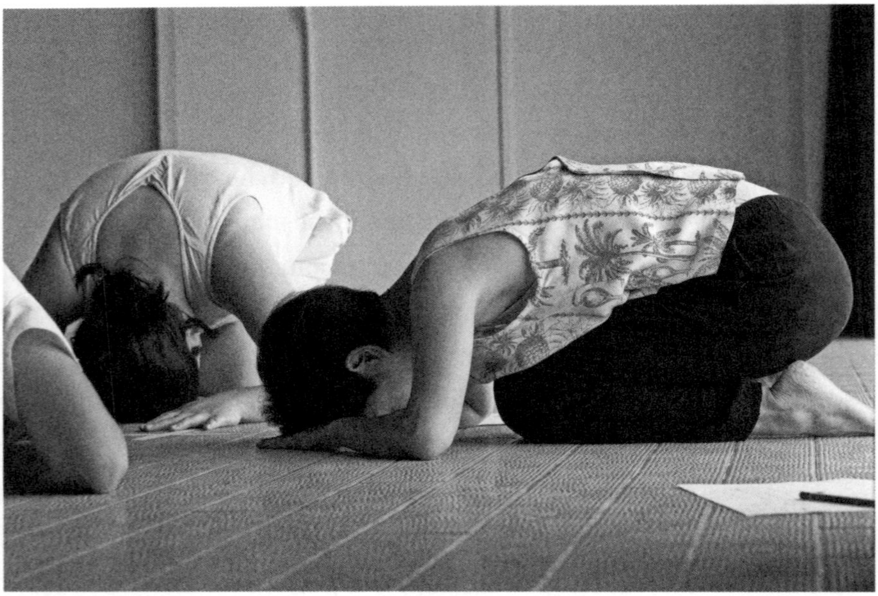

Raheleh Minoosh Zomorodinia, *Sensation*, 2016.
Alecia Neo, *Care Index* workshop, 2020.

Wantanee Siripattananuntakul, filming.
Yannick Dauby, recording.

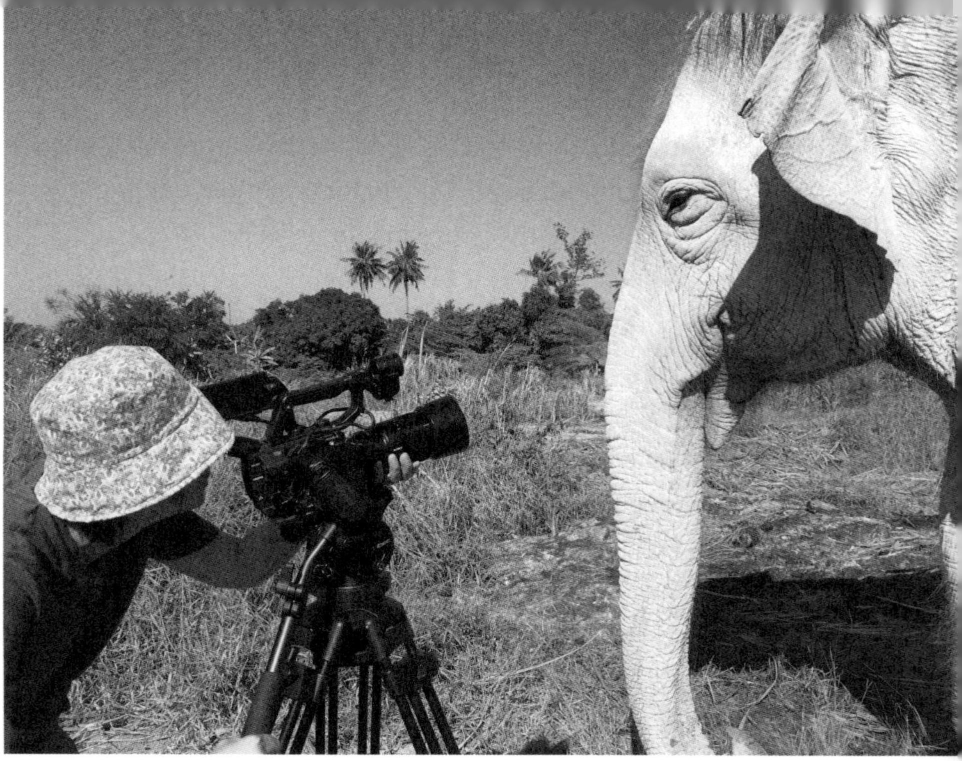

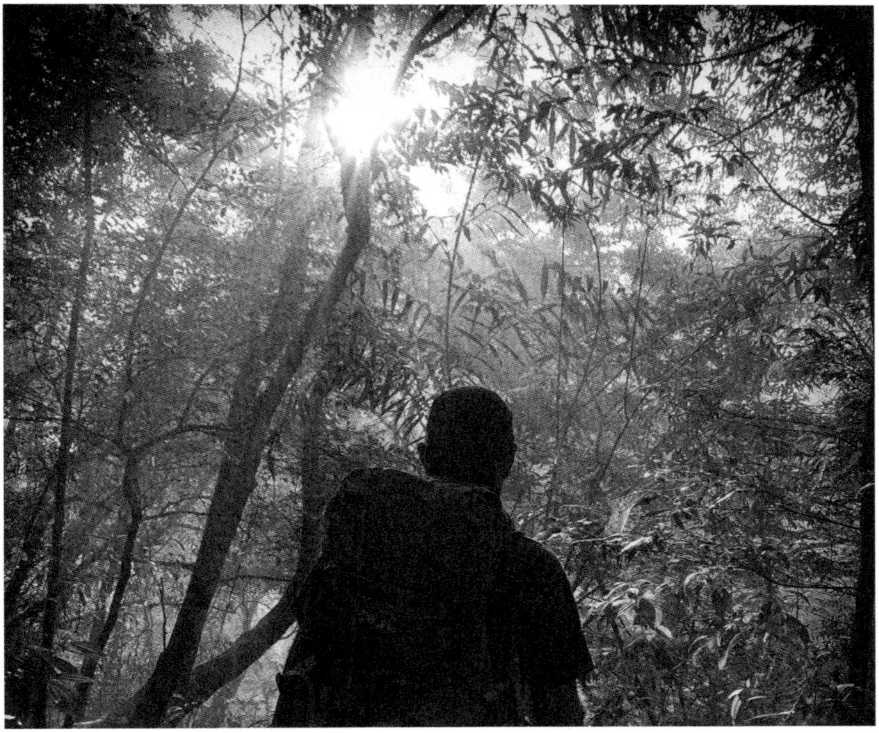

"Sold out," said Zero. So I chose Lion's Rock with a happy face instead.

"How are you these days? Do you feel your personal safety at stake?" I asked the investigative journalist in private.

"I have to keep going as if I were safe."

Our chat meandered into swimming. Between hiking, he said, he would jump into the sea when it showed. I told him my swim begins where no beach cuts the sea off the shore.

I forgot to ask how the tides were on his side this morning. Or maybe he already told me, and us.

As if.

Inherent in totalitarian rule, says Hannah Arendt, is the possibility that all inter-human relationships are destroyed. And yet, she entrusts the future to an "incredible, enduring tenacity" that could outlive "a palpable manufactured world."[3]

8

Peace. Something tyranny does not know, or, something it manufactures for its own use.

Peace – a tiny word. It elongates and lingers in the air.

For friends trying to bring peace out of a fractured world, the more it is held onto, the more it seems to slip away.

"Why peace at all?" Some cast doubts.

Too spiritual for the convenient life.

Too slow for the technology immersed life.

Too modest for the success-oriented life.

Too hidden for the image-hungry life.

Sometimes, the activity of listening is subjected to the same list of doubts.

"Why peace at all?" Some cast more doubts.

Too righteous or too mild, or both, for the roughness of life.

Too much waiting required.

Too much to be planned for.

There are worries that peace becomes a tool of arbitrary power employed as euphemism for top-down control and forced cooperation. There are worries that it sidelines differences, contests and conflicts which need deliberating, not silencing.

"In your call for peace, are you asking me to stop?" In this question is the imagination of refuge that peace promises for the future. In this question is also the desire and need that peace cares for us more than we care for it. We may even think we should leave it alone, as impossible to think with, until all conflicts are resolved. We don't think of peace as a formative response in time, as a process; we demand peace as result. We forget that peace might be an enduring uncertainty. In this question, we take courage from peace and peace makers, and we mistake courage as always already residing in ourselves needing not peace to attend to.

Peace puts us in debt. We calculate. We measure. We owe to it. We owe to such goods as truths to it. We are not sure if we could own up to it. Neither can we hold onto it. There is no icon that can carry all that peace is.

The more we think of nature as a metaphor for peace, the farther we are away from the peace of human making or unmaking. Nature is not quite at peace, which is its nature. In *On the Origin of Species* (1859), Darwin proposes that for natural selection to operate, the living world must have a certain "competitive character."[4] We give the "face of nature" the characteristic of being "bright with gladness," but "beneath this face and concealed by it" is the struggle for existence, with its death and destruction. "The face of Nature may be compared to a yielding surface, with ten thousand sharp wedges packed close together and driven inwards by incessant blows, sometimes one wedge being struck, and then another with greater force."[5] Are beings of nature conscious of battling each other? Does being conscious of determining who are the victors matter? Darwin says, as if to qualify or alleviate the way humans personify nature, presenting it as if it favors some over others, "[A] plant on the edge of a desert is said to struggle for life against the drought, though more properly it should be said to be dependent on the moisture.'"[6] This "Struggle for

Existence" therefore teaches us about mutual dependence, not survival of one at the expense of another. When we delegate peace to well-circulated images of nature in consumerist and mediatized cultures, we shed our responsibility in relating to peace as a human choice. This, I think, is the first ground to clear in preparing for peace.

The second ground is an ethic of being hospitable rather than hostile to peace. "Peace sounds too good to be true. Why bother?" Peace invites scepticism, which is sometimes healthy, sometimes not. Some say, "Aren't you for peace? Why do you act as if you are disturbing rather than making peace?" Such questions keep peace at a distance, as foreign territory, and as someone else's problem. To identify this someone else as a peacemaker and to burden her alone with peace is to think of peace as a flag someone else plants. Those who burden peacemakers for peace relate to peace the way peacemakers don't – peace is not a project with a beginning and end defined by clock time. It does not start and stop. It is a spark that sets something anew. It is a perpetually debatable value punctuating the human condition.

Peace is not an order that exists before anything else. It is not ready-made. It is instead a horizon with which we discern the edge of our fragility and vulnerability that touches upon and sits by each other. Despite this, it is worked for and worked with. Peace is a response. It is active. The absence of peace photography as a concept does not imply that visual images of peace – visions of peace – do not exist, as Frank Möller proposes.[7] Between phases of peace is not conflict or war, but uncertainty. Peace may come; peace may not come.

The ground to clear for peace involves more – perhaps peace is not a good in and of itself, but a condition for other goods to happen. It is modest and generous. As a gesture, it is not self-conscious. It resists the self-righteousness of what the good or claimers of the good sometimes become. Peace calls for dialogues that involve "participatory consciousness."[8] It is a way to attend to each other, a way to love. Peace is a coming together first.

If peace has a form, I imagine it may be that of a sphere. The glass ball that artist Sumei Tse conceives of – rolling in and out of our hands into the other's hands reflected and refracted back onto ours.[9] These are caring hands, groping hands, aware of the skin as physical boundary, but also the warmth from within that transmits, extends.

Peace is not just a state of truce. It doesn't have to defer to war in order to find a path to be. A colleague across the Pacific Ocean told me about Calgacus, the British chieftain and enemy of the Romans, who makes a speech before battle against the Romans: "They plunder, they butcher, they ravish, and call it by the lying name of 'empire.' They make a desert and they call it 'peace.'"[10] I would rather say, peace is when we resist putting a face to the enemy, however difficult sometimes. It may begin when we look within, when we ask whether we, too, house the potential animosity. When it meets our capacity for sloth that compels us to fix the enemy where we think it is, so that we keep reproducing it without recalibrating ourselves, peace tucks us into bed for a good night's sleep.

Confucius speaks of being "at peace," which Burton Watson, in his translation, interprets as a form of "nakedness." Other translations aside, it is interesting that Watson interprets the literal meaning of being "naked" as involving being "at peace with things."[11] It is both inner peace and peace in relation to that which is around. To be naked is to be vulnerable, and to be at ease with being vulnerable. Confucius sometimes uses another term "*an*" (安), meaning equanimity. I think of it as a close associate with the idea of peace.[12] Confucius also states: "The self-righteous villager is the thief of virtue."[13] In a similar way, some steal the language of peace to do otherwise. "Clever words are the disrupters of virtue."[14] Some disrupt peace to claim peace as theirs, as if it could be owned by anyone alone. Without peace as a shared condition, how could bringing the admirable out of others[15] be possible?

It is not easy to be at ease, to be at peace. It is more of a challenge when external conditions are at odds with one's chosen path. This saying from in the Analects has never stopped moving me:

> When Confucius was in Chen, he ran out of provisions and his followers were so weak that none of them could stand up. Zilu confront-

ed Confucius angrily, saying, Does the gentleman have to put up with such hardships? The Master said, The gentleman remains firm in the face of hardships. The petty man, when he encounters hardship, gives way to panic.[16]

Peace requires radical imagination, but it is also as ordinary as breath, coming and going in a rhythm we never flaunt, but ever nurture to vitalize ourselves with. Peace is something to return to, not an object to hold onto. It is a quality, not an event, as Jeanette Winterson speaks of love.[17] It is a quality of relations, a quality of being, and being with. It demands renunciation of a self that can only stand in front of others at an angle. It calls for a self that is always already in and of others, that sees through sight with insight.

"When the mind is utterly still without being forced or trained into quiescence, when it is silent because the self is inactive, then there is creation."[18] This stillness I think of as what peace gives. It releases us from all the business that misdirects or distracts us to short term petty victories over persons. It requires constant, arduous nurturing, detailed and caring attention.

Peace is not a silent chamber sheltering our fears or self-righteousness.

Peace is when I can cope. Peace is not perfection; it accommodates imperfection.

Peace is a regulator against my pride that I can live independent of others, an ethical life without others.

Peace is made, not received. It is not manufactured as a product, but sprouts out of good soil. It may thrive, it may perish.

Peace does not dampen anything we care about. It is a quiet, tenacious energy.

Peace is not an imperative, for no one can be forced into it. It is instead a commitment that allows for the recognition and deliberation of differences.

No one can monopolize peace, for peace makes itself known only when it arises, when hands touch and gently hold, when it lays bare its multiple origins.

"Especially compelling to me was something difficult to articulate but that underlay everything, an approach to life – an ease, an elegance, an absence of the unnecessary. Anything hurried, superficial, purely mercenary, or delusory was rejected. Central was a slowness allowing for the consideration of every choice. The state of the spirit, it is believed, reveals itself in small tasks, rituals – all the things that war interrupts."[19] This is journalist Anthony Shadid returning home.

Make peace the guest. May it become the host one day.

In hindsight, I realize I made of listening as sensitivity, just as I did the same of peace. Peace is when we break into laughter together.

TO CONCLUDE ON PARTING

> *March 30, 2022 (Facebook post)*
> By now the swirl has dispersed to become different formations of the night sky. Wherever you go, let the page be turned, our energy be shared, the same broadness above touch us, the same oceans around nurture us, and let us sustain such conditions that preserve the noble and dignified in the most ordinary – the air we breathe that stretches infinite miles yet never apart.

From here, I must begin again – however provisional the "we," who listen to be free.

NOTES

1. Ursula K. LeGuin. *Late in the Day: Poems 2010–2014*. Oakland, CA: PM Press. 2016:57.
2. George Steiner. *Real Presences*. Chicago: Chicago University Press. 1989: 63.
3. Hannah Arendt. *The Promise of Politics*. New York: Schocken Books. 2005: 161.
4. Nicholas Maistrellis. *Selections from Darwin's The Origin of Species: The shape of the argument*. Santa Fe: Green Lion Press. 2009: 27.
5. Maistrellis. 2009: 35.
6. Maistrellis. 2009: 32–33.
7. Roland Bleiker. (ed.) *Visual Global Politics*. Oxon: Routledge. 2018: 220.
8. David Bohm. *On Dialogue*. New York: Routledge. 2013.
9. https://edouardmalingue.com/wordpress/wp-content/uploads/2016/08/Su-Mei-Tse_E-catalogue.pdf
10. Agricola 32. See https://penelope.uchicago.edu/~grout/encyclopaedia_romana/britannia/monsgraupius/calgacus.html
11. Confucius. *The Analects*. Tr. Burton Watson. New York: Columbia University Press. 7:35 (「君子坦蕩蕩，小人長戚戚。」)
12. Confucius. 7:36 (「子溫而厲，威而不猛，恭而安。」)
13. Confucius. 17:13 (「鄉原，德之賊也。」)
14. Confucius. 15:27 (「巧言亂德，小不忍則亂大謀。」)
15. Confucius. 12:16 (「君子成人之美，不成人之惡。小人反是。)
16. Confucius. 15:2 (在陳絕糧，從者病，莫能興。子路慍見曰：「君子亦有窮乎？」子曰：「君子固窮，小人窮斯濫矣。」)
17. "Occupy Love", Feb 21, 2012 http://www.jeanettewinterson.com/journalism/occupy-love/
18. Krishnamurti, *Education and the Significance of Life*, 1981:125.
19. Anthony Shadid. *House of Stone: A Memoir of Home, Family, and a Lost Middle East*. Boston, New York: Mariner Books. 2013:6.

LUCIA FARINATI

Listening, empathy and difference: towards acts of public mourning and solidarity

My story acts here as a reflection on empathic listening outside the context of therapy. It looks at the role of listening in bereavement and how empathy might not always be possible. Empathic listening is often associated with the capacity to understand the emotions of others at a deep level and support them in a process of healing. But what happens when empathy sits outside the safe room of therapy? What kind of dialogic listening can take place instead of talking or narrative therapy?[1] Can art create a safe space for listening to narratives of trauma and loss?[2]

Every pain is important, yet every pain is different. "A hierarchy of grief could no doubt be enumerated" (Butler).[3] Grief, however, is treated differently across the globe. Especially in times of mass mortality and conflicts the conditions through which a certain life is grievable and which is not, which act of mourning can be public and which is banned, are constantly controlled by the State. Grief in this context furnishes a sense of political community of a complex order which again raises once more questions of equality and justice entangled with the capacity of registering people's voices, in other words, what can be understood as "political listening."

In her study *Listening, Conflict and Citizenship*, political theorist Susan Bickford argues that "political listening is not primarily a caring or amicable practice."[4] Although listening can often evoke ideas of empathy she posits political listening as a practice which is not prompted by friendship or consensus. "Political friendship is not emotional friendship based on love, intimacy and closeness but on respect, acknowledging others as different from us yet, like us, a unique who."[5] According to Bickford political listening requires both openness towards the other and self-involvement rather than self-abnegation or absence. Informed by an "intersectional" approach rooted in the work of feminists of color Bickford pictures listening as a journey or bridge to travel on together, as a political practice that leads towards solidarity.

Contrary to fictitious ideas of solidarity predicated by the State in terms of a "mutual us," solidarity is proposed here as "a separate space where political equality is enacted" (Bassel).[6] Listening is a challenge for solidarity and joint action in that "it treats the other as a partner in political action, treating the oppressed as actors and equals, and not merely as victims. Solidarity means regarding others as capable of taking an interest in the world and speaking for themselves, capable of political action, and therefore to be listened to and not just simply cared for."[7]

MY STORY

When I was 17, I lost my father tragically, and four years ago I lost both my mother and brother within a short space of time. Since my 30s I have experienced psychotherapy, holistic therapies, and more recently bereavement counselling. During the self-isolation of lockdown, I continued the bereavement process on my own, yet the trauma experienced by the death of millions of people made me feel that I was no longer alone. The impossibility for many people to gather at funerals or organize rituals of public mourning made me reflect on the role of listening and empathy in bereavement. How to mourn mass death? What does it mean to listen empathically in situations like the pandemic? Is empathy possible or helpful in traumatic situations?

In the past four years, I was convinced that my sister would understand my grief, as we had experienced the same losses. I assumed that she could feel and listen to my pain as her pain (in Italian *sentire* means both feeling and listening) and so we would become much closer to each other. However, I was wrong. She wanted distance and more time before allowing an encounter. While I felt almost rejected by her, I also realised that one of the biggest obstacles in the way of reaching my sister was my inability to create a safe space in order for her to speak out. I did not understand that my sister's pain was different from my own, that the bereavement process in relation to the same father, mother and brother was profoundly different for each of us. Instead of being reunited through loss, paradoxically loss became a barrier between us. Empathy in this scenario is not only impossible but may trigger negative emotions and the wrong kind of emotional responses. Every pain is important, yet every pain is different.

CONCLUSION

I understand that to regain the relationship with my sister, I don't need to feel or imagine her pain as my own, but to allow her grief to manifest itself as something different from my own. The possibility of reconstructing our sisterhood lies on the risky path of opening ourselves up, listening to each other's story not merely as a shared family history, but as two unique stories, distinct from each other. To allow this to happen we both need to embark on the journey of re-building a new home where it is possible to meet again, defeating the death anxiety ingrained in our thinking.

This reflection on difference, listening and solidarity goes beyond the framework of sisterhood determined by principles of sameness and/or identity politics: I am you, therefore you are me. Building on from an intersectional reflection on the politics of listening and mourning,[8] I would like to propose that pain acts here as a profound catalyst for understanding and recognizing difference. In cases of traumatic experiences empathy might not be possible or simply might not produce a space for resonance, reciprocal mutuality and symmetrical esteem (Honneth)[9] but might provoke instead distance, dissonance, conflict or simply silence. I therefore consider solidarity not as an assumed binary mutual relation but rather as a relational process that involves new forms of care and requires the "redistribution of risk and discomfort" in creating a safe space for listening and speaking (Dreher).[10]

The current situation of the pandemic seems a great opportunity to rethink the politics of mourning and listening as solidarity and care.[11] In contrast to individualized and privatized forms of grief, I see the act of mourning together as an act of public life, and indeed a political act in which it is possible to regain the space for freedom in solidarity with the living and the dead. To care for our lives as well as for what it is in the Others that we have lost, might be the first step.[12]

The earth is beneath our feet, the sky above,
Someone will hear this call.
For we can hear each other, and freedom is near ...

Fred Dewey, Calling All Freedom Ancestors![13]
London, 13 June 202

NOTES

1. See for example Alice Morgan, *What is narrative therapy?* Adelaide: Dulwich Centre Publications, 2000.
2. See for example, Sotelo Castro, Luis Carlos. 'Not Being Able to Speak Is Torture: Performing Listening to Painful Narratives'. *International Journal of Transitional Justice* 14, no. 1 (2020): 220–231.
3. Judith Butler, *Precarious life: The powers of mourning and violence*. London: Verso, 2006, p. 32.
4. Susan Bickford, *Listening, Conflict and Citizenship. The Dissonance of Demo- cracy*. Ithaca, N.Y.: Cornell University Press, 1996, p. 2.
5. Bickford, *Listening, Conflict and Citizenship*, p. 80.
6. Leah Bassel, 'Listening as solidarity', in *The politics of listening*, pp. 71–87. London: Palgrave Pivot, 2017.
7. Bickford, *Listening, Conflict and Citizenship*, p. 77.
8. Athena Athanasiou (2005). 'Reflections on the Politics of Mourning: Feminist Ethics and Politics in the Age of Empire', *Historein*, 5, 40–57: doi:https://doi.org/10.12681/historein.72
9. Axel Honneth, *The struggle for recognition: The moral grammar of social conflicts*. Cambridge: Polity Books, 1996.
10. Tanja Dreher (2009) 'Eavesdropping with permission: the politics of listening for safer speaking spaces', *Borderlands e-journal*, vol. 8, no. 1.
11. George Yancy (2020) *Judith Butler: Mourning Is a Political Act Amid the Pandemic and Its Disparities*, interview with Judith Butler, *Truthout*, 30 April 2020: https://truthout.org/articles/judith-butler-mourning-is-a-political-act-amid-the-pandemic-and-its-disparities/
12. A reflection on memory as 'a capacity to make the dead living' and sustains forms of collective resistance and care is offered by feminist Silvia Federici (2019) 'The Common is upon us. Principles of Health Autonomy. Forewords', in (ed.) Carenotes Collective, *For Health Autonomy. Horizons of Care Beyond Austerity – Reflections from Greece*, Brooklyn: Common Notions, 2020.
13. Fred Dewey, *The School of Public Life*, Berlin: Errant Bodies Press, 2014, p. 228.

BUDHADITYA CHATTOPADHYAY

is an artist, media practitioner, researcher, and writer. Incorporating diverse media, creative technologies and research, Chattopadhyay produces works for large-scale installation and live performance addressing contemporary issues. Chattopadhyay has received numerous residencies, fellowships, and international awards. He is the author of four books, including *The Nomadic Listener* (2020), *The Auditory Setting* (2021), and *Between the Headphones* (2021). Chattopadhyay holds a PhD from the Academy of Creative and Performing Arts, Leiden University, and an MA in New Media from the Faculty of Arts, Aarhus University. Currently, Chattopadhyay is a visiting professor at Critical Media Lab, Basel.

LUCIA FARINATI

is an independent researcher and a curator who lives in London. She studied on the Curatorial Programme at Goldsmiths University of London (2004), and was awarded a PhD from Kingston University on the subject of *Audio Arts* magazine (2020). Her research focuses on dialogic practices and methodologies investigating the role of listening at the intersection of art and activism, the history of the artist interview, and performativity in the context of sound and feminist archives. She has curated several sonic art projects under the collective name Sound Threshold. She is the co-author of *The Force of Listening*, Errant Bodies Press, 2017. www.soundthreshold.org

BRANDON LABELLE

is an artist, writer and educator, as well as founding initiator of The Listening Biennial and related Academy. His work focuses on questions of agency, community, pirate culture, and the poetic imagination, which results in a range of collaborative and para-institutional initiatives, including: Beyond Music Sound Festival (1998–2002), Surface Tension (2003–2008), Dirty Ear Forum (2013–), The Imaginary Republic (2014–19), The Living School (2014–16), Oficina de Autonomia (2017), Communities in Movement (2019–), among others. In 1995 he founded Errant Bodies Press, an independent publishing project. His publications include: *Dreamtime X* (2022), *Acoustic Justice* (2021), *The Other Citizen* (2020), *Sonic Agency* (2018), *Lexicon of the Mouth* (2014), *Diary of an Imaginary Egyptian* (2012), *Acoustic Territories* (2010, 2019), and *Background Noise* (2006, 2015).

KATE LACEY

is Professor of Media History and Theory in the School of Media, Arts and Humanities at the University of Sussex. Her research focuses on radio history, media publics, and listening as civic action. She has published widely, including *Feminine Frequencies: Gender, German Radio and the Public Sphere, 1923 to 1945* (University of Michigan Press, 1996) and *Listening Publics: The Politics and Experience of Listening in the Media Age* (Polity, 2013). She was a founding member of the Radio Studies Network and sits on the editorial boards of *The Radio Journal* and *The International Journal of Cultural Studies*.

ISRAEL MARTÍNEZ

is an artist based in Mexico. Seeking to generate a social and political critical reflection, and often exploring stealth as a communicative situation of deep relevance, Martínez works with sound to create pieces and projects materialized in multichannel audio installations, video, photography, actions or performances, texts, publications, and interventions in public spaces. In 2007, he was granted an Award of Distinction in Prix Ars Electronica, and in 2019, he was a winner of the CTM Radio Lab Call in Berlin. He has exhibited at Museo Nacional Centro de Arte Reina Sofía, MuseumsQuartier, MACBA, Moscow Biennale, TEA Tenerife Espacio de las Artes, Haus der elektronischen Künste Basel, Los Angeles Contemporary Exhibitions, among others. In 2012 he was part of the DAAD Artists-in-Berlin Program, and in 2014 of the residence program of MuseumsQuartier in Vienna.

SARA MIKOLAI

is a Sri-Lankan German dancer and choreographer from Berlin and is currently based in Colombo. With a background in Bharatanatyam, today she extends explorations of body and space in interdisciplinary formats, which take form in performance, sound, video, writing and installation works. Through a practice of listening and research, her work focuses on a critical and poetic engagement with epistemologies of dance through decolonial strategies, queer reclamations and ecological reflections. Sara graduated in Dance, Context & Choreography at HZT Berlin, as well as in the MFA in Performing Arts program at the Iceland University of the Arts, Reykjavik. She further holds a diploma in Bharatanatyam from the Oriental Fine Arts Academy of London. Currently she is engaged in the MPhil in Fine Arts program at the University of Peradeniya, in Kandy, Sri Lanka.

ALECIA NEO

is an artist and cultural worker. Her collaborative practice unfolds primarily through installations, lens-based media and participatory workshops that examine modes of radical hospitality and care. She is currently working on Care Index, an ongoing research focused on the indexing and transmission of embodied gestures and movements which emerge from lived experiences of care labour. Care Index has been recently presented at The Esplanade: Theatres by the Bay, The Listening Biennial, Assembly for Permacircular Museums (ZKM, Center for Art and Media Karlsruhe), New Season of Care (Asia-Art-Activism) and Presence of Mind (Gallery Lane Cove, NSW, Australia). She is the co-founder of Brack, an art collective and platform for socially engaged art. Active since 2014, her ongoing collaborations with disabled artists currently manifests as an arts platform, Unseen Art Initiatives.

DANIELA MEDINA POCH

(born in Bogotá, based in Berlin) is an artist and researcher who likes to write. Through site-specific, research-based work, her practice explores unconventional approaches to environmental intersectionality, debordering and de-othering. Observing everyday life correlations between language, identities and territories, her work aims to deconstruct hegemonic discourses and categories which perpetuate asymmetric power relations. Daniela is currently part of the MA program at Kunst im Kontext - Universität der Künste Berlin, CO-RE collective and the Neue Auftraggeber network. Her collective shows include Raupenimmersatism, SAVVY Contemporary, End to End – Transmediale 2020 C& Center of Unfinished Business, Berlin, VII Bienal of Performance, Galería Santa Fé, Bogota, and Fatídico Festivo, Blue Project Foundation, Barcelona, among others.

LUÍSA SANTOS

holds a PhD in Culture Studies by the Humboldt & Viadrina School of Governance, in Berlin, and an MA in Curating Contemporary Art by the Royal College of Art, in London. Luísa Santos is an Assistant Researcher, in Culture Studies / Artistic Studies, at the Faculty of Human Sciences of the Universidade Católica Portuguesa. An independent curator since 2009, she conducted research in curatorial practices at the Konstfack, in Stockholm, in 2013 and, since 2019, she is a research fellow at The European School of Governance (EUSG), in Berlin. At the CECC, in which she is a senior researcher, she takes the roles of coordinator and artistic director of the *4Cs: from Conflict to Conviviality through Creativity and Culture*, which she has initiated with a consortium of 8 European institutions in 2017. She has curated numerous exhibitions with artists such as Miguel Palma, Nikolaj Larsen, Yorgos Zois, Ângela Ferreira, Amira Hanafi, Marilá Dardot, Jeppe Hein, Jane Jin Kaisen, and Rouzbeh Akhbari. Since 2018, she is the co-artistic director of the nanogaleria, an independent curatorial project which she co-founded with Ana Fabíola Maurício.

JILL J. TAN

is a writer, artist, and researcher committed to collaborative practice and multimodal exploration through games, performance and poetics. As a PhD candidate in Anthropology at Yale University, she studies death and dying in Singapore, and works with the funeral profession. Jill also writes about dance and social forms of art. Jill's work appears in *Guernica, City and Society Journal, Brack, Ghost Proposal, Mynah Magazine, Palimpsest*, and the edited volume *Resistant Hybridities: Tibetan Narratives in Exile* (2020). Her multimedia hybrid poetics project "Notes on the bicentennial of a f/l/ound/er/ing (2019)" was awarded the 2022 Theron Rockwell Field Prize at Yale.

YANG YEUNG

is a writer on art and an independent curator based in Hong Kong. She founded the non-profit soundpocket in 2008 and is currently its Artistic Director. Her recent publications include "caring is a quality: on being touched by Alecia Neo's Care Index" (for Dance Nucleus, Singapore) and an essay on Francis Alÿs' solo exhibition *Wet feet __ dry feet: borders and games* (for Taikwun Contemporary, Hong Kong). She devotes herself to following how artists think, move, make and unmake sense of the world. She continues to work towards juxtaposing contemporary art with ideas from the ancient and modern classics she teaches at the Chinese University of Hong Kong.

THE LISTENING BIENNIAL READER
VOL 1: WAVES OF LISTENING

Edited by Brandon LaBelle
Published by Errant Bodies Press, Berlin / 2022
ISBN: 978–3–9823166–7–3

Design: fliegende Teilchen, Berlin
Print: druckhaus Köthen
Distribution: DAP, New York / les presses du réel, Dijon

Support has been received from:
Norwegian Artistic
Research Programme /
The Art Academy, Bergen, and
Oficina de Autonomia

www.listeningbiennial.net
www.erranbodies.org

Special thanks to Kat Austen, Miguel Buenrostro, Kate Donovan, Florence Freitag, and Michelle-Marie Letelier, for their input on wave epistemologies.